THE POLITICS OF PUBLIC UTILITY REGULATION

WILLIAM T. GORMLEY, JR.

:

The Politics of Public Utility Regulation

:

UNIVERSITY OF PITTSBURGH PRESS

Published by the University of Pittsburgh Press, Pittsburgh, Pa., 15260
Copyright © 1983, University of Pittsburgh Press
All rights reserved
Feffer and Simons, Inc., London
Manufactured in the United States of America

Library of Congress Cataloging in Publication Data

Gormley, William T., Jr., 1950–
　The politics of public utility regulation.

　Includes bibliographical references and index.
　1. Public utilities—United States.　I. Title.
HD2766.G64　　　1983　　　363.6'0973　　　82-42765
ISBN 0-8229-3479-5
ISBN 0-8229-5351-X (pbk.)

To my parents

Contents

viii : *Contents*

Acknowledgments

This project was truly a collective effort and I am pleased to acknowledge many debts.

I owe special thanks to Charles Williams of the University of Illinois-Chicago, who conducted a third of the interviews. More than anyone else, Charlie knows how much jet lag, indigestion, and gnashing of teeth this project involved. I am also indebted to John Hoadley of Duke University, who provided methodological advice on a wide variety of topics. Jack's advice was so lucid that I understood him 95 percent of the time, a record for me.

The quality of any large research project depends substantially on the talents of the research staff. In retrospect, I marvel at my good fortune in securing such an able team of research assistants: Carole Carlin, Cindy Hoffman, Jeff Loewinger, Laurel Munger, Saroja Reddy, Geoff Rendall, and Donna Warren. The timely completion of this project is a tribute to these research assistants and to the keyboard wizardry of three typists—Joyce Berlin, Mary Burton-Beinecke, and Marilyn Henry.

During the first two years of the project, I worked in Washington, D.C., thanks to John Logsdon of George Washington University's Science, Technology, and Public Policy Program, who kindly provided me with office space. This gave me quick access to government agencies, various experts and excellent restaurants. All were important!

Throughout the project, I received regular admonitions from a talented Advisory Board: Edward Berlin, Larry Kaseman, Bert Rockman, Tony Rosenbaum, and Harry Trebing. Their "friendly fire" was enormously helpful, although it usually took me a couple days to recover from their help.

Many colleagues here at Madison and elsewhere were kind enough to read a chapter or two and to offer valuable recommendations at critical junctures. I am indebted to Charles Anderson, Jeff Berry, Thad Beyle, Eric Brown, Richard Cole, Dennis Dresang, Murray Edelman, Daniel Elazar, Booth Fowler, Claire Fulenwider, Joel Grossman, Susan Hansen, Henry Hart, Michael Hayes, Bert Kritzer, Todd LaPorte, Leon Lindberg, Dick Merelman, David Magleby, Ira Sharkansky, Rod Stevenson, Jerry Thain, David Welborn, and Bruce Wallin for helpful comments along the way. I also received superb suggestions from Kenneth Meier, John Moore, and Carl Van Hour, each of whom read the entire manuscript.

I am grateful to Frederick A. Hetzel and his colleagues at the University of Pittsburgh Press, who succeeded in getting this book published before our next energy crisis. I am also grateful to Sandy Thatcher of the Princeton University Press for his helpful assistance.

This project was funded primarily by the National Science Foundation, through two grants (DAR-7812721 and DAR-8023993). The Wisconsin Alumni Research Foundation also provided financial support. Although NSF is in no way responsible for the contents of this book, it deserves much of the credit for supporting an admittedly ambitious undertaking. I am particularly grateful to Larry Rosenberg, who nurtured this project from the very beginning and offered many valuable suggestions along the way.

Selected portions of this manuscript have been adapted from journal articles I wrote, with permission of the publishers: "Nonelectoral Participation as a Response to Issue-Specific Conditions," *Social Science Quarterly*, vol. 62, no. 3 (September 1981), pp. 527–37, reprinted by permission of the University of Texas Press; "Alternative Models of the Regulatory Process," *Western Political Quarterly*, vol. 35, no. 3 (September 1982), pp. 297–317, reprinted by permission of the University of Utah, Copyright holder; and "Policy, Politics, and Public Utility Regulation," *American Journal of Political Science*, vol. 27, no. 1

(February 1983), pp. 86–105, reprinted by permission of the University of Texas Press.

Finally, I would like to thank my parents, who convinced me years ago that writing can be a pleasure and who taught me most of the words in this book.

THE POLITICS OF PUBLIC UTILITY REGULATION

: PART I :
The Scope of Conflict

Public utility regulation today is complex and conflictual. Solutions are seldom obvious, and decisions are seldom consensual. In the words of one southern regulator, this is a very "flustrating" situation. Flustrating though it may be to policy makers and participants, the public utility regulatory process is fascinating to students of politics and public policy. The stakes are high, the trade-offs are perplexing, the political challenges are varied, and the policy responses are diverse. In sum, public utility regulation provides an excellent opportunity to observe fifty political systems coping with very similar problems in very dissimilar ways.

Part 1 illuminates the scope of conflict. It looks at both insiders and outsiders, as individuals and as members of complex organizations. It examines disputes over both decisions and decision-making and suggests ways in which policy and process dilemmas are intertwined. It also lays the groundwork for part 2, which examines linkage mechanisms by using attitudinal, perceptual, and behavioral measures of concurrence, influence, and policy impacts.

Chapter 1 provides a broad overview of policy dilemmas in a political context. Public utility regulators play a crucial role in determining price signals, supply levels, and demand patterns. If they set prices too high, they impose a burden on consumers; but if they set prices too low, they deprive utility companies of capital to build new power plants. If they approve the construction of new power plants, they may threaten public health and safety; but if they reject proposals for new power plants, they run the risk of brownouts and blackouts. If they fail to encourage conservation, they aggravate supply problems; but if they promote conservation through higher prices, they exacerbate the rate burden of consumers. At times, public utility regulators must feel that they have been asked to untie a Gordian knot.

As they make these difficult choices, public utility regulators operate in a political environment whose features are discernible in the content of legislation, the recruitment of commissioners, the skills of the bureaucracy, the influence of regulated industries, and the scope of conflict. Although it is possible to generalize about the politics of public utility regulation, it is important to differentiate among states as well. Methods of selecting regulators and levels of public advocacy are especially likely to vary from state to state. These variations are the focal points of controversies over the public utility regulatory process. To some observers, inadequate public representation makes it unlikely that public utility commissions will be sufficiently responsive. To other observers, excessive politicization of the regulatory process makes it unlikely that regulators will be sufficiently responsible.

The first of these perspectives raises the specter of a crisis of accountability. It is often argued that broad, diffuse interests, such as consumer interests, will be underrepresented in policy-making. If so, public policy may be skewed in the direction of producer interests, because they are better organized and better represented. Chapter 2 focuses on levels of participation in public utility commission proceedings by two kinds of public advocates: grassroots advocates and proxy advocates. How active are they? How has their activity changed over time? What are their origins, goals, and incentives? What are their funding levels and funding sources? Is there a crisis of accountability? If so, how should that crisis be defined?

Ironically, increased public advocacy could be a problem itself if it contributes to a crisis of governance. Thus, some argue that an expansion of the scope of conflict dangerously politicizes the policy-making process. At best, this may lead to bargaining; at worst, it may lead to paralysis. In particular, regulators may be unable to render judgments that are detached, timely, and consistent. Chapter 3 focuses on the peculiar tensions faced by two kinds of regulators: political executives and career executives. How are regulators recruited? What professional and partisan predispositions do they bring to their jobs? Are public utility commissions truly independent of regulated industries, the governor, the public? Do commissions have the resources to address the difficult problems they face? Is there a crisis of governance? If so, how should that crisis be defined?

To answer these and other questions, several data bases are employed: (1) government documents on national trends in energy and telecommunications; (2) a questionnaire survey of public utility commissioners in all fifty states; (3) published data on policy outputs of all fifty states; (4) a content analysis of 356 commission documents from a sample of twelve states; and (5) interviews with 284 public utility regulators, public advocates, and utility company executives in the same twelve states. All uncited interviews were conducted expressly for this project.

Chapter 1 utilizes national figures on energy sources and rate levels. Chapter 2 relies on the questionnaire survey of commissioners, aggregate data from all fifty states, and interviews with 119 public advocates in twelve states. Chapter 3 relies on aggregate data from all fifty states, commission documents from twelve states, and interviews with 101 public utility regulators in twelve states. These multiple sources provide rich opportunities for analysis at the individual, organizational, and state levels.

: 1 :
Policy Dilemmas in a Political Context

For many years, state public utility commissions were virtually ignored by the public, the press, and the academic community. Commissioners occasionally appeared at hearings long enough to rubber-stamp utility company requests for a rate decrease, but such appearances were brief and painless. "I wonder what commissioners did thirty years ago," a California regulator muses. "They probably played a lot of golf." Today, in contrast, there is little time for golf or quiet reflection. Public utility commissions in the 1980s are beleaguered regulatory bodies that cannot seem to cope with the policy dilemmas confronting them. Public utility commissioners, once condemned to obscurity, are now scrutinized and criticized by citizens, reporters, and professors. Public utility commission staff members, once free to gossip and yawn, are now beset by conflicting demands, urgent deadlines, and onerous requirements. Clearly, the consensual years have come to an end.

In fact, the consensus that led to public utility regulation as we know it today was fragile from the very beginning. State public utility regulation developed in the early twentieth century as a result of a rather remarkable alliance. Progressive governors, such as Wisconsin's Robert LaFollette, viewed state regulation as an opportunity to pursue public interest goals through "scientific" regulation. The Progressives also preferred state regulation to control by corrupt local politicians. Utility companies, which might have been expected to oppose state regulation, found it less threatening than municipal ownership or the chaos of unregulated competition. Indeed, the National Electric Light Association, headed by Samuel Insull of Chicago, actively supported state regulation. The National Civic Federation, a coalition of corporate leaders, labor leaders, and civic reformers, shared the Progressives' disdain for local politicians and the utilities' skepticism toward public ownership. The result was a convergence of powerful interests. Without agreeing on the problem, these disparate groups nevertheless agreed that state regulation was the solution. Backed by such a formidable coalition, state public utility regulation swept across the country soon after Wisconsin and New York established the first public utility commissions in 1907.[1]

For over half a century, state public utility regulation was relatively tranquil. For the most part, the interests of utility companies and their customers coincided. Even the 1960s, turbulent in so many other respects, were marked by few conflicts over public utility regulation. With unit costs decreasing as larger plants were built, utility companies offered low rates to encourage consumption. Business and residential customers happily obliged. Yet this cycle of decreasing costs and lower prices was to end in the late 1960s and early 1970s.[2] With remarkable suddenness, utilities issues became much more complex and much more conflictual.

Although we are accustomed to thinking of conflict as a form of political behavior, conflictuality is a characteristic of issues as well. Simply put, some issues are more likely to generate conflict than others. Energy issues today are especially conflictual. One reason for this is our dependence on scarce fossil fuels and the vulnerability of our energy supply to international disruptions. The use of Middle Eastern oil as an economic and political weapon has triggered shortages, price increases, and enormous controversy. Another reason for conflict is growing awareness of the health and safety implications of extracting and transporting fuels and generating and transmitting electricity. Because health and safety can be costly, the environmental movement and the antinuclear movement have created new tensions, not just between utilities and the general public but among citizens as well. A third reason for conflict is our growing awareness of the distributive implications of policy choices. The emergence of antipoverty groups, consumer groups, and taxpayer groups in recent years has underscored the zero-sum nature of many policy choices. A fourth reason for conflict is that we have reached a technological plateau in the energy area. Economies of scale, which once enabled utilities to increase profits by lowering prices, have been exhausted. Instead, today's technologies offer an unappealing combination of higher costs, lower profits, and higher prices. Technology, once the solution to many of our most vexing problems, is now widely perceived as part of the problem.

If energy issues are much more conflictual than ever before, they are also much more complex. One reason for this is technological uncertainty. Nuclear power is perhaps the most dramatic example of a highly unpredictable technology. The possibility of a major accident, a prolonged shutdown, or both makes it extremely difficult to plan for the future. A second reason for complexity is the electric utility industry's reliance on highly capital-intensive construction projects with long lead times. This makes it difficult, but essential, to estimate the cost of capital with precision, especially in an inflationary period. It also limits adaptability to changing conditions. Finally, the behavior of consumers is very difficult to anticipate. Despite numerous studies, we simply do not know how consumers will react to price increases, new rate structures, or political speeches characterizing conservation as a patriotic duty.[3] In broader terms, we are uncertain about current energy supplies, current energy reserves, the relationship between tax incentives and energy development, the relationship between tax incentives and energy conservation, the relationship between prices and energy demand, the costs of technological development, and the speed of technological innovation. The only certainty, it seems, is uncertainty.

Like energy issues, telecommunications issues have become terribly complex. The decision of the Federal Communications Commission (FCC) to introduce competition into the terminal equipment and private line markets has blurred the distinction between monopolistic and competitive services. The sharing of equipment between AT&T and its local operating companies has made it difficult to distinguish between the costs of local service and the costs of interstate service. Yet, these ambiguities have permitted regulators to dampen conflict by keeping local exchange rates relatively low, despite rapidly rising costs at the local level. Technological advances, such as microwave relay and satellite transmission, have kept down the costs of interstate services. Although the costs of local service have climbed dramatically, those cost increases have been masked by cross-subsidies from interstate services. All of this may change, now that AT&T has agreed to divest itself of its local telephone companies.[4] As cross-subsidies are eliminated and the goal of universal service is threatened, bitter conflicts are likely to erupt. During the 1970s, however, telecommunications issues were overshadowed by energy issues.

Although energy policy and telecommunications policy are made by a wide variety of federal, state, and local agencies, state public utility commissions have especially significant responsibilities. Public utility commissions perform many critical functions, the most visible of which is to determine the rates charged by investor-owned (or private) utilities for services provided within their jurisdiction. The rate-setting of state public utility commissions should be differentiated from that of related government agencies. Municipal governments set rates for municipally owned (or public) utilities. The Federal Energy Regulatory Commission (formerly the Federal Power Commission) sets rates for wholesale and interstate power sales. The Federal Communications Commission sets rates for interstate telephone calls. All but one or two public utility commissions regulate electric, natural gas, and telephone utilities. Most also regulate water, sewer, and transportation companies. However, jurisdictions do vary. The Texas Public Utility Commission, for example, does not regulate natural gas utilities. The Virginia State Corporation Commission, in contrast, regulates not only all major utilities but also banks, insurance companies, even worm farmers.

Although the rate-setting process differs from state to state, it always involves the determination of revenue requirements and rate structures. A utility company's revenue requirements are the total funds that the utility may collect from ratepayers. Revenue requirements are calculated by multiplying the utility company's rate base by an allowed rate of return and adding this product to the utility company's operating costs. The *rate base* is the total value of the utility company's capital investments (including its power plants, transmission lines, and other property), which may or may not include construction work in progress (CWIP). The allowed *rate of return* is a profit sufficient to pay interest on accumulated debt and to provide a "fair" return to investors. A fair return is determined through a comparable earnings test (where a utility company's earnings are measured against those of a firm facing comparable risks), a discounted cash flow approach (where a utility company's capital costs are estimated by analyzing conditions in the financial market), or some other method. *Operating costs* include expenses for fuel, labor, management, maintenance, and advertising. The costs of taxes and depreciation are also part of the utility's revenue requirements.

If revenue requirements concern the total size of the pie, rate design concerns how the pie will be sliced. First, costs must be allocated among several classes of customers, including residential, industrial, and commercial customers. In general, the allocation of costs among classes of customers is based on the actual costs of providing service to each class. Such costs include fixed costs (which the utility incurs regardless of the level of use) and variable costs (which depend on the level of use). In computing costs, however, it is not obvious what pricing principles should apply.[5] Once costs have been allocated among classes of customers, rate structures must be devised within each class. Again, there is disagreement on how the costs of service should be calculated. There is also disagreement on whether public utility commissions should give consideration to such goals as economic development, energy conservation, and social equity.

Beyond rate-setting, public utility commission jurisdictions vary considerably from state to state. In some states, public utility commissions must approve proposals for new power plants before construction can begin. In other states (for example, California, New York, Massachusetts), that function is performed by a special siting board or energy commission, whose membership may or may not overlap with that of the public utility commission. Even where a public utility commission lacks explicit jurisdiction over power plant siting, however, it can exercise enormous influence over such decisions. Public utility commission decisions on the sale of stocks and bonds determine whether a utility company can raise the money it needs to finance a new plant. Public utility commission constraints on the utility company's rate of return determine how profitable a new capital investment will be. Public utility commission policies on rate design and load management have a profound impact on demand patterns, which determine whether a new power plant is needed in the first place. Thus, public utility commissions have substantial control over rates, supply, and demand. From a policy perspective, public utility regulation may be viewed as an attempt to integrate these three variables. That task has proven exceedingly difficult in recent years.

POLICY DILEMMAS

Rates

The Arab oil embargo of 1973–1974 triggered a sharp upward spiral in energy rates that shows no signs of abating. As a result of the embargo and subsequent price increases by the Organization of Petroleum Exporting Countries (OPEC), the Arab oil cartel, the price of imported oil climbed dramatically. The United States, which depended on foreign oil for one-third of its domestic oil consumption in 1973, was vulnerable to OPEC price increases.[6] Because over one-tenth of all electricity in this country is generated by oil-fired plants (see table 1), increases in the

Table 1
U.S. Electricity Generation, by Source of Power
(1981)

Source of Power	Proportion of Total Electricity Generation
Coal	51.2
Oil	10.7
Nuclear	13.2
Gas	14.0
Water	10.2
Total	99.3

Source: National Electric Reliability Council, *Electric Power Supply and Demand* (Princeton, July 1981), p. 70.

price of oil inevitably meant increases in the price of electricity. Between January 1974 and January 1981, the average price of electricity to residential users of 500 kilowatt-hours of electricity per month rose 131 percent.[7]

The Arab oil embargo also precipitated a sharp increase in natural gas rates. In most respects, natural gas is an excellent substitute for oil. Like oil, natural gas is used to heat many American homes. It is also used to generate over one-eighth of this country's electricity. As oil became more expensive, natural gas also became more expensive. Between January 1974 and January 1981, the average price of natural gas to residential users of 100 therms of natural gas per month rose 253 percent.[8]

There were, to be sure, other causes of rising energy rates in the 1970s, including rising wages, rising capital costs, and declining economies of scale. Indeed, the 1970s were generally inflationary. Nevertheless, the rate of inflation for energy far outstripped the rate of inflation for other items.[9] The rate of inflation for energy utilities also exceeded the rate of inflation for telephone utilities. Although the costs of providing local telephone service increased during this period, cross-subsidies from interstate services, where costs were relatively stable, permitted local telephone rates to remain relatively stable as well. From January 1974 to January 1981, local telephone exchange rates rose by only 22 percent (see table 2).[10] Thus, energy rate hikes far exceeded telephone rate hikes over the same period.

Table 2
Residential Utility Bills, 1974–1981
(National Averages)

Utility	1974	1975	1976	1977	1978	1979	1980	1981
Electricity	$14.10	$17.93	$19.26	$20.86	$22.19	$23.05	$27.50	$32.61
Natural gas	11.33	13.79	16.74	20.88	23.59	28.83	34.93	40.05
Telephone	7.85	8.28	8.75	9.22	9.30	9.35	9.41	9.57

Sources: Electricity—U.S. Department of Energy (monthly rates for residential customers using 500 killowatt-hours of electricity per month). Natural gas—U.S. Department of Labor (monthly rates for residential customers using 100 therms of natural gas per month). Telephone—National Association of Regulatory Utility Commissioners (monthly rates for residential customers purchasing a one-party flat rate exchange service).

High energy rates hurt all consumers but especially the poor. Although the poor generally consume less energy than other members of society, they must allocate a larger percentage of their budget to energy bills. As Grier puts it, "Utility bills . . . have always been difficult for many of the poor to meet. But with energy prices rising recently at double-digit rates—far faster than the general rate of inflation—energy has now become one of the largest items in low-income households' budgets."[11] According to one government study, the poorest U.S. households (with annual incomes less than $1,800) spend more than 25 percent of their income on energy, while the richest U.S. households (with incomes of $27,000 or more) spend only 6 percent of their income on energy.[12]

With energy rates climbing rapidly, many of the poor are unable to pay their bills on time. In many states, they are subject to late payment penalties if they fail to do so. Some of the poor are unable to pay their utility bills at all. In some states, their service may be disconnected, even during the harshest days of winter. Public utility regulators, though concerned, are generally reluctant to provide special protection for the poor, which they regard as a legislative responsibility. One regulator, for example, explains the practical difficulties with a winter shutoff ban:

It is terribly frustrating to go through a very tense meeting with consumer groups demanding that you say, ban cut-offs. And you say, "Well, do you want to ban cut-offs for everybody? What happens to the person who has adequate income and doesn't pay?"—"Oh, no, not him, we want you to discriminate and just do it only for people who need it." Well, we don't have any such authority to discriminate on those grounds. First, we have no idea what income is. We do not know the income of our utility customers. We can't tell the utility to look into their income. That would violate all the standards of a democratic society as we know it. So, by law, we are prohibited from collecting income data, and we cannot discriminate according to the income category of consumers. And yet, that's explicitly the demand that is made upon us. . . . They don't let us for a week forget that income distribution problem. Now, sad to say, there's very little we can do about it that's constructive. But you try to explain that, you get a lot of hostility. And they view it, rightfully so, as a badminton game where the legislature passes it back to us and we pass it back to the legislature, and nobody deals with the problem.

Unfortunately, what is at stake in this badminton game is nothing less than human life. Whatever the practical arguments in favor of shutoffs, their consequences can be tragic indeed. Two Detroit children died in a fire apparently caused by candles used to light their apartment after Detroit Edison shut off their electricity.[13] Another Detroit child perished in a fire apparently caused by a defective electric space heater used to warm his bedroom after Michigan Consolidated Gas shut off the gas to his apartment.[14] Some consumers, well aware of the threat that disconnection poses, resist efforts to terminate their service. In one widely publicized incident, a Los Angeles woman reacted to a visit by a Southern California Gas serviceman with orders to disconnect her service by striking him on the arm with a shovel and chasing him away. When the serviceman returned with two policemen, the woman reportedly brandished a knife. In full view of her twelve-year-old daughter, the police shot the woman to death.[15] These incidents underscore the potentially tragic consequences of high utility rates.

Although high rates make it difficult for consumers to satisfy their energy needs, low rates make it difficult for utility companies to maintain a reliable energy supply. Without sufficient revenue from ratepayers, utility companies cannot attract capital from other sources. Without such capital, utility companies cannot finance the construction of new power plants. To raise capital for plant construction, a utility company relies on two methods of external financing: issuing stock (common or preferred) and selling bonds (long-term or short-term). Both avenues have proven increasingly difficult in recent years. According to Joskow and MacAvoy, the earned return on common stock equity has come perilously close to falling below prospective returns in the bond market.[16] If that occurs, investors will cease to buy utility company stock. Even before that happens, investors will be difficult to attract.[17] Investors have no reason to prefer stocks to bonds if the rate of return on stocks, which include an element of risk, is not substantially higher than the yield on new long-term debt. Moreover, utility stocks have become even riskier and less attractive as a number of major utility companies, including Consolidated Edison and General Public Utilities, owner of Three Mile Island, have failed to make dividend payments.

Under such circumstances, utility companies are tempted to borrow money. Yet the bond market has presented its own problems. Alarmed by the growing difficulties of utility companies, financial analysts downgraded the bonds of many electric utilities. From 1974 through June 1977, there were 184 changes in the ratings of electric utility debt by Moody's and Standard & Poor's, the two major ratings services. In all, 35 issues were upgraded and 150 were downgraded.[18] Those utility companies with downgraded bonds were forced to offer higher interest rates on new bond issues.

This creates a predicament for public utility regulators. If they allow utilities to raise rates enough to finance the sale of new stocks and bonds, they aggravate the already staggering rate burden of consumers. If, instead, they fail to do so, they deprive utilities of the opportunity to raise capital in an already troubled financial market. Of course, the inability of utilities to raise capital is a major problem only if new power plants are needed—a hotly debated point to which we now turn.

Supply

To support their plea for new power plants, utility company officials raise the specter of a major power failure, such as that which crippled New York City on July 13, 1977. As a result of lightning which struck Consolidated Edison's power lines, 9 million residents of New York City and Westchester County were without power for four to twenty-five hours. The power failure triggered a looting spree in which as many as two thousand stores were ransacked or set on fire. Nearly four thousand people were arrested. Total losses were estimated at over $1 billion.[19]

Although no utility is completely immune from the possibility of overloaded circuits, a utility company can better avert a power failure if it has a substantial "reserve margin" that can be called upon during emergencies. In the long run, high reserve margins may be beneficial to ratepayers: if a plant failure occurs, utilities may be able to fall back on their reserves rather than purchase expensive power from another source. In the short run, though, high reserve margins usually mean high rates, since ratepayers must normally pay for construction and maintenance costs. Most electric utility companies have reserve margins of about 20 percent.[20] However, there is widespread disagreement over whether such reserve margins are too low or too high. In a Kansas City Power and Light Company case, the Missouri Public Service Commission decided that a reserve margin greater than 20 percent is too high; in a Dayton Power and Light Company case, the Ohio Public Utilities Commission decided that the same reserve margin is not too high.[21]

Just as there is disagreement over whether new power plants are needed, there is also disagreement over the appropriate source of power, assuming that new power plants are to be built. One solution is to rely more heavily on coal, which currently accounts for one-half of all electricity generated in the United States. Coal was the linchpin of the Carter administration's energy development program, which called for converting coal into oil and gas through a crash effort to produce synthetic fuels. It is easy to understand the Carter administration's enthusiasm for coal, since the United States possesses an estimated 27 percent of the earth's coal reserves.[22] Coal might serve as a "bridge" to a more stable energy future.

Much of America's coal reserves, though, are accessible only through deep mining, an extremely hazardous occupation. Such coal generally lies east of the Mississippi, in such states as Pennsylvania, Illinois, Indiana, Ohio, and Kentucky. Because of its location near the nation's major population centers, eastern coal is easier to transport to the populous parts of the country that need it the most. However, most eastern coal is high in sulfur content. High-sulfur coal, when burned, spews harmful sulfur dioxide into the atmosphere. Furthermore, the Environmental Protection Agency (EPA) has required utilities to install expensive pollution control devices, "wet scrubbers," when using high-sulfur coal. If eastern coal is used with wet scrubbers, as the EPA insists it must be, electric rates will skyrocket.

That leaves western coal, generally low in sulfur. When such coal is burned, much less sulfur dioxide is emitted. Most western coal is close to the surface and can be extracted through strip mining, rather than deep mining. Unfortunately, though, strip mining leaves deep, ugly scars on the earth's surface that require costly reclamation efforts. Moreover, transportation costs are high, because western coal, located primarily in such states as North Dakota, Montana, and Wyoming, must be transported long distances, usually by rail. The railroads, in an economic slump, have tried to recoup some of their losses by charging high rates for the transportation of coal. Thus, coal, whether western of eastern, is not without its drawbacks, both environmental and economic.

An alternative solution is to rely more heavily on nuclear power, which currently accounts for approximately one-eighth of the electricity generated in the United States. Nuclear power is an integral part of the Reagan administration's energy program, which calls for the development of a breeder reactor designed to produce more nuclear fuel than it uses. The Reagan administration is enthusiastic about nuclear power because nuclear technology is already far advanced. Like coal, nuclear power might provide a temporary solution to this country's energy needs.

However, nuclear power faces an uncertain future in the wake of the Three Mile Island accident, which intensified public apprehension over the safety of nuclear power.[23] Since March 1979, when the Three Mile Island cooling system failed, only three new nuclear power plants have been licensed to operate by the Nuclear Regulatory Commission (NRC).[24] Indeed, enthusiasm for nuclear power was waning well before the Harrisburg accident. In 1978, only two new nuclear power plants were ordered, and a number of others were canceled.[25] Persistent questions about the safety of nuclear power remained unanswered. The probability of a major accident was unknown. The effects of low-level radiation on humans were unclear. Even more decisive were economic considerations. The completion of a nuclear power plant was taking more than eleven years, during which time construction costs and interest rates were increasing. Still more difficult problems loomed ahead, including the disposal of radioactive waste and the decommissioning of nuclear plants.

Troubled by both safety and economic considerations, some state regulatory bodies took a provisional stand against nuclear power. The Wisconsin Public Service Commission imposed a moratorium on nuclear plant construction in that state until questions concerning waste disposal, fuel supply, and decommissioning costs were satisfactorily resolved. The California Energy Commission banned new nuclear power plants in California until the nuclear waste disposal problem was solved.[26] Other public utility commissions (for example, Missouri and Oregon) struck a more indirect blow at nuclear power by excluding construction work in progress from the rate base of electric utilities, thereby making it difficult for utilities to raise money to finance capital-intensive power plants.[27] Despite the support of the Reagan administration, nuclear power is widely perceived as both expensive and hazardous.

A less hazardous source of power is solar energy. In contrast to coal and nuclear power, solar energy is inexhaustible, clean, and safe. According to some observers, it offers the hope of a veritable promised land.[28] Certainly, there is much that public utility commissions could do to promote solar energy. For example, commissions might encourage residential customers to purchase solar heating units by offering them low-interest loans financed by utility companies. Or commissions might encourage utilities to lease solar units by promising a larger rate base or a higher rate of return as an inducement.[29] The Harvard Business School's Energy Project estimates that solar energy could meet between one-fifth and one-fourth of this country's energy needs by the year 2000.[30]

Others are much less optimistic, given the wide variety of economic, technological, and legal barriers that solar energy faces.[31] Despite tax incentives, "active" solar systems, with mechanical moving parts, are still too expensive for most homeowners. Nor is that likely to change in the near future. Breakthroughs in photovoltaic technology could reduce the costs of solar household systems, but such breakthroughs are likely to be postponed by reduced federal support for solar research and development. Moreover, even if costs were considerably lower, the absence of solar access legislation discourages many homeowners from installing units whose access to the sun could be blocked by nearby construction. In short, it is doubtful that solar energy can solve our short-term energy needs. That leaves only one alternative to new coal-fired or nuclear plants—energy conservation.

Demand

Through substantial conservation efforts, the need for new power plants can be sharply reduced. There are at least three ways in which public utility regulators could promote energy conservation: (1) by adopting rate designs that discourage consumption, especially during peak-demand periods; (2) by encouraging industrial and commercial customers to produce their own electricity through cogeneration; and (3) by encouraging residential customers to weatherize and insulate their homes.

During the 1970s, a number of state public utility commissions considered rate designs that promote energy conservation. Indeed, under the Public Utility Regulatory Policies Act of 1978, state public utility commissions were required to "consider and determine" whether a variety of energy conservation measures should be adopted. These include: (1) inverted rates, which charge more per kilowatt-hour as consumption increases; (2) time-of-day rates, which charge more per kilowatt-hour during peak demand hours; (3) seasonal rates, which charge more per kilowatt-hour during peak demand seasons (usually the summer); and (4) rates for interruptible service, which charge less per kilowatt-hour to customers who agree to have their service temporarily interrupted when demand reaches dangerously high levels.

After considering these and other rate structure reforms, public utility commissions have reached sharply different conclusions. A number of commissions have retained "declining block" rate structures which encourage consumption by charging less per kilowatt-hour as consumption increases. Other commissions have adopted rate structure reforms so halfhearted that they are doomed to fail. The Massachusetts Department of Public Utilities, for example, adopted time-of-day rates with differentials between peak and off-peak rates so small that they are unlikely to shift consumption patterns. The Georgia Public Service Commission adopted inverted rates, only to reverse itself after these rates drew the bitter opposition of all-electric residential customers. Instead of redesigning the rate schedule to provide separate rates for all-electric homes, the Georgia Commission simply eliminated the inverted rate design. Only a handful of states have been exceptionally innovative in rate structure reform. These states include Wisconsin, California, New York, and Michigan.

Another way to encourage energy conservation is by promoting cogeneration, which involves the simultaneous production of heat and electricity, usually at an industrial site.[32] In the process of generating low-temperature steam for heating, many industries also generate high-temperature steam. Instead of discharging the latter into the air as waste, industries could harness it and use it to produce electricity.[33] With the price of electricity supplied by investor-owned utilities climbing sharply, many industries would be delighted to generate their own electricity. However, two obstacles remain: high back-up rates and low buy-back rates.

Through cogeneration, industries may be able to meet some, but not all, of their electric needs. When their own electricity falls short, they need back-up electricity from an investor-owned utility. But investor-owned utilities have discouraged cogeneration by charging high back-up rates to cogenerators. Buy-back rates also pose problems. Through cogeneration, industries may be able to meet more than their own electric needs. When that happens, they naturally would like to sell their excess electricity to an investor-owned utility. Here also, investor-owned utilities have discouraged cogeneration by offering low buy-back rates to cogenerators. The Federal Energy Regulatory Commission now requires state public utility commissions to ensure that back-up rates and buy-back rates are set at reasonable levels. However, there is much room for disagreement over what constitutes a reasonable rate. Also, public utility commissions have been slow to recognize the potential for cogeneration by commercial customers.[34]

A third area where public utility commissions could be doing much more is in utility company financing of energy conservation efforts. At the present time, most utility companies have a vested interest in energy consumption because reduced consumption means reduced earnings. One way to break that cycle would be to provide utility companies with incentives to promote conservation by giving them a chance to make a profit on home insulation investments. For example, the Oregon Public Utilities Commission allows its electric utilities to include the costs of interest-free home insulation loans to all-electric customers in the rate base. Thus, Pacific Power & Light and other Oregon electric companies are permitted to earn a profit on their home insulation investments. The Oregon Public Utilities Commission justifies this arrangement on the grounds that home insulation is properly viewed as an attractive alternative to new plant construction. In the words of one staff member, "It's cheaper to buy kilowatt-hours through insulation and weatherization than through thermal generating."

The Energy Conservation and Production Act (ECPA), approved by Congress in 1978, barred utilities from including conservation investments in their rate base and severely limited the ability of utilities to make loans for conservation efforts.[35] ECPA also prohibited utilities from installing conservation equipment. Apparently, members of Congress feared that utilities might engage in anticompetitive practices. However, the 1980 synfuels bill substantially eliminated these restrictions, while authorizing the Federal Trade Commission and the Department of Energy to prevent anticompetitive practices. Utilities may now finance conservation efforts, install conservation equipment through independent contractors, and include conservation investments in their rate base, if their public utility commission allows it. Nevertheless, with the exception of a few northwestern commissions, public utility commissions have moved very slowly to give utility companies a stake in the conservation of nonrenewable energy resources through home insulation. Overall, few public utility commissions have aggressively seized opportunities to promote energy conservation.

Can conservation solve our energy problems? According to the Harvard Business School Energy Project, the United States could reduce its energy consumption by 30 to 40 percent without reducing its standard of living.[36] However, that estimate may well be overly optimistic.[37] Even if the Harvard Energy Project is correct, energy conservation should not be viewed as a cost-free alternative. In the short run, energy conservation may mean even higher rates for those who are least able to afford it—namely, residential customers. If public utility commissions encourage business customers to shift their consumption from peak to off-peak hours, residential customers will be responsible for a larger share of peak demand, which is more expensive. Depending on how costs are allocated, this could result in higher residential rates. If public utility commissions encourage business customers to cogenerate, residential customers will be responsible for a larger share of the utility's fixed costs, which could translate into higher rates. If public utility commissions encourage residential customers to invest in home insulation, other residential customers may be asked to finance the utility's carrying charges.[38] In the long run, all of this may reduce the need for expensive and dangerous new power plants. In the short run, however, it may aggravate the already staggering rate burden of those who are least able to pay.

The Political Context

There are few obvious solutions to public utility regulatory problems. Instead, there is considerable disagreement over ends, means, and the relationship between the two. This situation is not unique to public utility regulation but rather is characteristic of a broader class of policy problems. When issues are highly complex and highly conflictual, policy dilemmas are extremely difficult, both technically and politically. Indeed, the political context in which regulation occurs is part of the problem, not because politics undermines policy analysis but because policy analysis depends on clear signals from those who have a legitimate stake in public policy. Unfortunately, those

signals are seldom clear when issues are both complex and conflictual.

Politicians, frightened by all the controversy, find that words
are safer than actions. As consensus evaporates, coalition-
building becomes more difficult and the urge to legislate di-
minishes. Regulators, who have no choice but to act, attempt to
justify their actions by emphasizing their expertise, accountability, or both. Regulators also fight for additional staff resources to help them cope with a growing regulatory burden.
Although regulatory commissioners often seek "acceptable"
solutions to policy problems, regulatory staff members often
seek "correct" solutions, although they frequently disagree on
which solutions are correct. The result is likely to be considerable ingenuity at the policy formulation stage, and considerable
frustration at the policy adoption stage. Regulated industries,
whose credibility is undermined by public criticism, seek to
legitimize their requests by inundating commissions with paper. Sometimes this strategy succeeds. When it fails, regulated
industries may threaten all sorts of dire possibilities—unreliable service, economic stagnation, even financial collapse—if
their demands are not met. Finally, citizens, who suddenly discover that much is at stake, demand better representation in the
regulatory process. They appeal for a "public interest" solution
to policy problems, although it soon becomes apparent that even
"public interest groups" disagree on where the public interest
lies.

These, then, are the basic outlines of the politics of public
utility regulation. First, legislative language establishes the
degree of discretion with which regulators make their choices.
Second, the method of selecting regulators determines who does
the choosing. Third, the professional skills of the regulatory
bureaucracy affect the quality of policy analysis. Fourth, the
ability of regulated industries to control the flow of information
establishes the adequacy of the record on which decisions are
based. Fifth, the scope of conflict determines the extent to which
diverse viewpoints are represented. In short, the politics of public utility regulation encompasses administrative discretion,
the quality of regulators, the professionalism of the regulatory

bureaucracy, the flow of information from regulated industries, and public access. Each of these variables is shaped by complexity and conflictuality. Yet each is also manipulable to some extent.

Legislative Delegation of Authority

As numerous scholars have pointed out, the legislative branch delegates substantial authority to administrative agencies.[39] Instead of adopting clear, specific, enforceable statutes, the legislative branch prefers vague mandates to serve "the public interest, convenience, or necessity" or to make decisions that fall within a "zone of reasonableness." The legislative branch has been especially reluctant to enact clear laws for regulatory agencies which, in contrast to social benefit agencies (such as Health and Human Services or the Veterans Administration), impose penalties for which legislators would prefer not to be blamed.

The failure of the legislative branch to adopt clear statutes is particularly notable in the case of older "economic" regulatory agencies, as opposed to newer "social" regulatory agencies. In delegating authority to social regulatory agencies, the legislative branch has established certain standards that must be met, within the boundaries of administrative discretion. For example, the Environmental Protection Agency must meet specific deadlines in achieving clean air and clean water, both of which are defined in relatively specific terms. In delegating authority to economic regulatory agencies, however, the legislative branch has merely asserted that key values must be weighed by administrators. Public utility commissions, for instance, must strike a balance between investors' right to a fair return and consumers' interest in low rates. The precise nature of that delicate balance is left to the discretion of the regulatory agency.

Despite the growing salience of utilities issues, state legislatures have shown little or no interest in adopting specific statutes that circumscribe the behavior of public utility commissions. Although many utility-related bills are introduced at the beginning of a legislative session, very few survive. Of those that do eventually secure passage, few are significant. There is much huffing and puffing, of course, but not much consequential activity. For example, a study of the Maryland State Legislature revealed that 215 utility-related bills were introduced between 1976 and 1979. Of these, only 33 were passed, and only 2 could be described as major pieces of legislation.[40]

With growing public interest in utilities issues, there has been a tremendous increase in legislative rhetoric. There has also been an increase in oversight by legislative committees specializing in energy policy, environmental policy, or administrative rules and regulations. Yet there has been very little collective action. When issues are extremely complex and extremely conflictual, legislators are likely to conclude that retrospective criticism by individual legislators is safer than prospective action by the legislature as a whole.

Nor is this situation as pathological as it may seem. For the most part, public utilities issues are best resolved by specialized agencies which have the expertise to deal with them. The determination of an appropriate rate of return for a regulated utility requires an understanding of economics and finance. The determination of appropriate policies concerning tax payments and plant depreciation requires an understanding of accounting. The determination of appropriate reserve margins requires an understanding of electrical engineering. Under such circumstances, legislative activism could result in what Jones describes as "speculative augmentation" or "policy beyond capability."[41] Although legislators sometimes go overboard, substantial delegation of legislative authority is a necessity in regulatory policy.

Ironically, those issues best addressed by the legislative branch in theory are least likely to be addressed in practice. The legislative branch, whose explicit purpose is to allocate resources through law, is clearly better able to resolve broad questions of social equity than a specialized institution designed to administer or interpret the law in a particular policy domain. Yet, as Lowi has pointed out, the legislative branch is especially loath to confront "redistributive" issues that approximate a zero-sum game.[42] Such issues, which pit the rich against the poor, are extremely divisive and erosive of political support. If one assumes that legislators are committed first and foremost to the goal of reelection, such activity by legislators is highly unlikely.

In the public utilities area, this means that state legislatures are unlikely to address policy dilemmas caused by the impact of high utility rates on the poor. Given legislative inertia, public utility regulators must either ignore social equity considerations altogether (a callous choice) or incorporate such considerations into pricing decisions (which might be deemed discriminatory pricing by the courts). This has become a shameless shell game, with dire consequences for the poor, especially in Frostbelt states, where adequate energy in the wintertime is essential to survival. Although there are compelling reasons for the legislative branch to delegate complex, technical problems to public utility commissions, there is no excuse for legislative failure to address questions of social justice.

The Selection of Commissioners

A persistent criticism of regulatory agencies over the years has been that the quality of regulators could be much better.[43] Cushman summarizes the problem succinctly: "Ours may be a government of laws and not of men, but the success of the regulatory commission rests with the men who compose it."[44] Regrettably, the regulatory appointments process has often been viewed more as an opportunity to dispense patronage than as an opportunity to appoint high-minded public servants to office. A U.S. Senate committee study of the Federal Communications Commission and the Federal Trade Commission (FTC), for instance, revealed an appointments process favorable to mediocre office seekers. The U.S. Senate committee concluded that the regulatory appointments process "tends to eliminate the person with talents for imaginative, aggressive regulation."[45]

In eleven states, public utility commissioners are popularly elected, either statewide or by district. In most states, however, public utility commissioners are appointed by the governor. In the past, such appointments often reeked of spoils system politics. Public utility commission posts were widely regarded as sinecures, and loyalty was the litmus test for appointment. Today, in contrast, it is widely recognized that a public utility regulator needs the patience of Job, the wisdom of Solomon, and the optimism of Sisyphus. Although few contemporary regulators measure up to such standards, the quality of commission appointees has improved sharply in recent years. Many of the new appointees are skilled professionals with impressive credentials. A growing number of commissioners, for example, are economists or specialists in public finance.[46]

Nevertheless, as utilities issues have become more conflictual, commission appointments have become more controversial. To many, the problem is not competence but accountability. One commonly suggested solution to this problem is direct popular election of commissioners. The presumed advantage of direct election is that it promotes responsiveness to the public as a whole, rather than to special interest groups. However, direct popular election of commissioners encourages behavior that trivializes the concept of accountability. Like members of Congress, elected public utility commissioners curry the favor of constituents through casework and other responses to particularized demands. In Mississippi, for example, popularly elected commissioners spend much of their time listening to individual constituents complain about their own private misfortunes. Not long ago, a woman called because her washing machine had broken down. She was promptly connected to one of the commissioners, who patiently explained that, although the commission lacked jurisdiction over washing machines, he hoped she would call again. This pattern confirms Fenno's observation that "constituents may want good access as much as good policy from their representative."[47] In Georgia, where the commissioners are elected, similar problems arise. Recently a well-publicized commission meeting was canceled when the commission could not obtain a quorum to conduct business. Commissioner Billy Lovett, who had previously agreed to attend the meeting, changed his mind when he received an invitation to address some constituents in Watkinsville.[48]

These examples suggest that electoral accountability manifests itself more in constituent services than in public policy decisions. Yet the direct election of commissioners is likely to have public policy consequences as well. In particular, it encourages extremism, sometimes of the left, sometimes of the right. In states where public utilities issues are very salient, elected commissioners may pursue short-term consumer interests at the expense of energy independence, the financial integrity of utility companies, environmental protection, and the long-term interests of consumers. In states where public utilities issues are not very salient, elected commissioners may rubber-stamp rate hikes because their "popular mandate" protects them from the criticisms of citizens' groups and reporters. In studying congressional behavior, Fenno has observed that "members of Congress feel a good bit more accountable . . . to some constituents than to others."[49] In particular, members of Congress are often more accountable to their "reelection" constituency (or a subset of that constituency) than to their geographic constituency. Similarly, elected public utility commissioners are often accountable to very few people through public policy decisions because they are accountable to so many people through constituent services.

In contrast to elected commissioners, appointed commissioners devote more time to policy analysis, and less time to constituent relations. However, some fear that regulators appointed by the governor are likely to march to his drumbeat. This fear seems unfounded. To begin with, the governor's incentives to interfere with public utility regulation are weak. Public utilities issues are complicated, messy, and controversial. In the words of one regulator, "There's almost nothing to be gained by a governor getting involved." Besides, there is a long-standing taboo against gubernatorial interference in the affairs of independent regulatory agencies. As Fesler observed many years ago, the "independent" regulatory commissions, though rarely independent from outside pressure groups, have in fact been very independent of their political sovereigns, including the governor and the state legislature.[50] According to Wilson, this is still true today: "Whoever first wished to see regulation carried on by quasi-independent agencies and commissioners has had his boldest dreams come true."[51]

Bureaucratic Professionalism

Independent though they may be of both the chief executive and the legislative branch, regulatory commissions nevertheless depend on both for appropriations. This can have important implications for the level of agency funding—and for the level of bureaucratic professionalism. More than a decade ago, the Ash Council argued that regulatory agencies lack sufficient resources to deal with the problems that confront them.[52] Several years later, Welborn concluded that the problem remained: "The budgets of regulatory agencies are small and tight. . . . Appropriations have increased in recent years, yet the increments have not been equal to rising work loads."[53] Certainly, the capacity of the bureaucracy to deal with difficult problems depends in large part on its resources. Technical expertise is needed if the bureaucracy is to confront complex issues with timeliness and precision. Legal expertise is needed if the bureaucracy is to confront conflictual issues effectively in formal agency proceedings and in court.

Yet more than organizational size is at issue here. Each profession brings with it a peculiar world view, a set of predispositions, and certain blind spots. In Mosher's words, "Those within each profession—or many of them—have some common ways of perceiving and structuring problems and of attacking and solving them; they are likely to share their views of the world and of the place of their profession in it; they are likely also to share a common, and more or less unique, bundle of technical skills, knowledge, and vocabulary."[54] Thus, if the level of resources determines a bureaucracy's ability to cope with different kinds of problems, the mix of professionals determines how it copes with such problems.

Although completely reliable data are not available, the hiring practices of public utility commissions appear to have changed during the 1970s. In general, public utility commissions tended to hire more economists (to develop rate structures based on marginal cost pricing principles) and more lawyers (to preside over rate hearings and draft legally defensible opinions). In contrast, commissions were less likely to hire accountants and engineers.[55] Although these developments created conflicts between professions in some states, such disagreements were muted by adroit political leadership and by bureaucratic expansionism.[56] Since public utility commissions were expanding, it was possible to hire new professionals without displacing older professionals.

During the 1970s, public utility commission budgets increased dramatically. Five years after the Arab oil embargo of 1973, commission budgets had doubled in California, Illinois, Florida, and many other states.[57] One reason for this phenomenal growth was the sudden emergence of complex, conflictual issues that demanded urgent attention. Another reason was that public utility commissions were less dependent on general revenues than other state agencies. Instead, they relied heavily on special fees paid by utility companies. Thus, when state politicians began to slash agency budgets in order to reduce taxes, they felt less compelled to reduce public utility commission budgets.

Although the capacity of public utility commission staffs to deal with troublesome policy problems clearly grew in the 1970s, the regulatory burden of the commissions also grew. As economies of scale vanished and costs increased, utility companies filed frequent rate hike requests to prevent their revenues from eroding. As early as 1971, many commissions were in deep trouble. In Joskow's words, "many state commissions found themselves extremely overburdened with pending rate of return cases. . . . To compound the problems even further, regulatory agencies found that once they had processed a rate of return case and established new prices for the firm, a new price increase request was filed almost immediately."[58] The situation worsened as the number of rate cases increased dramatically. Despite the augmentation of staff resources, commissions were besieged and sometimes overwhelmed. The problem was exacerbated in some respects by the enormous resources of utility companies, whose information was detailed and helpful, but suspect.

Industry Influence

A number of scholars have argued that regulated industries dominate regulatory policy-making.[59] Indeed, some have suggested that regulatory agencies are actually "captured" by the industries they are supposed to regulate.[60] These criticisms apply much more to older "economic" regulatory agencies, such as public utility commissions, than to newer "social" regulatory agencies, such as the Environmental Protection Agency and the Occupational Safety and Health Administration. The social regulatory agencies regulate so many industries that they are not easily dominated by one. The economic regulatory agencies are more susceptible to industrial domination because their jurisdiction is much more limited. As critics have pointed out, the "independence" of independent regulatory commissions sometimes means independence from everyone but the regulated industries. In McConnell's words, "Originally, independence was conceived quite simply as a matter of independence from partisan politics. . . . Unfortunately, what was achieved was not freedom from all politics, but freedom only from party and popular politics. The politics of industry and administration remained."[61]

Nevertheless, it is easy to exaggerate the grip of regulated industries on regulatory agencies. For example, some have argued that many regulators are overly sympathetic to regulated industries because they used to work for such industries. According to Common Cause, over half of the Nixon-Ford appointees to federal regulatory agencies entered federal service through the "revolving door" between regulated industries and the regulatory agency.[62] This argument breaks down, though, for two reasons. First, Common Cause's overly broad definition of prior employment (encompassing people who once represented a regulated industry indirectly through a law firm or consulting firm) substantially exaggerates the extent of the revolving door phenomenon. Second, the impact of a regulatory commissioner's employment background on his or her voting behavior, though noticeable, is rather weak in comparison to such factors as political party identification.[63] It is possible, of course, that regulators are affected more by the prospect of future employment with a regulated industry than by the actual experience of prior employment with such an industry. It is also possible that agency staff members, whose actions are less subject to public scrutiny, are more likely than commissioners to succumb to "revolving door" pressures. Until such evidence is forthcoming, however, the revolving door seems a weak explanation for regulatory agency performance.

If regulated industries dominate the regulatory process, it is through the control of information, not personnel. As Cramton has noted, government institutions are highly responsive, but only to the inputs they receive.[64] Those inputs—in the form of legal briefs, statistical compilations, feasibility studies, and customer surveys—come primarily from regulated industries, which spend enormous amounts of money on formal presentations in regulatory agency proceedings. According to a U.S. Senate report, AT&T spent $1 million in a single year on one FCC rate case; eleven airlines spent $2.8 million in a single year for outside legal fees incurred in Civil Aeronautics Board rate cases.[65] Regulated industry officials also frequently communicate informally with regulatory officials. A Common Cause study of federal regulatory commissioners' office contacts revealed that 46 percent of such contacts were with regulated industry representatives, while only 4 percent were with representatives of public interest groups or individual citizens (the remaining contacts were with members of the press, congressional officials, foreign visitors, and others).[66] These contacts, both formal and informal, enhance the influence of regulated industry officials.

Public utility regulators probably have fewer informal contacts with regulated industry officials than do their federal counterparts. Most public utility commission decisions take place within the context of rate cases—quasi-judicial proceedings in which ex parte communications, or off-the-record contacts, are normally restricted. Wisconsin's Administrative Procedure and Review Act, for instance, prohibits ex parte communications between a party to a contested case and a hearing examiner "or any other official or employe of the agency who is involved in the decision-making process." When such an ex parte communication occurs, the hearing examiner or agency official is required to place on the record the actual submission, if written, or a summary thereof, if oral, as well as a written or oral summary of responses made.[67] Such restrictions make it very risky for utility company officials to engage in ex parte contacts during a rate case.

In other respects, however, utility companies dominate the flow of information to public utility commissions. In rate cases, utility companies spend enormous sums of money on legal advice, technical assistance, and clerical support. In three recent California rate cases, for example, one company spent between

$300,000 and $400,000; a second spent $500,000; and a third spent $2 million. Aided by such expenditures, utility companies furnish voluminous amounts of information to public utility commissions, including demand forecasts, supply projections, cost of capital estimates, and many other special exhibits. Unfortunately, few public utility commission staffs have the time or expertise to challenge utility company information—for example, by developing alternative energy demand forecasts of their own. As a result, public utility commissions are often overwhelmed by the information utility companies provide.

Public Access

It is widely acknowledged that certain interests tend to be underrepresented in regulatory policy-making.[68] This argument has three variations: (1) certain interests are unlikely to crystallize into groups; (2) certain groups are unlikely to participate in the policy-making process; and (3) certain participants in the policy-making process are unlikely to be effective. Underrepresented interests, though diverse,[69] are thought to include consumers and the poor.

Olson, for example, has argued that consumers are less likely to be represented in the policy-making process than producers.[70] Members of small groups, such as employees of regulated firms, have ample incentives to participate in policy-making or to finance such participation. From their vantage point, the benefits of participation (higher wages, job security, and so forth) outweigh the costs (lobbying and litigation expenses). This is especially true when costs can be shared with investors, consumers, or both. In contrast, members of a large group, such as consumers, lack incentives to coalesce or participate. The costs of collective action are too high to warrant involvement by anyone who does not have a strong economic stake in the outcome. The benefits of successful collective action are so diffuse that everyone will share in them, whether they have participated or not. Thus, the logic of collective action favors small groups over large groups, producers over consumers, regulated industries over the general public.

The poor also face serious obstacles. Although the poor have stronger incentives to organize than other consumers, they have difficulty maintaining an effective organization. Because they have been powerless for so long, the poor are wary of suggestions for organizational control or interorganizational coordination. Consequently, they find it difficult to manage internal conflict or to form a coalition with other groups.[71] Even more than other underrepresented interests, the poor lack financial resources. To overcome this handicap, they often resort to protest, but protest is seldom an effective political resource. As Lipsky has noted, "Relatively powerless groups cannot use protest with a high probability of success."[72]

Despite these obstacles, citizens' groups have become increasingly active and important participants in the public utility regulatory process. The overall level of public participation in public utility commission proceedings rose sharply in the 1970s, as a wide variety of citizens' groups intervened on behalf of consumers, the poor, and other underrepresented interests. Some citizens' groups, distressed by the impact of new power plants on the environment, supported energy conservation as an alternative to new construction. Other citizens' groups, upset by steadily rising rates, pleaded for rate relief. Parallel to this development, some state legislatures responded to public concern by institutionalizing public representation in the form of an office of consumer counsel or a consumer protection board. Although such offices already existed in some states (Maryland and Indiana, for example), the mid-1970s witnessed a sharp increase in the number of state public advocacy offices,[73] which were empowered to represent consumers in public utility commission proceedings and, in most instances, the courts.

In retrospect, it seems clear that the 1970s ushered in a new era of public utility regulation—an era of public salience, public discontent, and public advocacy. Nevertheless, it is important to qualify this observation in two respects. First, the level of public advocacy in public utility commission proceedings varies dramatically from state to state, as we shall see in the next chapter; second, the effectiveness of public advocacy varies from issue to issue and from group to group, as we shall see in subsequent chapters. Thus, the "publicizing" of public utility regulation in the 1970s was neither uniform nor uniformly effective.

Instead, it may be described as a partial and partially successful process of adaptation to the exacerbation of old policy problems and the emergence of new ones.

CONCLUSION

Over the past decade, utilities issues have become much more complex and much more conflictual. Energy issues have become especially exasperating. If regulators allow rates to increase dramatically, they impose a terrible burden on lower-class and middle-class consumers; if they resist rate hike requests, they run the risk of power failures, bankruptcies, or both. If regulators encourage reliance on coal or nuclear power, they invite certain threats to public health and safety; if they encourage reliance on solar energy, they entrust our future to an unproven technology with little likelihood of solving short-term problems. Energy conservation seems to be the best solution to these dilemmas, but it requires consumers to make adjustments they may not be willing to make unless high prices compel them to do so. And that brings us back to the rate problem again.

As utilities issues have become more complex and more conflictual, the politics of public utility regulation has changed. Legislators and governors have become more aware and more vocal, although they have avoided significant collective action. The expertise of public utility commissioners has improved, although their accountability has been questioned. The size and professional composition of the regulatory bureaucracy has changed, with economists and lawyers playing an increasingly important role as public utility commissions have grown. Utilities, facing new economic and political challenges, have generated more paper than ever before. Most significantly, the scope of conflict has expanded. Public participation in public utility commission proceedings—through citizens' groups—has increased. Representation of consumer interests by state officials has also increased. Although these trends have not been across the board, they constitute the single most important change in public utility regulatory politics in years. Why is public advocacy high in some states, low in others? Why do people participate in the public utility regulatory process, despite the dearth of selective incentives? What are the purposes of public advocates? What are the structural characteristics of public advocacy organizations? These are some of the questions that will be addressed next.

: 2 :

Grassroots Advocates and Proxy Advocates: The Quest for Accountability

Democratic theorists have long argued that the public needs to be represented in the political process.[1] According to some contemporary theorists, representation through the electoral process is enough.[2] According to others, however, public representation must be an ongoing process if meaningful accountability is to be achieved.[3] There are at least three rationales for public advocacy on a more or less continuous basis. First, it is argued that citizens have a right to be heard on issues that affect their lives. Second, it is argued that public input helps decisionmakers to reach better decisions. Third, it is argued that representation promotes public acceptance of controversial decisions. In short, public advocacy is thought to improve the fairness of the decision-making process, the quality of decisions, and the legitimacy of political authorities.

On the other hand, public representation beyond the electoral process poses potential threats. Indeed, a number of objections have been raised to public advocacy in administrative proceedings.[4] First, it is said that public advocates oversimplify technical issues by resorting to demagogic appeals to the general public and by peddling simplistic remedies. Second, it is said that public advocates disrupt the administrative process through delays aimed at preventing the timely resolution of policy controversies. Third, it is said that public advocates are not truly accountable to the constituencies they claim to represent. To sum up, public advocates are thought to oversimplify policy problems, disrupt the administrative process, and misrepresent their claims to authority.

Although the question of public representation is troublesome enough in most issue areas, it is especially troublesome in an area as complex as that of public utility regulation. Many issues determined by public utility commissions—concerning a proper rate of return on equity, construction work in progress, marginal cost pricing, and so on—are extremely technical. Pitkin has suggested that public consultation may be less appropriate in areas where technical expertise is involved.[5] Yet, as Nelkin and Pollak have pointed out, even technical decisions involve "substantive issues" which "embody highly controversial political and social values."[6] To leave such decisions to "experts" is to guarantee that the values of experts will predominate. Under such circumstances we must strike a balance between competence and participation. We cannot leave technical decisions entirely up to political elites or scientific experts without input from the public. On the other hand, public advocates must be knowledgeable if they are to contribute to sound decisions.

FORMS OF PUBLIC ADVOCACY

The goals of participation and competence are promoted in different ways by the two most widely used nonelectoral methods for achieving public representation in public utility commission proceedings. The first involves direct participation before the regulatory agency by organized citizens' groups. This approach emphasizes the need for citizens to speak for themselves rather than through intermediaries. It may be referred to as a "grassroots advocacy" approach, because it relies on grassroots citizens' groups to advocate underrepresented interests. Grassroots advocacy embodies what Dennis Thompson calls "the principle of participation" in that it actually brings the public into the policy-making process as participants.[7]

The second method involves representation before the regulatory agency by government officials from another agency who are paid to represent underrepresented interests, such as those of consumers. This approach emphasizes the need for persuasive spokespeople for underrepresented interests. It may be described as a "proxy advocacy" approach, because it relies on government officials to serve as proxies for underrepresented interests. Proxy advocacy embodies what Thompson calls "the principle of competence" in that it engages competent public officials to make a convincing case on behalf of the public.[8]

Grassroots advocacy and proxy advocacy have both become increasingly important features of the public utility regulatory process. How do patterns of public advocacy vary from state to state? Do public advocates participate in similar cases? Do they pursue similar goals? Why is public advocacy high in some states but not others? What impels people to choose public advocacy as a career? What incentives do public advocates have to continue their involvement? These are some of the questions to be addressed in this chapter. As Pitkin has written, "A representative government requires that there be machinery for the expression of the wishes of the represented, and that the government respond to these wishes unless there are good reasons to the contrary."[9] The purpose of this chapter is to assess the machinery that exists for expressing the wishes of the represented. Subsequent chapters will explore the extent to which government responds to those wishes, as opposed to others.

Variations Across States

How do patterns of public advocacy in public utility commission proceedings vary from state to state? To answer that question, I conducted a mailed questionnaire survey of all 188 state public utility commissioners during January and February 1979. The commissioners were asked to furnish estimates (on a scale of 1 to 10) of the level of activity by different types of intervenors (including grassroots advocates and proxy advocates) in their state's electric, natural gas, and telephone cases during the 1974–1978 period. Responses were obtained from 83.5 percent of the commissioners after one letter and a reminder letter three weeks later. At least one response was obtained from each of the fifty states and the District of Columbia. Within each state, commissioners' estimates were averaged to create a single estimate. An estimate greater than the midpoint of the scale (5.5) was defined as high activity; an estimate lower than the midpoint was defined as low activity.[10]

As table 3 indicates, public advocacy patterns are strikingly diverse. The questionnaire survey reveals that there are four types of states, relatively equal in number: (1) grassroots advocacy states—in approximately 20 percent of the states, grassroots advocates are very active but proxy advocates are not; (2) proxy advocacy states—in approximately 20 percent of the

Table 3
Activity Levels of Intervenors Before
Public Utility Commissions

Proxy Advocates

	Low	*High*
High	Arizona California Colorado Delaware Idaho Illinois Maine South Carolina Texas West Virginia Wisconsin	Arkansas Connecticut District of Columbia Hawaii Maryland Massachusetts Michigan Minnesota Missouri New Mexico New York North Carolina Rhode Island Vermont Virginia
Low	Alaska Iowa Kansas Louisiana Mississippi Nebraska Nevada North Dakota Oklahoma Oregon South Dakota Tennessee Utah Wyoming	Alabama Florida Georgia Indiana Kentucky Montana New Hampshire New Jersey Ohio Pennsylvania Washington

Grassroots Advocates

states, proxy advocates are very active but grassroots advocates are not; (3) dual advocacy states—in approximately 30 percent of the states, both grassroots advocates and proxy advocates are very active; and (4) acquiescent states—in approximately 30 percent of the states, neither grassroots advocates nor proxy advocates are very active.

How valid are commissioners' estimates of intervenor activity levels? That question has been answered by gathering public utility commission documents in a stratified sample of twelve states, including three in each of the four quadrants. The states were chosen by merging nominations from a panel of five experts[11] with estimates from commissioners in all fifty states and the District of Columbia. Each panelist recommended three states thought to fit each of the four quadrants. The three states mentioned most frequently by the panel for each of the four categories were tentatively included in the sample. The panel's classification of states was then compared with the commissioners' estimates. Where discrepancies existed,[12] states upon which the panel and the commission agreed were substituted for the panel's top choices. This process yielded the following sample of twelve states: three grassroots advocacy states (California, Illinois, Wisconsin); three proxy advocacy states (Florida, Georgia, New Jersey); three dual advocacy states (Massachusetts, Michigan, New York); and three acquiescent states (Mississippi, North Dakota, Wyoming).

In each of the twelve states, opinions and orders for major electric, natural gas, and telephone rate cases during the 1974–1978 period were obtained. A major rate case was defined as one involving a utility company that served more than 5 percent of the state's residential customers.[13] For each state, I calculated the percentage of major rate cases in which different types of public advocates intervened. Comparisons of actual and estimated activity levels confirmed the validity of the commissioners' estimates. The Pearson's correlation coefficient was .878 for grassroots advocacy activity, .964 for proxy advocacy activity. Thus, estimated activity levels can be used with considerable confidence in their validity.[14]

Although aggregate figures are useful indicators of overall activity levels, they do disguise two important facts: (1) the level of participation by public advocates varies by type of case; and (2) the level of participation by public advocates has changed over time.

As table 4 indicates, public advocates are more likely to participate in electric cases than in other kinds of cases. This is altogether understandable. As noted in chapter 1, electric rates rose much more sharply than local telephone rates during the 1970s. Natural gas rates also increased dramatically, but many Americans heat their homes by other means (such as oil or electricity). Also, the generation of electricity raises especially troublesome health and safety questions. Both grassroots advocates and proxy advocates are more likely to participate in electric cases. In other respects, however, they behave a bit differently. Whereas grassroots advocates are somewhat more likely to participate in natural gas cases than in telephone cases, proxy advocates are somewhat more likely to participate in telephone cases than in natural gas cases. It should be noted, though, that the number of natural gas cases far exceeds the number of telephone cases. Thus, although proxy advocates participate in a greater proportion of telephone cases than natural gas cases,

Table 4
Public Advocacy in P.U.C. Proceedings by
Year and Type of Case

	1974	1975	1976	1977	1978	1979	*Average*
Grassroots advocates							
Electric	55.6%	58.8%	52.6%	56.0%	94.7%	71.4%	63.4%
cases	(15/27)	(20/34)	(10/19)	(14/25)	(18/19)	(15/21)	(92/145)
Gas	40.9%	52.8%	42.3%	58.8%	60.9%	53.8%	51.1%
cases	(9/22)	(19/36)	(11/26)	(10/17)	(14/23)	(7/13)	(70/137)
Telephone	60.0%	35.3%	40.0%	55.6%	42.9%	57.1%	47.3%
cases	(6/10)	(6/17)	(6/15)	(10/18)	(3/7)	(4/7)	(35/74)
Proxy advocates							
Electric	33.3%	38.2%	52.6%	44.0%	68.4%	66.7%	48.3%
cases	(9/27)	(13/34)	(10/19)	(11/25)	(13/19)	(14/21)	(70/145)
Gas	13.6%	36.1%	26.9%	29.4%	52.2%	53.8%	34.3%
cases	(3/22)	(13/36)	(7/26)	(5/17)	(12/23)	(7/13)	(47/137)
Telephone	30.0%	29.4%	33.3%	38.9%	28.6%	71.4%	37.8%
cases	(3/10)	(5/17)	(5/15)	(7/18)	(2/7)	(5/7)	(28/74)

they participate in a greater absolute number of natural gas cases. In this sense, they resemble grassroots advocates.

Table 4 also reveals that public advocates have become increasingly active in the public utility regulatory process. These changes are especially dramatic in the case of proxy advocates. In 1974, proxy advocates participated in 33.3 percent of the electric cases, 13.6 percent of the natural gas cases, and 30.0 percent of the telephone cases. Five years later, proxy advocates participated in 66.7 percent of the electric cases, 53.8 percent of the natural gas cases, and 71.4 percent of the telephone cases. Grassroots advocates also increased their activity during this period but more gradually, partly because grassroots advocates were already rather active in 1974. Perhaps these differences in the evolution of grassroots advocacy and proxy advocacy reflect more fundamental differences in the purposes of these alternative forms of public advocacy. To explore that possibility, it is necessary to examine the concepts of grassroots advocacy and proxy advocacy in greater detail.

Grassroots Advocacy

A grassroots advocacy group may be defined as a private organization that promotes interests unrelated to the occupations of its members. Expressed a bit differently, a grassroots advocacy group is nongovernmental, nonbusiness, and nonlabor, although it may receive funds from governmental, business, or labor sources. A grassroots advocacy group may attempt to represent the entire public, the majority, the least advantaged, or an even smaller segment of the public. For that matter, it may attempt to represent more affluent members of the community.

The concept of a grassroots advocacy group, though similar to that of a public interest group, is not identical with it. Schattschneider defines a public interest group as one that promotes "common interests shared by all or by substantially all members of the community."[15] However, many of the citizens' groups that participate in administrative, legislative, and judicial proceedings do not purport to speak for the public as a whole. Instead, they only claim to speak for a particular constituency—the poor, the elderly, the handicapped, and so forth. Because these groups are often underrepresented in policy-making, they have much more in common with public interest groups than with special interest groups. Yet use of the "public interest group" concept requires that certain underprivileged groups be classified as special interests.

The concept of a grassroots advocacy group bypasses this problem since it does not require one to assess how many people are likely to benefit from a particular policy. Thus, the concept of a grassroots advocacy group is considerably broader than the concept of a public interest group. A citizens' group that favors lower electric rates for the elderly is not a public interest grcup, but it is a grassroots advocacy group. A citizens' group that favors lower electric rates for all-electric customers (a relatively small proportion of total customers) is not a public interest group, but it is a grassroots advocacy group. A legal aid society, which represents poor people, is not a public interest group, but it is a grassroots advocacy group.[16]

The concept of a grassroots advocacy organization is sufficiently broad to encompass a diverse range of private groups other than business and labor groups. However, it is too broad to capture important differences among such organizations. What kinds of grassroots advocacy groups participate in public utility commission proceedings? Interviews with grassroots advocates in the stratified sample of twelve states reveal that four types of groups predominate: environmental groups, antinuclear groups, consumer groups, and low-income groups.

1. Environmental groups include such national organizations as the Environmental Defense Fund, the Natural Resources Defense Council, the Sierra Club, and Friends of the Earth. They also include local groups, such as Wisconsin's Environmental Decade and the West Branch Conservation Society (New York). These organizations support environmental protection and energy conservation. They often oppose the construction of new power plants, and they favor rate structures likely to discourage energy consumption. They also support greater emphasis on renewable energy sources.

2. Antinuclear groups include such organizations as the Clamshell Alliance (New England), the Badger Safe Energy Alliance (Wisconsin), and Mid-Hudson Nuclear Opponents (New York). As their names imply, these organizations oppose

the development of nuclear power. Usually, they oppose a particular power plant or the nuclear power proposals of a particular company. Their stated reasons for opposition include both safety and economic considerations.

3. Consumer groups include such organizations as Toward Utility Rate Normalization (California), the Illinois Public Action Council, Mass Fair Share (Massachusetts), the Michigan Citizens Lobby, and Long Island Consumer Action (New York). These organizations strive to keep residential utility rates as low as possible without a reduction in the quality of service. They oppose utility rate hike requests and challenge various expenses utility companies propose to pass on to ratepayers, including construction work in progress, advertising expenses, and "phantom" taxes.[17] They also argue that residential consumers should pay less and business consumers should pay more.

4. Low-income groups include neighborhood associations (such as the South Austin Coalition Community Council in Chicago), senior citizens' groups (such as the New Jersey Federation of Senior Citizens), coalitions of the poor and elderly (the Wyoming Energy Advocacy Coalition), and numerous legal aid societies. They support special protection for the poor through customer service regulations and rate designs that favor the low-income consumer. They advocate less austere security deposit, late payment, and disconnection policies that recognize the special cash flow problems of the poor. Some also support lifeline rates, which charge less per unit for small amounts of energy than for larger amounts. A lifeline rate is a special kind of inverted rate,[18] designed to help the poor or the elderly meet essential energy needs.

Although grassroots advocacy groups have separate identities, they often work closely together in public utility commission cases. There is, for example, a natural affinity between environmental groups and antinuclear groups, both of which are willing to countenance higher rates for the sake of public health and safety. There is also a natural affinity between consumer groups and low-income groups, which are troubled by the impact of rate inflation on consumers generally and the poor in particular. They are more willing to tolerate some threats to health and safety. They are also less enthusiastic about energy conservation through higher prices.

These lines of cleavage are common, but they sometimes dissolve. Many of the campus-based Public Interest Research Groups (PIRGs), for example, support safe, clean energy at low rates, with special protection for the very poor. In this respect, PIRGs have much in common with all four types of citizens' groups. They believe that a balance must be struck between energy that is safe and clean, and rates that are fair and reasonable. PIRGs also represent the specific interests of their student constituents from time to time. For example, the Public Interest Research Group in Michigan PIRGIM) opposed a Michigan Bell Telephone proposal for directory assistance charges. Such charges, PIRGIM contended, would discriminate against college students, who are more transient than other members of society and who are thus less likely to be listed in a telephone directory.

Although some grassroots advocacy groups, such as PIRGs, cannot be categorized, most can. Table 5 provides a classification of grassroots advocacy groups that intervened in public utility commission proceedings during a recent one-year period in the sample of twelve states.[19] The groups were categorized on the basis of the stated priorities, values, and activities of grassroots

Table 5
Grassroots Advocacy Groups
(N = 72)

Environmental Groups (N = 7)

Friends of the Earth (Calif.)
Environmental Defense Fund (Calif.)
Natural Resources Defense Council (Calif.)
Citizens for a Better Environment (Ill., Wis.)
Sierra Club (N.Y.)
West Branch Conservation Assn. (N.Y.)
Wisconsin's Environmental Decade

Antinuclear Groups (N = 10)

People Against Nuclear Power (Calif.)
Georgians Against Nuclear Energy
Clamshell Alliance (Mass.)
Plymouth County Nuclear Information Committee (Mass.)
New Bedford Safe Energy Alliance (Mass.)

Table 5 continued

Great Lakes Energy Alliance (Mich.)
Rochester Safe Energy Alliance (N.Y.)
Mid-Hudson Nuclear Opponents (N.Y.)
Safe Haven (Wis.)
Badger Safe Energy Alliance (Wis.)

Consumer Groups (N = 21)

Consumers Lobby Against Monopolies (Calif.)
Toward Utility Rate Normalization (Calif.)
Coalition for Economic Survival (Calif.)
Florida ACORN
Georgia Consumer Center
Illinois Public Action Council
Southern Counties Action Movement (Ill.)
Organization of the Northeast (Ill.)
Mass Fair Share (Mass.)
Michigan Coalition on Utilities and Energy
Michigan Citizens Lobby
Long Island Consumer Action (N.Y.)
Genessee Valley Peoples Power Coalition (N.Y.)
Concerned Consumers of Mid-Hudson (N.Y.)
People Outraged with Energy Rates (N.Y.)
New York State Peoples Power Coalition
Long Island Ratepayers Assn. (N.Y.)
New York Consumer Assembly
Citizens Committee for Metroplan (Wis.)
Citizens Committee for Better Telephone Service of Delafield (Wis.)
Wisconsin's Citizens' Telephone Coalition

Low-Income Groups (N = 23)

Seniors for Political Action (Calif.)
Seniors for Legislative Issues (Calif.)
Miami Legal Services (Fla.)
Georgia Poverty Rights Organization
Operation PUSH (Ill.)
South Austin Coalition Community Council (Ill.)
Legal Assistance Foundation of Chicago (Ill.)
Northwest Community Organization (Ill.)
Land of Lincoln Legal Assistance Foundation (Ill.)
Mass Law Reform Institute (Mass.)
Franklin Community Action Corp. (Mass.)
Wayne County Legal Services (Mich.)
New Jersey Federation of Senior Citizens
Legal Aid Society of New York
Brooklyn Legal Services (N.Y.)
Westchester Legal Services (N.Y.)
Public Utility Law Project (N.Y.)
Legal Aid of North Dakota

Table 5 continued

North Dakota Community Action Assn.
Project Involve (Wis.)
Legal Action of Wisconsin
Legal Services of Laramie County (Wyo.)
Wyoming Energy Advocacy Coalition

Other (N = 11)

Deaf Counseling Advocacy Referral Agency (Calif.)
Campaign for Economic Democracy (Calif.)
California Solar Energy Assn.
California PIRG
Public Interest Economics West (Calif.)
SUNRAE (Calif.)
Mass. PIRG
PIRGIM (Mich.)
New Jersey PIRG
NYPIRG (N.Y.)
Center for Public Representation (Wis.)

advocates. This classification of grassroots advocacy groups yields three unexpected findings.

First, the number of active grassroots advocacy groups is surprisingly large in a number of states. In California, at least fifteen grassroots advocacy groups intervened in California Public Service Commission cases within one year. In New York, at least sixteen grassroots advocacy groups intervened in New York Public Service Commission cases within one year. Even in smaller states, the number of active grassroots advocacy groups is often quite high. In Massachusetts, for example, at least seven grassroots advocacy groups intervened in Massachusetts Department of Public Utilities cases within one year. These findings contradict Olson's assertion that large, diffuse interests will not organize for collective action, owing to a lack of selective incentives.[20] They are more consistent with arguments that "purposive incentives" or "expressive benefits" motivate some individuals to organize and participate on behalf of large, diffuse interests.[21]

Second, environmental groups constitute a surprisingly small percentage of public advocates in the utilities area. Of seventy-two grassroots advocacy groups active in public utility commission proceedings in the twelve states, only seven, or 9.7 percent, are environmental groups. Although environmental groups are frequently mentioned as active participants in the public utility regulatory process,[22] these references are due more to the prominence of a few highly visible national citizens' groups (the Environmental Defense Fund, Friends of the Earth, the Sierra Club) than to the overall activity of environmental groups. Some of the most prominent grassroots advocacy groups in the country are environmental groups, but environmental groups are not among the most active participants in public utility commission proceedings.

Third, low-income groups are surprisingly well represented in public utility commission proceedings. Of seventy-two grassroots advocacy groups active in public utility commission proceedings, twenty-three, or 31.9 percent, are low-income groups. As observers have argued, the poor do face formidable organizational obstacles, including internal conflicts and uneasy relations with other groups.[23] Also, sharp cutbacks in federal funding for the Legal Services Corporation will undoubtedly limit the activities of legal aid societies in the 1980s. During the 1970s, however, legal aid societies often represented low-income groups in public utility commission proceedings.

Proxy Advocates

In contrast to grassroots advocates, proxy advocates are public officials. A proxy advocacy group may be defined as a governmental organization that represents all or most residents of a particular jurisdiction before another governmental organization. The idea seems to be that you set a bureaucrat to catch a bureaucrat. However, proxy advocates are not ordinary bureaucrats. Unlike regulatory commissioners, who make policy, proxy advocates merely recommend policy. Unlike regulatory agency staff members, who recommend policy to their superiors, proxy advocates recommend policy to public officials at another agency. In short, proxy advocates are public officials whose mission is to represent the public on policy questions decided by another administrative agency.

Proxy advocates should not be confused with government officials who represent their agency or a variety of agencies in another agency's proceedings. When the General Services Administration intervenes in public utility commission proceedings in an effort to minimize rates charged to federal agencies, it is intervening on behalf of federal agencies, not residential ratepayers. When municipalities intervene in public utility commission proceedings in an effort to minimize rates charged to municipal governments, they are intervening on behalf of local governments. Lower rates for local governments, of course, could eventually mean lower taxes for citizens. However, they could also mean higher rates for residential customers. Unless public officials directly represent residents of a particular jurisdiction, they are not proxy advocates.

The concept of proxy advocacy also needs to be differentiated from that of an ombudsman, the Scandinavian concept of a buffer between the bureaucracy and the public. Like proxy advocates, an ombudsman is a government official who represents members of the public. However, he focuses much more on bureaucratic red tape than on policy problems. He facilitates more than he advocates. He investigates complaints by aggrieved individuals, regardless of whether those complaints are symptomatic of a deeper administrative crisis. In short, the ombudsman's concerns are much more particularistic than the proxy advocate's.[24]

The concept of proxy advocacy has received very little attention from political scientists, largely because it is relatively new. Over the past few years, however, proxy advocates have proliferated to the point where they constitute an identifiable group of public officials. In the utilities area, they even have their own organization, the National Association of State Utility Consumer Advocates, formed in May 1979. What kinds of proxy advocates participate in public utility commission proceedings? There are basically two: attorneys general and consumer counsels.

1. *Attorneys general.* In approximately thirteen states, attorneys general have intervened on behalf of consumers in public utility commission proceedings.[25] In a few states, such as Michigan and Massachusetts, the attorney general has actively participated in the public utility regulatory process as a public advocate since the late 1960s. In the overwhelming majority of

states, the attorney general is elected by the people.[26] Consequently, the possibility arises that the attorney general will be a member of one party, while the governor, who appoints public utility commissioners in most states, will be a member of another party. Indeed, this situation exists in approximately one-third of the states.[27] When it does, public utility commission proceedings may serve as battlegrounds for interparty conflicts.

In many states, the attorney general has explicit statutory authority to intervene in public utility commission proceedings on behalf of consumers. In North Carolina, for example, the attorney general is empowered "to intervene, when he deems it to be advisable, in the public interest in proceedings before any courts, regulatory officers, agencies and bodies, both State and Federal, in a representative capacity for and on behalf of the using and consuming public."[28] In other states, the attorney general relies on common law powers to justify intervention in public utility commission proceedings. Without explicit statutory authority, however, some attorneys general have failed to convince the courts that they have the right to intervene in administrative proceedings on behalf of consumers.[29]

The participation of the attorney general in a public utility commission proceeding, incidentally, does not necessarily mean that the attorney general is functioning as a proxy advocate for the public. In many states, the attorney general is legal counsel to state administrative agencies, including the public utility commission. Thus, when the attorney general participates in public utility commission proceedings in Georgia, Mississippi, Wyoming, and many other states, he does so strictly as legal counsel to the public utility commission.

In other states, the attorney general plays both roles simultaneously. In Michigan, for example, the attorney general's Special Litigation Division represents the public in Public Service Commission proceedings and the courts, while the attorney general's Public Service Division represents the Public Service Commission staff. This awkward arrangement involves clearcut conflicts of interest, not easily remedied by the expedient of relatively autonomous divisions. The attorney general's very selection of personnel to play these conflicting roles guarantees that he or she will influence the quality of representation provided to the public utility commission, on the one hand, and the public, on the other hand. Unless the attorney general is equally zealous in recruiting and retaining attorneys for both divisions, the process can easily become unfair.

2. *Consumer counsels*. In approximately eighteen states, specially created offices of consumer counsel have intervened on behalf of consumers in public utility commission proceedings.[30] Most of these offices were created in the mid-1970s, although the Maryland and Indiana offices have existed for many years. In most instances, the consumer counsel is appointed by the governor, which means that the consumer counsel and the governor are almost always of the same party. In a few states, the consumer counsel is appointed by the state legislature. In Florida, for example, the public counsel is appointed by a special state legislative auditing committee.

Legislation creating offices of consumer counsel usually specifies that the office is to represent all consumers in proceedings before the public utility commission. Typically, such language is interpreted to mean that the office of consumer counsel must represent residential, commercial, and industrial consumers. Occasionally, a statute specifies a narrower constituency. The Georgia statute, for example, requires the Consumers' Utility Counsel to represent residential and small business customers in particular. Most offices of consumer counsel are also empowered to intervene in the courts and before federal agencies when utilities issues are at stake.

Although several grassroots advocacy groups frequently intervene in the same utility rate case, two proxy advocates seldom intervene in the same case. Indeed, the presence of a bona fide proxy advocate in the utilities area discourages the emergence of other utility-oriented proxy advocates in the same state. If an office of consumer counsel represents consumers in public utility commission proceedings, the attorney general normally remains on the sidelines. If the attorney general represents the public in public utility commission proceedings, pressure to create an office of consumer counsel is less intense. There are a few exceptions to this pattern. In New York, the Consumer Protection Board and the attorney general have intervened simultaneously before the Public Service Commission since 1979, when a new attorney general, Robert Abrams, took office.[31] In Florida, the people's counsel and the attorney general both played active roles in the Public Service Commission's review of the "Daisy Chain" scandal, in which Florida Power purchased oil at inflated prices in return for kickbacks to the company's chairman.[32] Nevertheless, it is widely believed that only one state government office should attempt to represent consumers through intervention in public utility commission proceedings. Joint appearances by proxy advocates could unravel as inexorably as in Shakespeare's *Twelfth Night*, where Viola is mistaken for her brother Sebastian. Eventually, one party is likely to be deemed an impostor!

Whatever form it takes, proxy advocacy is a governmental response to the perception of political market failure. Proxy advocacy is based on four premises: (1) that citizens lack incentives to organize on their own behalf; (2) that citizens lack the knowledge to understand where their best interests lie; (3) that citizens lack the resources to participate effectively in complicated regulatory proceedings; and (4) that individual citizens' groups are often unrepresentative of the public as a whole. Although most of these premises are arguable, the first is often false. Clearly, a substantial number of citizens' groups have participated in public utility commission proceedings in a substantial number of states. What accounts for the presence of highly active grassroots advocates in some states but not others? What accounts for the presence of highly active proxy advocates in some states but not others? Aggregate data from all fifty states and the District of Columbia help to answer these questions.

ORIGINS OF PUBLIC ADVOCACY

Although proxy advocacy has received virtually no attention in the literature, a number of explanations have been offered for state-level variations in citizen participation. Elazar has argued that citizen participation is high in "moralistic" states where participation is considered a civic duty, low in "traditionalistic" states where political elites are expected to make decisions.[33] According to Elazar, different "political cultures" have developed as people with distinctive ethnic and religious backgrounds have settled in different parts of the country. In general, states along the northern tier are moralistic, and southern states are traditionalistic. In a test of Elazar's hypothesis, Sharkansky has found that traditionalistic states are indeed characterized by lower levels of voter turnout.[34] Others have noted that electoral participation is weak in states where interparty competition is weak.[35]

Unfortunately, these variables, which help to explain interstate variations in electoral participation, do not help to explain variations in nonelectoral participation. Neither political culture nor interparty competition is a good predictor of grassroots advocacy activity in public utility commission proceedings. The Pearson's correlation coefficient between interparty competition[36] and grassroots advocacy activity, though in the expected direction, is weak ($r = .114$). The Pearson's correlation coefficient between political culture[37] and grassroots advocacy activity is also in the expected direction but weak ($r = -.094$).

These state-level findings are consistent with Hansen's community-level finding that general political structure variables explain only 8 percent of the variance in "communal participation" or participation aimed at influencing broad social issues.[38] As Hansen puts it, "Information on a community's political structure does not help us as much in predicting nonelectoral participation as it does with voting."[39] Thus, the question remains: if general political structure variables do not explain variations among states or communities in nonelectoral participation, what variables do?

Issue-Specific Catalysts

A key problem with such variables as interparty competition and political culture is that they do not take into account the specific frustrations that trigger political demands in a particular policy area.[40] To identify the frustrations that stimulate grassroots advocacy activity in public utility commission proceedings, it is necessary to recall that most active grassroots advocacy groups are consumer groups or low-income groups whose overriding concern is high energy rates. Although energy rates have risen sharply throughout the United States since the OPEC oil embargo of 1973–1974, some states have suffered more than others. Northeastern states, heavily dependent on expensive oil and distant from natural gas fields, have been particularly hard hit. Western states, more reliant on cheaper hydroelectric power and closer to natural gas fields, have experienced lower rates. In 1976, while New York state residents were paying $29.87 per month for 500 kilowatt-hours of electricity, Washington state residents were paying $7.58. During the same year, while residents of Massachusetts were paying $3.64 for 1,000 cubic feet of natural gas, residents of Wyoming were paying $1.18. Thus, although the energy crisis is national in scope, it has hurt some states severely, others much less. Interstate disparities have been so striking that one might expect greater grassroots advocacy activity in states where residential utility rates have been higher.

As expected, there is a positive relationship between residential electric rates and participation by grassroots advocates in public utility commission proceedings ($r = .377$, $p < .01$). There is also a positive relationship between residential natural gas rates and grassroots advocacy activity ($r = .363$, $p < .01$). Since residential electric rates and residential natural gas rates are intercorrelated ($r = .507$), it is appropriate to create an energy rates index variable that measures both electric and natural gas rates.[41] Such an index is especially useful when two or more variables are so highly interrelated that their separate effects on a third variable are difficult to measure. The correlation between energy rates and grassroots advocacy activity is .407 ($p < .005$).

To recapitulate, a key problem with general political structure variables is that they fail to take into account specific frustrations that may stimulate nonelectoral participation. A second problem is that they fail to take into account the specific political characteristics of the decision-making body—in this instance, the public utility commission. One characteristic of state public utility commissions that could affect the level of nonelectoral participation is the method of selecting public utility commissioners. Stewart has argued that popular election of agency officials is properly viewed as an alternative to a system of interest representation based on expanded public participation in administrative and judicial proceedings.[42] Both are means of holding agency officials accountable to broader publics. Direct election accomplishes this by expanding the scope of conflict to the entire electorate. Expanded public participation in administrative and judicial proceedings accomplishes this by affording spokespeople for underrepresented interests access to the decision-making process between elections.

If direct election of agency officials and expanded public participation are alternative means to the same end, there should be less public participation in states where agency officials are elected. As expected, there is a relationship between method of selection of public utility commissioners and nonelectoral participation ($r = -.418$, $p < .001$). The negative sign means that grassroots advocacy groups are less likely to participate in public utility commission proceedings in states with elected commissioners. Perhaps grassroots advocacy groups assume that elected agency officials can be trusted to safeguard their interests.

What are the effects of energy rates and method of selection, while controlling for other variables that also influence the level of nonelectoral participation? What percentage of the variance in nonelectoral participation do energy rates and method of selection explain? Through multiple regression analysis, the effects of energy rates, method of selection, and other variables on nonelectoral participation can be estimated. Included as control variables in the multiple regression equation are two economic variables—urbanization and industrialization—which historically have shown some relationship to the level of rates.[43] Urbanization is defined here as the percentage of each state's population living in urban areas. Industrialization is defined as the percentage of each state's work force employed in the manufacturing sector. A third control variable, per capita income, was also considered because of studies that show a relationship between per capita income and voter turnout.[44] However, per capita income was not included in the multiple regression equation because it is only weakly related to nonelectoral participation ($r = .100$). Similarly, political culture and interparty competition were omitted from the equation because of their weak relationship to nonelectoral participation.

As table 6 indicates, the relationship between energy rates and nonelectoral participation is statistically significant ($p < .05$) even after controlling for the effects of economic variables. The relationship between method of selection and nonelectoral participation is also statistically significant ($p < .05$) after the same controls are applied. Other relationships, in contrast, are weak.

Energy rates and method of selection together explain nearly 28 percent of the variance in nonelectoral participation. Although much of the variance remains unexplained, the explanatory power of the two issue-specific variables is striking when compared to that of several political structure variables in Hansen's community-level study of nonelectoral participation. In that study, five general political structure variables explained only 8 percent of the variance in nonelectoral participation, as opposed to 26 percent of the variance in voter turnout.[45] This suggests that to understand variations in nonelectoral participation, it is necessary to look beyond general political structure variables to issue-specific variables, including both sources of discontent in public policies and sources of contentment in the political structure.

Under certain circumstances, grassroots advocacy groups will organize to participate in public utility commission proceedings. But what if they fail to organize? Do proxy advocates rush to champion those interests which citizens are unable or unwill-

Table 6
Public Advocacy as a Response to Method of Selection,
Energy Rates, and Other Variables
(N = 50)

Variable	Grassroots Advocacy		Proxy Advocacy	
	Standardized b	F	Standardized b	F
Method of selection[a]	−.343	6.70[b]	−.138	1.01
Energy rates	.341	6.16[b]	.357	6.33[b]
Urbanization	−.072	0.27	.070	0.24
Industrialization	.058	0.19	.138	1.01
	F = 4.61	R² = .29	F = 3.60	R² = .24

a. Method of selection is a dichotomous variable; 0 signifies an appointed commission and 1 signifies an elected commission.
b. $p < .05$.

ing to promote themselves? If so, there should be a negative relationship between grassroots advocacy and proxy advocacy, with low grassroots advocacy encouraging high proxy advocacy. Yet, as table 3 indicated, this is not the case. In fact, there is a slight tendency for proxy advocacy to be high where grassroots advocacy is high and for proxy advocacy to be low where grassroots advocacy is low. Clearly, proxy advocacy is not a mere substitute for grassroots advocacy.

What, then, accounts for proxy advocacy? As table 6 suggests, proxy advocacy and grassroots advocacy have somewhat similar origins. Like grassroots advocacy, proxy advocacy is higher in states with high energy rates. If one looks at unstandardized b's, however, one discovers a stronger relationship between energy rates and proxy advocacy (b = .145) than between energy rates and grassroots advocacy (b = .077). This supports the proposition that grassroots advocacy is more multifaceted than proxy advocacy. Whereas grassroots advocacy is a response to a variety of concerns about the environment, nuclear power, and the level of rates, proxy advocacy is more exclusively a response to high energy rates. This also suggests that a higher percentage of the variation in levels of grassroots advocacy might be explained if one had statewide measures of public concern about environmental and nuclear issues.

Although issue-specific catalysts help to explain the origins of grassroots advocacy and proxy advocacy groups, they do not explain why particular people devote years of their lives to such groups. What motivates people to choose public advocacy as a vocation? What motivates a homemaker or a retired tailor to donate large chunks of time to a citizens' group that seeks to influence their state public utility commission? What motivates a talented lawyer or engineer to accept a job with an office of consumer counsel when a corporate law firm or utility company would pay twice as much? To answer these questions, it is necessary to shift our attention from the organization to the individual.

Personal Incentives

To understand why people devote themselves to an organization, Salisbury urges us to consider the perspective of exchange theory.[46] This perspective suggests that people affiliate with an organization because they derive some rewards from that affiliation. A leader secures organizational benefits, which he shares with those who value such benefits. If a leader has sufficient incentives to persist and others have sufficient incentives to donate time, money, or both, the organization may succeed. In the absence of such incentives, however, the organization will quickly atrophy.

What incentives induce otherwise level-headed individuals to endure the drudgery, penury, and misery of grassroots advocacy? One possibility, of course, is that these people are just plain crazy. Consider the following exchange:

Q: Why did you join your organization?
A: God knows! I've been trying to figure that out for the last two years.

Or consider the following:

Q: What incentives are there for you to remain within your organization?
A: I guess I'm just an idiot. Must be! I don't get paid for what I do.

Perhaps these public advocates are genuinely puzzled by their own behavior. Still, public advocacy seems too deliberate to be a whimsical flight of fancy.

What rational incentives do people have to commit themselves to a grassroots advocacy organization? According to Clark and Wilson, people join organizations because of material incentives, solidary incentives, purposive incentives, or some combination of the three.[47] Material incentives are tangible rewards with monetary value—a job, a good salary, and so on. Solidary incentives are tangible rewards that flow from social interaction with respected colleagues in a congenial atmosphere. Purposive incentives are intangible rewards derived from the stated purposes of the organization.[48]

Interviews with seventy-seven grassroots advocates and thirty-five proxy advocates in twelve states suggest that some incentives are more compelling than others. As table 7 reveals, grassroots advocates are motivated more by purposive incentives (community service, policy influence) than by solidary incentives (good colleagues, professional autonomy) or material incentives (monetary rewards, career advancement). Many grassroots advocates also mention interesting work.[49] Since grassroots advocates are generally not well paid, very few cite a good salary as an incentive. Nor do many mention good colleagues as a reason for joining or remaining. (Many grassroots advocacy organizations are so small that collegial interaction is minimal.) Overall, purposive incentives appear to be more important to grassroots advocates than other incentives. These findings coincide with similar findings by Jeffrey Berry, who interviewed professional staff members of national public interest groups. In Berry's words: "Although solidary incentives cannot be ignored for some members of some groups, it is the more ideological, policy-oriented motivations of individuals that make it possible for most public interest groups to exist."[50]

In contrast to grassroots advocates, proxy advocates are motivated more by material incentives, less by purposive incentives. These differences are especially evident if one looks at reasons for joining, as opposed to reasons for remaining. Although very few grassroots advocates mention material incentives as reasons for joining their organizations, nearly one-fourth of all proxy advocates do. And though approximately one-half of all grassroots advocates cite community service or policy influence

Table 7
Personal Incentives of Public Advocates

	Grassroots Advocates (N = 77)		Proxy Advocates (N = 35)	
	Reasons to Join	Reasons to Stay	Reasons to Join	Reasons to Stay
Interesting work	52.0%	46.7%	62.9%	62.9%
Community service	30.0	23.4	8.6	8.6
Policy influence	20.8	42.8	17.1	42.9
Personal convenience	18.2	4.0	40.0	2.9
Career advancement	5.2	20.8	11.4	28.6
Good colleagues	5.2	7.8	2.9	20.0
Professional autonomy	3.9	22.1	2.9	14.3
Monetary rewards	0.0	7.8	11.4	5.7

Note: Column percentages do not add up to 100% because respondents often mentioned more than one incentive.

as original goals, only about one-fourth of all proxy advocates cite such goals as factors from the start.

Over time, though, there is a tendency toward convergence. Material incentives become more important for grassroots advocates, purposive incentives become more important for proxy advocates, solidary incentives become more important for both. Of equal or greater interest, changes occur within each of these categories. The importance of community service declines or remains the same, while the importance of policy influence increases dramatically. For both grassroots advocates and proxy advocates, purposive incentives become more focused, more specific. At the same time, solidary incentives become more organization-specific. At grassroots advocacy organizations, where staffs tend to be very small, public advocates come to appreciate the pleasures of autonomy. At proxy advocacy organizations, where staffs are larger, public advocates come to appreciate the joys of collegiality. Finally, material incentives become less immediate as public advocates come to accept delayed gratification. For both grassroots advocates and proxy advocates, career advancement increases in importance. Monetary rewards, never important to begin with, remain unimportant. Even proxy advocates, who are better paid than grassroots advocates, seldom cite money as a reason for continuing with their organization. Yet, if money is not especially important as a personal incentive, it may be extremely important as an organizational resource.

Funding of Public Advocacy

It is often argued that broad, diffuse interests, such as consumers, are incapable of organizing or participating.[51] In the context of public utility regulation, that argument does not hold up. If there is a crisis of accountability, it is not so simple as public choice theorists suggest. The public is often represented in public utility commission proceedings by grassroots advocacy groups, proxy advocacy groups, or both. However, participation in itself may not be enough. Even if public advocates participate, do they have the resources to participate effectively? Even if they participate effectively, do they have the incentives to represent a diverse range of interests? One way to answer these questions is to look at the funding of public advocacy groups.

Successful public advocacy may well depend on adequate financial resources. If so, there is cause for concern. As students of administrative law have argued, many citizens' groups lack the financial resources to participate effectively in administrative proceedings.[52] In Cramton's words: "For public interest groups cost is a considerable obstacle to effective participation in formal agency proceedings."[53]

To determine resource levels, respondents were asked to estimate their organization's total annual budget and the percentage of that budget allocated to utilities issues. Because public advocacy organizations vary substantially in the percentage of their total budgets allocated to utilities issues, a comparison of raw budget figures would be misleading. Grassroots advocacy groups, which tend to be multipurpose organizations, are more likely than proxy advocacy groups to allocate a very small percentage of their total resources to utilities issues. To correct for this, all raw budget scores have been adjusted to reflect the percentage of the budget allocated to electric, natural gas, and telephone issues combined. As table 8 indicates, proxy advocates are much better funded than grassroots advocates. Among grassroots advocacy organizations, forty-five of seventy, or 64.3 percent, spend less than $25,000 a year on utilities issues, whereas only two of seventy, or 2.9 percent, spend more than $250,000 a year. All six proxy advocacy organizations spend more than $250,000 a year on utilities issues. Clearly, the financial resources of proxy advocates are far superior to those of grassroots advocates.

Table 8
Financial Resources of Public Advocates

Resources Devoted to Utilities Issues	Grassroots Advocacy Organizations (N = 70)	Proxy Advocacy Organizations (N = 6)
$ 0–9,999	41.4% (29)	0.0% (0)
$ 10,000–24,999	22.9% (16)	0.0% (0)
$ 25,000–99,999	25.7% (18)	0.0% (0)
$100,000–249,999	7.1% (5)	0.0% (0)
$250,000+	2.9% (2)	100.0% (6)

Yet funding levels cannot be viewed in isolation from funding sources. The power of the purse is widely regarded as the wellspring of the legislature's political power over administrative agencies.[54] It is less commonly observed that the legislature's power depends largely on the absence of alternative funding sources for administrative agencies. An organization that depends exclusively on legislators for funds will not deliberately antagonize its legislative benefactors. In contrast, an organization that has the option of raising funds through a variety of methods will be less constrained.

To determine the extent of such financial dependency, respondents were asked to identify their organization's funding sources.[55] As table 9 indicates, all six proxy advocacy organizations in the sample depend exclusively on the government or a governmentally mandated fee system for their funding. All six receive funds from their state legislatures or from utility companies under an arrangement approved by their state legislatures.[56] Three of the six also receive funds from the federal Department of Energy.[57] In contrast, grassroots advocacy organizations receive funds from a wide variety of sources, including individual contributions, membership fees, foundation grants, federal agencies, state agencies, and the Legal Services

Table 9
Funding Sources of Public Advocates

Funding Source	Grassroots Advocacy Organizations (N = 69)	Proxy Advocacy Organizations (N = 6)
Individual contributions	40.6% (28)	0.0% (0)
Membership dues	31.9% (22)	0.0% (0)
Private foundation	20.3% (14)	0.0% (0)
Federal government	18.8% (13)	50.0% (3)
State government	14.5% (10)	66.7% (4)
Utility companies[a]	0.0% (0)	33.3% (2)
Legal Services Corp.	13.0% (9)	0.0% (0)
Church	5.8% (4)	0.0% (0)
Students	5.8% (4)	0.0% (0)
Other	23.0% (16)	0.0% (0)

a. Utility company contributions to proxy advocacy organizations are not voluntary but rather are mandatory fees assessed by the New Jersey and Massachusetts legislatures.

Corporation. A grassroots advocacy group that antagonizes key legislators may still secure funds from other sources; a proxy advocacy group that antagonizes key legislators invites severe financial reprisals. As a result of these differences in funding arrangements, proxy advocates are more constrained politically than grassroots advocates.

Conclusion

Despite impediments, public advocates have been active participants in public utility commission proceedings in nearly three-fourths of the states. These public advocates are grassroots advocates in some instances, proxy advocates in others. Grassroots advocates encompass a large number of environmental, antinuclear, consumer, and low-income groups. The proportion of environmental groups is surprisingly small; the proportion of low-income groups is surprisingly large, although that may be changing. Proxy advocates include the attorney general in some states, a consumer counsel in others. An attorney general and a consumer counsel seldom intervene in public utility commission proceedings in the same state.

In general, public advocacy is high in states with high energy rates and appointed public utility commissioners, low in states with low energy rates and elected commissioners. These variations confirm that nonelectoral participation has issue-specific roots. However, issue-specific conditions stimulate public advocacy only because a substantial number of individuals are sufficiently motivated to pursue public advocacy work. Their incentives are often, though not always, purposive in nature.

The presence of active public advocacy groups in public utility commission proceedings does not in itself guarantee accountability. These groups may participate, but not effectively. Or they may participate effectively but not on behalf of the full range of underrepresented interests. Even if public advocacy groups help to promote accountability, problems of governance may remain. Indeed, public advocacy activity may contribute to a crisis of governance by making it difficult for public utility commissions to avoid the pitfalls of dissensus and delay. These and other problems of governance are dealt with in chapter 3.

: 3 :

Political Executives and Career Executives: The Perils of Governance

A number of commentators have suggested that contemporary political institutions suffer from "overload," or a diminishing ability to cope with rising expectations and growing demands. According to these observers, there is a widening gap between what we expect the government to provide us and what the government is able to provide us.[1] As Anthony King puts it: "Americans used to write of 'Big Government' as though the State, in becoming all-embracing, would become all-powerful. Today our image of government is more that of the sorcerer's apprentice. The waters rise. The apprentice rushes about with his bucket. The waters rise even faster. And none of us knows when, or whether, the magician will come home."[2]

At first glance, the bureaucracy seems aptly suited to handle troublesome problems of governance. On the demand side, the bureaucracy is more insulated from political conflicts than the legislature or the chief executive. On the supply side, the bureaucracy possesses greater expertise to deal with complex policy problems. Yet the bureaucracy has special weaknesses as well. To ensure its survival, it must cultivate a constituency. Thus, it is not so removed from the political arena as it might appear. Furthermore, expertise is of limited use in many situations. When asked to balance competing interests or values, bureaucrats cannot hide behind a shield of neutral competence.

There is growing recognition of the fact that the bureaucracy, like other political institutions, faces formidable problems of governance.[3] It is not clear, though, how those problems ought to be defined. What exactly does it mean to say that the bureaucracy finds it difficult to govern? Are bureaucrats demoralized and dispirited because success is so elusive? Is the bureaucracy fragmented and beset by internal divisions? Is the bureaucracy manipulated by its sovereigns, the chief executive and the legislature? Is the bureaucracy paralyzed by indecision and unable to act in a timely manner? Is the bureaucracy, though able to act, vulnerable to second-guessing by the courts?

Chapter 3 addresses these questions through an analysis of public utility commissions in twelve states. The analysis relies primarily on interviews with thirty-eight commissioners and sixty-three top-level staff members.[4] The chapter focuses on the recruitment of public utility regulators, lines of cleavage within commissions, relations between public utility regulators and their sovereigns, and the ability of regulators to avoid administrative delay and judicial review. In broader terms, this chapter asks whether there is evidence of demoralization, fragmentation, interference, paralysis, or inconclusiveness.

RECRUITMENT

The regulation of public utilities is an essential public task, but it is not always a pleasant one. In recent years, public utility commissioners have been forced to mediate disputes between construction-minded utility executives and conservation-minded environmentalists, between investors upset by low dividends and consumers upset by high rates, between business customers who threaten to leave their state and voters who threaten to leave their party. A public utility commissioner today is about as popular as a baseball umpire. At best, he is taken for granted; at worst, he is an object of scorn and derision. Indeed, one commissioner, a former umpire, says the two jobs require identical outlooks: "I use my umpire background a lot as commissioner. Call 'em as you see 'em. Let the chips fall where they may. . . . Never change your decision. Stick by it, right or wrong. . . . Call 'em fast. If you don't, it's just flop a coin, you blind son of a gun. Call 'em fast and have it over with."

Although the job of a public utility commissioner is difficult in most states, it is especially vexing in states where utilities issues have become highly politicized. In Illinois, for example, consumer groups are very upset with high utility rates, and commissioners are not permitted to forget it. The family of the chairman looked outside their window one Sunday to find over a hundred demonstrators conducting a prayer vigil outside their home. Another commissioner found himself "mau-maued" by an angry crowd of about four hundred people at a public forum where he had been asked to present his views. On more than one occasion, the Illinois Commerce Commission has had to suspend its proceedings so that irate citizens could express their views. Many of these protests are organized by the Illinois Public Action Council (IPAC), an amalgamation of sixty-four citizens' groups, labor groups, and community organizations. In keeping with the philosophy of Saul Alinsky,[5] who radicalized many of IPAC's leaders, IPAC maintains ferocious public pressure on the Illinois Commerce Commission through a combination of confrontation politics and clever public relations. As a result, Illinois commissioners find themselves closely scrutinized by the media, the public, and a wide variety of citizens' groups.

Public utility commission staff members are considerably less visible than commissioners, but they have their problems as well. Political executives, who are not protected by civil service, know that they can be dismissed or demoted if they lose the favor of the chairman or the other commissioners. Career executives, who are protected by civil service, know that their promotion opportunities depend on the perceptions of their superiors. In either case, staff members often find it difficult to serve several masters at once.

As with commissioners, the staff members' fortunes vary from state to state. The job of a staff member is especially exasperating in states where commissioners are sharply divided on the issues. In Georgia, for example, commissioners with very different philosophies feud publicly with one another and with members of the staff. On one occasion, Commissioner Billy Lovett raised the hackles of colleagues when he publicly claimed credit for various accomplishments of the Georgia Public Service Commission. Hugh Jordan, executive director of the commission, subsequently disputed Lovett's claims in a newspaper interview. Lovett, furious, accosted Jordan in the halls, grabbed him by the collar, and warned him not to call him a liar again. Understandably, this incident did little to improve staff morale.

Personal Incentives

Given the torments that public utility regulators must endure, one might well wonder what possesses a person to become a public utility regulator in the first place. To determine this, public utility commissioners and top-level staff members were asked why they joined the commission. As table 10 indicates, many regulators joined the commission because they viewed public utility regulation as a challenging, exciting field. In fact, four out of every ten regulators cite interesting work as a reason for joining the commission.

A substantial number of commissioners joined the commission in response to a convincing personal request, usually by the governor. Approximately four out of every ten commissioners cite such a personal request. These commissioners, like Barber's

Table 10
Personal Incentives of Public Utility Regulators

	Commissioners (N = 34)		Staff Members (N = 60)	
	Reasons to Join	Reasons to Stay	Reasons to Join	Reasons to Stay
Interesting work	42.3%	52.2%	37.9%	49.9%
Convincing request	38.2	0.0	6.5	0.0
Policy influence	20.0	37.0	8.1	21.9
Career advancement	17.0	8.2	26.0	13.7
Community service	11.1	13.6	1.6	16.5
Personal convenience	5.5	8.7	41.3	20.1
Good colleagues	2.6	8.7	11.5	11.6
Monetary rewards	0.0	11.3	6.6	26.3
Professional autonomy	0.0	2.6	4.9	11.4
None	0.0	18.2	0.0	1.8

Note: Column percentages do not add up to 100% because respondents often mentioned more than one incentive.

"reluctant" legislators,[6] accepted their position out of a sense of duty. It is important to emphasize, though, that they were persuaded not by family and friends but by the governor. Once the governor leaves office, "reluctant" commissioners may no longer have incentives to remain. Even if they have such incentives, the new governor may lack incentives to reappoint them!

In contrast to commissioners, staff members seldom cite a convincing personal request as a reason for joining the commission. Rather, they mention convenience, happenstance, the need for a job. As one staff member recalls, "I developed a bad habit of calorie intake. I needed to eat!" Approximately four out of every ten staff members were motivated in part by personal convenience. A substantial number of staff members also cite career advancement as a motivation. Over the years, state regulatory agencies have been training grounds for federal regulatory agencies. There are also opportunities for advancement at the state level as vacancies occur. Approximately one out of every four staff members cites such considerations.

Of course, reasons for joining the commission may not coincide with reasons for remaining. To determine why people stay at the commission, regulators were asked: "What incentives are there for you to remain at the commission?" As table 10 indicates, public utility commissioners seldom cite career advancement as a reason for remaining. Although some commissioners have used the commissionership as a springboard to higher office,[7] many have concluded that service on the public utility commission is a political liability. Indeed, approximately one out of every five commissioners cannot think of a single reason to stay. Some commissioners find that they are not thick-skinned after all, that they are unable to cope with a tarnished public image. Consider the following lament from a commissioner who craves the public esteem he once enjoyed: "I was very active in the community. . . . I was on the Boy Scout board, United Fund board, Red Cross board, did all the things, Mr. Nice Guy. And the way some of the citizens' groups treat me now, you know, it's just not worth it. It's not worth it to me, it's not worth it to my family."

Clearly, a substantial minority of commissioners are demoralized and disaffected. If this continues, it could lead to more rapid turnover among commissioners. At the moment, the median tenure of public utility commissioners is 4.2 years—a figure roughly comparable to that of federal regulatory commissioners.[8] That could change, though, if commissioners become increasingly dissatisfied with their public image.

Not surprisingly, staff members stay at the commission longer than commissioners. Among staff members, the median tenure is 10.3 years. In contrast to commissioners, staff members are better able to cite reasons to stay. Career executives, who are protected by civil service, can at least find comfort in their job security. State civil service offers them a steady income, good fringe benefits, a good pension plan, and job security. Political executives, who are not protected by civil service, lack the same kind of job security. However, many political executives are former career executives with "bumping rights" which permit them to resume their old posts as career executives if they lose their new ones as political executives. Thus, the typical political executive can be demoted but not dismissed.

Personal Characteristics

Despite the drawbacks of public utility regulation as a vocation, thousands of people continue to serve as commissioners and top-level staff members. Who are today's regulators? According to Lincoln Smith, today's commissioners differ markedly from some of their "tobacco-drooling, lethargic" predecessors. In particular, they are more likely to be female, more likely to be black, less likely to be lawyers.[9] Smith is correct, but it is important not to exaggerate these changes. Although the ranks of female commissioners have grown, women still constitute only 19 percent of all commissioners, and an even smaller percentage of chairpersons.[10] Furthermore, some changes have not yet penetrated the upper echelons of public utility commission staffs. Of sixty-three top-level staff members interviewed for this project, only one was a woman and none was black. Also, although there are fewer lawyers than before, lawyers still predominate among commissioners.

As public utilities issues grow in complexity, governors appear to be appointing more economists and others with a business background to public utility commissions. Nevertheless, commissioners with a business background are still outnumbered by commissioners with a legal background. Whereas 28.6 percent of the commissioners interviewed for this project have a business background, 45.7 percent have a legal background. Among staff members, lawyers are less numerous (30.2 percent). Because staff members are expected to provide technical judgments, a greater proportion of them have a background in engineering, business, or accounting (see table 11).

One of the most persistent criticisms of regulatory agencies is that many of their personnel come from the industry they are supposed to be regulating. This phenomenon, known as the "revolving door," is thought to promote favoritism toward regulated industries. In fact, only 8.8 percent of the commissioners interviewed for this project had ever worked for a utility company. Furthermore, that industry experience was often negligible. For example, one commissioner worked as a telephone company representative for one year immediately after receiving her bachelor's degree. She hated her job so much that she decided to go to law school. The background of staff members tells a very different story. Among top-level staff members, 31.2 percent had worked for a utility company. This finding is noteworthy, for it suggests the need to differentiate between commissioners and staff members in estimating the extent of the revolving door phenomenon.

The 1980 elections swept into power a number of Republican governors, who are likely to appoint Republicans as public utility commissioners, subject to minority party representation provisions in many states.[11] During the time of this study, how-

Table 11
Professional Background
of Public Utility Regulators

	Commissioners (N = 35)	Staff Members (N = 63)
Law	45.7% (16)	30.2% (19)
Business	28.6% (10)	20.6% (13)
Engineering	0.0% (0)	30.2% (19)
Accounting	5.7% (2)	12.7% (8)
Other	20.0% (7)	6.3% (4)

ever, commissioners were overwhelmingly Democratic. Among commissioners, 65.8 percent were Democrats, 29 percent were Republicans, and 5.3 percent were independents. Among top-level staff members, 39.3 percent were Democrats, 21.3 percent were Republicans, and 39.3 percent were independents. In short, although regulators as a whole were twice as likely to be Democrats as Republicans, staff members were considerably more likely to be independents. Presumably, independent staff members can better adapt to a changing political background as parties and commissioners come and go.

Overall, this review of personal characteristics suggests modest differences between commissioners and staff members. Commissioners are more likely to be lawyers, less likely to be independents, and less likely to have worked for a utility company. However, the more important point is that neither commissioners nor staff members are homogeneous groups, judging from their personal characteristics. If personal characteristics have attitudinal consequences, then commissioners will disagree on some issues and staff members will disagree on some issues. Such disagreements could complicate the problems of coordination and control that any bureaucracy faces.[12] Thus, a key question is whether regulators who differ in their personal characteristics also differ in their opinions on the problems that public utility commissions confront.

LINES OF CLEAVAGE

Do personal characteristics have implications for policy attitudes? To determine this, public utility regulators were asked to agree or disagree with twenty statements concerning policy choices faced by public utility commissions. These statements will be considered in greater detail in chapter 4, when the policy preferences of commissioners are compared with those of staff members, utility company executives, and public advocates. For the moment, it suffices to consider whether different personal characteristics coincide with different policy preferences. Were there a greater number of black or female regulators, it would be useful to see whether policy preferences differ by race or sex. The sample does not include a sufficient number of blacks or women for this kind of analysis, but it does permit an inquiry into the effects of party, professional background, and industry background. Since one's party identification might influence one's choice of a profession or an employer, it seems advisable to control for political party when considering the last two variables.

Political Party

Several surveys of federal bureaucrats indicate noteworthy differences between Democrats and Republicans. In a study of federal bureaucrats during the early days of the Nixon administration, Aberbach and Rockman found that Democrats were more supportive of government provision of social services.[13] In a study of federal bureaucrats during the Ford administration, Cole and Caputo found that Republicans were more favorable to the programs and policy goals of the "new federalism."[14] In a study of regulatory commissioners and top-level staff members during the Ford administration, Quirk found that Democrats were more likely than Republicans to hold anti-industry attitudes.[15]

As table 12 indicates, partisan differences within the state bureaucracy are discernible as well, but only if southern regulators are excluded from the analysis. If one looks at all respondents, there are no statistically significant differences between Democrats and Republicans. If, however, one looks at regulators outside the South, three statistically significant differences emerge. First, Democrats are more enthusiastic about reimbursing citizens' groups for the costs of their participation in public utility commission proceedings. Second, Democrats are less likely to assert that public utility commissions move too slowly in making decisions. Third, Democrats are more supportive of seasonal rate structures, which promote energy conservation when peak demand is highest by charging more per unit of energy during peak months (usually summer), less during off-peak months. On other issues, Democrats tend to be more supportive of direct popular election of public utility commissioners, less willing to sacrifice environmental protection for economic prosperity, and more enthusiastic about inverted rates, which tend to benefit the poor (who consume less energy), and which also encourage energy conservation. In broader

Table 12
Regulators' Policy Preferences by Political Party

	Party (all regions)			Party (excluding South)		
	Democrats (N = 49)	Independents (N = 26)	Republicans (N = 24)	Democrats (N = 27)	Independents (N = 23)	Republicans (N = 22)
1. Investor-owned utilities are generally more efficient than publicly owned utilities.	82.9%	95.2%	88.9%	68.8%	94.4%	88.2%
2. There is already enough citizen involvement in public utility commission decisions.	31.1	40.0	52.2	20.8	45.5	52.4
3. Investor-owned utilities have a tendency to provide misleading information to regulators.	40.9	33.3	30.4	30.4	33.3	23.8
4. Utility companies should be allowed flexibility to design rates, provided that they are not discriminatory.	60.9	53.8	59.1	56.0	60.9	60.0
5. Construction work in progress should not be included in the rate base of utility companies.	47.4	33.3	41.2	52.4	31.3	46.7
6. Popular election of public utility commissioners is not a good idea.	69.6	90.5	82.6	100.0	89.5	81.0
7. Utility companies are allowed excessive rates of return on common stock equity.	2.3	0.0	0.0	0.0	0.0	0.0
8. Some environmental damage must be tolerated for the sake of economic prosperity.	75.0	83.3	82.6	60.0	81.0	85.7
9. Citizens' groups that participate in pubic utility commission proceedings ought to be reimbursed for the costs of their participation.	41.5	44.0	27.3	72.7	45.5	20.0**
10. Residential ratepayers pay less than their fair share of the costs of service.	51.2	76.2	52.2	47.6	73.7	47.6

Statement						
11. Public utility commissioners move too slowly in making decisions.	50.0	77.3	75.0	40.0	80.0	72.7*
12. Public utility commissioners should promote greater competition in the sale of electric power to large industrial customers and to retail distribution systems.	44.4	53.3	37.5	55.0	61.5	35.7
13. Public utility commissioners should not rely on utility company estimates of future energy demand.	72.1	81.8	69.6	72.0	78.9	66.7
14. An inverted rate structure, with residential customers paying more per kilowatt hour as they consume more, is a good idea.	47.5	50.0	31.8	58.3	46.7	25.0
15. The desirability of alternative modes of electricity generation is best determined by utility company management.	33.3	23.8	47.6	32.0	22.2	50.0
16. Mandatory time-of-day rates for residential customers should not be implemented at the present time.	47.4	59.1	73.9	45.0	57.9	76.2
17. Electric and gas companies should not be allowed to shut off service during the winter to apartment buildings whose landlords refuse to pay their bills.	56.8	76.2	60.0	70.8	88.9	61.1
18. Rates for interruptible service are impractical for residential customers.	55.9	65.0	81.8	56.3	61.1	85.0
19. A fuel adjustment clause is a good idea.	87.8	95.2	87.5	81.0	94.7	86.4
20. Seasonal rates should be adopted for both residential and business customers.	86.1	73.7	61.9	95.0	75.0	57.9*

Note: The percentages here refer to the proportion of respondents in each category who agree with each statement. A single asterisk indicates that $p < .05$; a double asterisk indicates that $p < .01$.

terms, Democrats appear to be more committed to an open (though possibly slower) regulatory process, to environmental protection (though possibly at the expense of economic prosperity), and to rate structures that promote conservation and redistributive values. It is difficult to generalize about independents, who appear to be closet Democrats on some issues, closet Republicans on others. Outside the South, though, independents seem to agree more with Republicans on revenue requirements issues, more with Democrats on rate structure issues.

Professional Background

The effects of professional background on political attitudes have received some attention through empirical research. In a study of federal bureaucrats, Plumlee concluded that "there appear to be no major differences between executives with legal backgrounds and those from other backgrounds on the basis of policy-relevant attitudes."[16] Plumlee reached this conclusion after finding no statistically significant differences between lawyers and nonlawyers along three dimensions: efficacy, cynicism, and liberalism. In a study of 4,400 faculty members at 161 colleges and universities, Ladd and Lipset found that people with a legal background are virtually indistinguishable from those with a business or engineering background.[17] Thus, the conventional wisdom seems to be that lawyers do not differ from nonlawyers in their policy preferences.

Yet, as table 13 indicates, professional background does make a difference. In four of twenty cases, differences between lawyers and nonlawyers[18] are statistically significant at an acceptable level. Furthermore, these differences remain statistically significant after controlling for political party.[19] Indeed, if controls are applied for political party, two more relationships are statistically significant: first, lawyers are more likely to believe that citizens' groups should be reimbursed for the costs of their participation in public utility commission proceedings; and, second, lawyers are less likely to believe that the desirability of alternative modes of electricity generation is best determined by utility company management.[20]

Across a range of issues, lawyers are more sympathetic to various underrepresented interests, including consumers in general (lawyers are more opposed to the inclusion of construction work in progress in the rate base of utilities), residential consumers (lawyers are less likely to agree that residential consumers pay less than their fair share of the costs of service), the poor (lawyers are more supportive of inverted rates), and environmentalists (lawyers are less willing to countenance environmental damage for the sake of economic prosperity). Of course, a cynic might argue that lawyers have a vested interest in the viewpoint that certain interests need to be better represented.[21] After all, this viewpoint sparked the creation of the Neighborhood Legal Services program, a boon not only to the poor but to lawyers as well. This was also the impetus for the creation of consumer protection offices, many of which are staffed primarily by lawyers. Thus, it is not surprising to find that lawyers are more likely to support government reimbursement of expenses (including legal fees) incurred by citizens' groups that participate in public utility commission proceedings. Happily for lawyers, the interests of due process coincide with the pecuniary interests of the legal profession.

Nevertheless, it is important to recall that the lawyers who take these positions are lawyers at public utility commissions, whose headaches are likely to intensify as citizens' groups challenge their commission in court. They are not lawyers in search of clients but gainfully employed attorneys who must rebut the arguments of other attorneys in the hearing room and in court. Whether there are too many or too few lawyers at public utility commissions is difficult to say. However, those who advocate that there should be fewer lawyers[22] ought to keep in mind that members of other professions, including engineers, accountants, and economists, are less supportive of underrepresented interests. Thus, the replacement of lawyers by nonlawyers is likely to have important policy consequences.

Industry Background

The "revolving door" between regulated industries and regulatory agencies has received a considerable amount of attention.[23] It is widely assumed that regulators who once worked for a regulated industry are more likely to favor industry in their attitudes and behavior. However, recent studies have begun to challenge conventional views of the revolving door. In a study of four federal regulatory agencies, Quirk found only "scant evidence" that direct industry employment is associated with pro-industry attitudes.[24] In a study of FCC commissioners, I found a relatively weak relationship between industry experience and pro-industry voting behavior.[25] Both Quirk and I have found - that "indirect" industry experience (for example, through a law firm that represents regulated industries, among other clients) is not associated with pro-industry attitudes or behavior.[26]

As table 13 indicates, public utility regulators who formerly worked for a utility company do not differ from other regulators in their policy preferences. Of twenty policy statements, there are no statistically significant differences between the two groups. This remains true after controls have been applied for political party.[27] Moreover, the tendencies that do exist are sometimes in an unexpected direction. For example, people with industry experience are actually less likely to believe that utilities should have flexibility to design rates. Those with industry experience are also less likely to believe that commissions should rely on utility company estimates of future energy demand.

It is possible, indeed likely, that people who worked for a utility company will have a certain sympathy toward utility companies, but it is equally likely that they will be tougher critics of utility company arguments. Former utility company employees will know where to find skeletons in the closet, and they may choose to rattle them from time to time. In practice, these two tendencies may cancel each other out.

It is important to emphasize that the data reported here refer only to the "entry" stage of the revolving door. As Quirk has shown, regulators at three of four agencies anticipate enhanced job opportunities if they take pro-industry policy positions.[28] In this complicated game of musical chairs, no one wants to be caught without a seat. Nevertheless, although the "exit" stage of the revolving door needs to be closely watched, the "entry" stage does not appear to pose a serious problem.

To sum up, the conventional wisdom fares well in some instances but not others. As expected, Democrats differ from Republicans, at least outside the South. Contrary to popular belief, lawyers also differ from nonlawyers. However, regulators who once worked for a utility company do not differ from other regulators.

In many respects, disagreement among public utility regulators is a healthy sign. As Downs has suggested, a certain amount of dissensus within the bureaucracy is likely to promote innovation.[29] It may also enhance the ability of public utility commissions to respond to competing points of view. Even if a commission chooses to reject a particular viewpoint, it may be advantageous to formulate a response to that viewpoint at an early stage rather than being surprised by it at a commission hearing. In this respect, dissensus within a commission can serve as a kind of early warning system.

Nevertheless, it must be conceded that differences between Democrats and Republicans pose a potential problem, especially in states with civil service systems that permeate the highest echelons of the bureaucracy. In such states, commissioners of one party may find that their policies are obstructed by top-level staff members of another party or no party. The danger here is that Democrats, Republicans, and independents will be unable to work together. The result may be public policy that is incoherent or inconsistent over time.

Differences between lawyers and nonlawyers also pose a potential problem. In most states, economists, engineers, and accountants formulate public utility commission policies, while lawyers write commission opinions and defend them in court. If lawyers disagree with the policies they are asked to explain and defend, they may be rather weak advocates for the commission and its point of view. This is to suggest not that lawyers will deliberately sabotage a public utility commission's case for a particular policy but that they will be more eloquent in defense of policies they support. Thus, a consumer-minded lawyer may be more vigorous in defending his agency against the utility company's charge that the rate of return is too low than against the consumer advocate's charge that the rate of return is too high.

As for differences between regulators who formerly worked for a utility company and regulators who did not, they appear to be very weak indeed. Utility companies may influence public

Table 13

Regulators' Policy Preferences by Professional, Industry Background

	Professional Background		Industry Background	
	Lawyers (N = 35)	Nonlawyers (N = 63)	Worked for Utility Company (N = 22)	Didn't Work for Utility Company (N = 73)
1. Investor-owned utilities are generally more efficient than publicly owned utilities.	78.3%	92.3%	87.5%	87.7%
2. There is already enough citizen involvement in public utility commission decisions.	31.3	40.0	30.0	40.0
3. Investor-owned utilities have a tendency to provide misleading information to regulators.	43.3	34.5	38.9	37.3
4. Utility companies should be allowed flexibility to design rates, provided that they are not discriminatory.	39.1	59.0	50.0	58.8
5. Construction work in progress should not be included in the rate base of utility companies.	61.5	31.9*	29.4	46.3
6. Popular election of public utility commissioners is not a good idea.	89.6	74.6	85.0	75.8
7. Utility companies are allowed excessive rates of return on common stock equity.	0.0	1.8	0.0	1.5
8. Some environmental damage must be tolerated for the sake of economic prosperity.	61.3	86.7*	68.2	82.1
9. Citizens' groups that participate in public utility commission proceedings ought to be reimbursed for the costs of their participation.	55.2	31.0	30.0	40.6

Statement				
10. Residential ratepayers pay less than their fair share of the costs of service.	41.4	67.3*	66.7	51.6
11. Public utility commissioners move too slowly in making decisions.	51.6	70.7	57.1	67.7
12. Public utility commissioners should promote greater competition in the sale of electric power to large industrial customers and to retail distribution systems.	36.8	51.0	61.5	44.5
13. Public utility commissioners should not rely on utility company estimates of future energy demand.	83.9	68.4	88.9	72.1
14. An inverted rate structure, with residential customers paying more per kilowatt hour as they consume more, is a good idea.	67.9	34.6**	47.1	41.9
15. The desirability of alternative modes of electricity generation is best determined by utility company management.	23.3	42.2	38.9	32.8
16. Mandatory time-of-day rates for residential customers should not be implemented at the present time.	48.2	62.5	73.6	53.2
17. Electric and gas companies should not be allowed to shut off service during the winter to apartment buildings whose landlords refuse to pay their bills.	58.6	64.3	47.4	64.1
18. Rates for interruptible service are impractical for residential customers.	66.7	65.5	52.9	70.2
19. A fuel adjustment clause is a good idea.	86.7	91.1	88.9	87.9
20. Seasonal rates should be adopted for both residential and business customers.	79.2	72.6	80.0	73.7

Note: The percentages here refer to the proportion of respondents in each category who agree with each statement. A single asterisk indicates that $p < .05$; a double asterisk indicates that $p < .01$.

utility commissions in important ways, but not through the "entry" stage of the revolving door. Of course, utility company influence through the revolving door is only one possible form of outside manipulation. Interference by the governor or the state legislature could undermine the independence of public utility commissions just as easily.

INDEPENDENCE

When state public utility commissions were first created, they were designed to be largely independent of the governor and state legislators, who were thought to be too "political" for the technical tasks of regulation. Whether public utility commissions are or should be independent has been disputed for years.[30] On the positive side, independence promotes the value of neutral competence. Yet, as Kaufman notes, neutral competence has occasionally been deemed less important than other values, such as executive leadership and representativeness.[31] One result of these intellectual twists and turns is a state bureaucracy much like the city of Troy, with old foundations submerged but never fully replaced. Another result is a literature rife with conflicting images of the governor and the state legislature.

The Governor

There are sharp disagreements over the governor's role as "chief administrator." To some observers, the governor stands astride state government like a colossus. As Beyle and Williams put it, "The governor is the prime mover of significant politics and administration at the state level."[32] Sabato also views the governor as a dominant figure. Indeed, Sabato argues that the governor has become increasingly powerful in recent years, as a result of constitutional amendments, reorganizations, and, oddly enough, the growth of civil service.[33] Others see the governor's role as more limited. In a survey of state administrators from all fifty states, Wright found that the governor was perceived as exercising less control than the state legislature. Wright also found that gubernatorial control of the bureaucracy varies sharply across states.[34] In an important extension of Wright's work, Weinberg found that gubernatorial control of the bureaucracy varies within states as well. Some state agencies are easily managed by the governor; others are not.[35] Together, Wright and Weinberg make a case for a governor who is weaker in practice than in theory. To evaluate these contrasting perspectives in the context of public utility regulation, we may examine the governor's ability to shape public utility commission policies through commission appointments, legislative initiatives, and public appeals.

The governor's most important power over public utility commissions is the power to choose commissioners. In thirty-seven states, the governor appoints public utility commissioners, sometimes with the advice and consent of the state senate, sometimes without. In most of these states, the governor designates the chairperson of the commission. In most of these states, the governor may remove a commissioner for cause.[36] Yet there is less to these powers than meets the eye. In most states with an appointed commissioner system, commissioners are appointed to staggered terms. Thus, the governor cannot immediately replace his predecessor's appointees with his own. Moreover, states with appointed commissioners usually have legal requirements for minority party representation. Under these provisions, the governor is barred from filling all commission vacancies with members of his own party. Public utility commissioners are further insulated from the governor by the traditional view of public utility commissions as "independent" regulatory agencies. This norm provides considerable protection to outspoken commissioners, as one commissioner explains:

> Here I can say anything I like. As a matter of fact, some guy charged me before the governor, and the governor's office called me and said, "Hey, did you write that?" I said, "You're goddamned right I did!" "Well, we just asked you." I said, "Well, okay. Now you know." So they just told the guy, well, I have a right to say what I like.

Unable to control his commission appointees as much as he might wish, a governor can always propose legislation. Although substantive gubernatorial initiatives in the utilities area are rare, a governor occasionally plunges head first into the thicket. For example, New Hampshire governor Hugh Gallen pushed a bill through the state legislature outlawing the inclusion of construction work in progress (CWIP) in the rate base of New Hampshire's electric utilities. More commonly, governors have championed procedural reforms designed to improve the public utility regulatory process. In Florida, for example, Governor Reubin Askew advocated that the state's elected commissioners be replaced by appointed commissioners and that the number of commissioners be expanded from three to five. In 1978, the Florida State Legislature enacted both reforms into law. In New York, Governor Hugh Carey persuaded the state legislature to establish a state energy office and to increase the size of the Public Service Commission from five to seven commissioners.

However, the legislative route is strewn with abandoned ideas, as more than one governor has discovered. Shortly after his election, Governor Lee Dreyfus of Wisconsin proposed a sweeping overhaul of the public service commission, including the establishment of an elected commissioner system and the transfer of most public service commission staff members to a revamped state energy office. Three years after the governor submitted his proposal, the legislature had not approved a single part of it. Not surprisingly, the governor shifted his attention to other issues.

Disappointed by commissioners and legislators alike, a governor can always appeal to the people. With popular support, he might be able to reverse his fortunes at the commission or the legislature. By and large, however, governors have adopted a very low public profile in the utilities area. The single most important reason is that governors have few incentives to get involved. More often than not, utilities issues have the characteristics of a zero-sum game: there are clear winners but also clear losers. Under such circumstances, the cagey governor remains aloof from the fray, not because he is uninterested, not because he respects the integrity of an "independent" commission, but because it behooves him to remain silent. One public utility regulator sums up the governor's situation:

> If you look at the design of the public utility law, it's clearly designed to put some distance between the commission and

partisan politics. But I suspect the real operative factor is that there's almost nothing to be gained by a governor getting involved. We are in some sense, under current circumstances, the real heavy in the social scene today. And the governor cannot escape criticisms for his appointments and the actions of his appointees, in fact, of the commission as a whole, whether he appointed them or not. But if he speaks out, what's he going to do? Is he going to speak out and criticize? Well, that's pretty tough, since he made some of the key appointments. . . . So is he going to speak out in favor? What does he gain by that? Then he has to accept responsibility for all the bad decisions. And they are bad from the public's point of view, in most cases. So I think that the incentive for every politician is to maintain that distance.

The State Legislature

If the governor's control of the bureaucracy is limited, perhaps the legislature's is greater, as Wright suggests.[37] In fact, it cannot be denied that state legislatures have acquired new stature in recent years. The state legislator's job has become a full-time occupation in most states, and legislative staffs have grown in size and skill. According to Alan Rosenthal, state legislatures are more productive, effective, and interventionist than ever before.[38] Yet one wonders whether the incentives of individual legislators have changed as rapidly as the resources of legislative institutions. When Barber interviewed state legislators in the 1960s, he found that half were "spectators" or "reluctants" with minimal interests in lawmaking; another one-sixth were "advertisers" with a decidedly short-term perspective.[39] Clearly, state legislatures have become much more professional. On the other hand, it is difficult to imagine spectators, reluctants, or advertisers controlling the bureaucracy in any meaningful way. To assess these contrasting perspectives, we may consider several potential legislative levers over the bureaucracy: statutes, appropriations, oversight, and advice and consent.

When public utility commissions were first established, state legislatures across the country required them to provide "reasonable" rates to consumers, a "fair" return to investors.[40] To this day, that regulatory framework, vague enough to justify almost any decision, remains intact. Although numerous bills concerning utility regulation have been introduced by state legislators, very few have passed. The fact of the matter is that, for most state legislators, the introduction of a bill suffices. Constituents want to know what their representative has done about a policy problem, not what the legislature has done. If he acts but the legislature does not, a legislator can simply assert that his benighted colleagues were too obtuse to recognize a good policy proposal. He can then portray himself as a voice of reason in the legislative wilderness, whose reelection is essential if truth and justice are to prevail. Of course, a real "lawmaker" may insist on carrying the legislative process through to its logical conclusion. However, legislative leadership has become increasingly difficult, owing to the fragmentation of legislative power and the growing autonomy of individual members.

There are, to be sure, some instances of lawmaking in the utilities area. During the 1970s, most state legislatures adopted or modified fuel adjustment clauses, designed to expedite the recovery of fuel costs incurred by utility companies. With rising fuel costs accounting for over two-thirds of rate hikes, state legislatures felt it best to handle such issues apart from general rate cases. Later, some state legislatures tightened fuel adjustment clauses to control abuses. The Virginia Legislature required the state Corporation Commission to hold quarterly review hearings and annual project hearings on fuel costs. The North Carolina Legislature mandated a fuel cost recovery delay of at least three months to stimulate efficiency. Other states inaugurated detailed audits of fuel expenses.[41]

Many state legislatures also created state energy offices, consumer protection offices, or both. Some state legislatures addressed the growing difficulties of the poor by passing lifeline rates[42] or by easing termination-of-service procedures to give the poor additional time to pay their utility bills in the winter. For the most part, however, state legislatures adopted very few statutes that affect public utilities.

Next to the power to legislate, the most celebrated legislative power is the "power of the purse." Through the appropriations process, state legislatures can influence administrative agencies in important ways. However, public utility commissions are less vulnerable to the vicissitudes of budgetary politics than other administrative agencies. In most states, public utility commissions are funded exclusively or primarily by special fees and charges imposed on utility companies. In fact, only five public utility commissions rely exclusively on general tax funds.[43] Because public utility commissions are not competing with other administrative agencies for scarce resources, legislatures have been less inclined to trim commission budget requests. Indeed, public utility commission budgets have grown substantially in recent years.

The capacity of state legislatures to control the bureaucracy through oversight has improved dramatically over the past decade. Two-thirds of the state legislatures now have statutory authority to review proposed rules and regulations before their adoption.[44] Thus, in Wisconsin and many other states, public utility commission rules must be approved by the state legislature before they can take effect. To place this in perspective, however, it is important to note that the most important public utility commission decisions are made in rate-making proceedings, which are not subject to legislative review.

Many state legislatures also provide for periodic review of administrative agencies through sunset laws. In 1980 the Florida State Legislature's review of the Public Service Commission led to major revisions of the commission's decision-making process. Nevertheless, sunset review is more an organized encounter between legislators and bureaucrats than a form of legislative control. As a result of Florida's sunset review, for example, the Public Service Commission secured authority to conduct management audits, won permission to conduct investigatory hearings behind closed doors, and acquired substantial control over its regulatory trust fund. Thus, sunset review is not necessarily a threat to the independence of public utility commissions.

A final mechanism for legislative control is the advice and consent process. In most jurisdictions where the governor has the power to appoint commissioners, the senate has the power to advise on and consent to such appointments. Occasionally, the legislative branch withholds its consent. In Idaho, for example, the state senate rejected two of Governor John Evans's nominees to the public utility commission. However, this is rare. In general, state legislatures approve gubernatorial nominees to regulatory agencies as regularly as Congress approves presidential nominees to federal regulatory commissions.[45] At the state level, as at the federal level, there is a much stronger accent on consent than on advice.

Overall, the picture that emerges is remarkably consistent with the view that regulatory agencies are "independent" of the governor and the state legislature. The problem with many recent assessments of gubernatorial and legislative power is that they focus on resources rather than incentives, the trappings of power rather than its exercise. There is no denying that utilities issues have become politicized in recent years. Yet politicization does not necessarily mean that politicians will be attracted to these issues as bees to honey. On the contrary, politicization erodes the incentives of many politicians to get involved.

The independence of public utility commissions is not a principle to which politicians have solemnly committed themselves, but neither is it a myth. Public utility commissions remain independent not because politicians respect their integrity but because they recognize a political liability when they see one. Public utility commissions today have little to fear from the governor or the state legislature. Both are bogeymen whose power to scare vanishes with the light of day. In fact, the more crucial actors are those who intervene openly in public utility commission proceedings. A wide variety of interest groups have applied pressure to public utility commissions, especially in rate cases. If the independence of public utility commissions is threatened, this is where the threat may lie.

Overload

In the electric utility industry, overload occurs when a utility company is unable to meet customer demand for its product. Frequently, this results in a power failure, with civilization as we know it coming to a screeching halt. Alternatively, a utility company may secure help from another utility company through a power pool. In government, overload occurs when a political institution cannot cope with the various demands placed upon it. If the institution is a regulatory agency, overload may manifest itself in regulatory lag (delay in reaching a decision), judicial review (the transfer of problems to the courts), or both. In either case, there is a sense in which the administrative process has failed.

Regulatory Lag

Regulatory lag is the time it takes for a regulatory agency to reach a decision. In a utility rate case, that is usually the time between a company's rate hike request (the filing date) and the commission's action on that request (the decision date). According to many utility company executives, regulatory lag is a growing problem for the industry.[46] In a period of rapidly rising costs, utility companies are eager to receive prompt rate relief. The longer a rate case lasts, the greater the likelihood that cost estimates submitted by the company will be obsolete by the time they are approved. If so, the utility company will be unable to earn its allowed rate of return. This can undermine investor confidence and increase the cost of capital. One utility executive, whose company waited nineteen months for a commission decision, sums up his frustrations:

> The most important issue that we face . . . is the problem of getting timely rate increases. Our last rate case, I think, was a good example of the problem. . . . We filed that case in March of 1977, and we did not get our order until September of 1978. So nineteen months had expired, and there's just no way that a company can earn its authorized rate of return, or near its authorized rate of return, with that kind of time delay.

What causes regulatory lag? According to Stewart, regulatory lag is a direct result of the expansion of the scope of conflict to previously underrepresented groups, such as environmentalists and consumers.[47] As agencies have liberalized opportunities for intervention by citizens' groups in their proceedings, citizens' groups have insisted that time be set aside for their views to be heard. In addition, citizens' groups have insisted on formal administrative procedures, which are more time-consuming than informal procedures. Although Stewart is concerned about this trend, he readily concedes that citizens' groups are acting rationally:

> Unorganized interests may remain at a considerable disadvantage in the informal processes of agency decision-making because their comparative lack of cohesion and financial resources prevents them from having as effective representation as organized concerns. It may therefore be to the advantage of unorganized interests to force administrative decision-making into the formal mode, even if their chances of ultimately prevailing are slim. The delay costs that can be imposed on opponents by resort to formal proceedings present tactical advantages that lawyers are unlikely to forego.[48]

If Stewart's assessment is correct, then public utility commission cases should be taking longer, given the influx of public participants in recent years. This should be especially true of rate cases, which have been particularly inviting targets. To determine whether regulatory lag has increased in recent years, public utility commission orders were obtained for major rate cases decided in twelve states during the 1974–1979 period.[49] Commission orders were examined to determine the length of each case, from filing date to final decision date.[50] Where either date was unclear, the commission or the company was asked for clarification. These procedures yielded a data base consisting of 246 major rate cases, including 120 electric cases, 104 natural gas cases, and 57 telephone cases.[51]

As table 14 indicates, regulatory lag has actually decreased in recent years. Moreover, this is true of all three types of rate cases: electric, natural gas, and telephone. By 1979, the average electric rate case lasted 8.2 months; the average natural gas rate case lasted 10.3 months; and the average telephone rate case lasted 9.8 months. Information gathered by Merrill Lynch suggests that the average length of a rate case may have declined still further in 1980.[52]

Public utility commissions and state legislatures have coped with the problem of regulatory lag in a variety of ways. The most common approach has been the adoption of fuel adjustment clauses and purchased gas adjustment clauses, which provide for automatic or relatively automatic increases in rates as fuel costs increase. By removing the single most important reason for electric and natural gas rate hikes from the rate case, public utility commissions and state legislatures have made rate cases considerably more manageable and less time-consuming.

Another common approach has been the adoption of deadlines for decision-making. At the present time, forty-one states have deadlines for decision-making in rate cases.[53] In New York, for example, the Public Service Commission must reach a decision within eleven months after a utility company files a rate hike request. If a decision is not reached by that time, the proposed rates automatically go into effect. Such a deadline provides strong incentives to act expeditiously.

A third, less frequently used, approach involves the settlement of a rate case. In New Jersey, rate cases are often resolved in this manner, through negotiations involving the utility company, the Department of Public Advocate, and the Board of Public Utilities. In Michigan, some natural gas rate cases have been settled through bargains struck by the company, the attorney general, the Public Service Commission, and other interested parties. A prerequisite to settlement appears to be the

Table 14

Regulatory Lag: Months Elapsed Between
Filing Date and PUC Decision Date
(Major Rate Cases)

	1974 (N = 43)	1975 (N = 66)	1976 (N = 49)	1977 (N = 43)	1978 (N = 49)	1979 (N = 31)
Electric cases	12.8	10.6	12.5	9.7	12.4	8.2
Natural gas cases	11.6	8.7	10.3	11.4	11.1	10.3
Telephone cases	16.5	10.4	8.4	14.8	11.1	9.8

Note: A major rate case was defined as one involving a utility company that serves more than 5 percent of a state's residential customers. In Florida and Massachusetts, where an unusually large number of small utilities provide service, only utilities serving more than 25 percent of the state's residential customers were included. The grouping of cases is by PUC decision date.

involvement of a proxy advocacy agency that can credibly claim to represent consumers. Without the approval of such an agency, bargains struck between a commission and a utility company might well lack legitimacy in the eyes of the public.

A fourth approach, adopted by the New Mexico Public Service Commission, involves a cost-of-service indexing arrangement to provide for automatic increases in rates to compensate for revenue shortfalls. Thus, rates go up automatically if the earned rate of return on equity falls considerably below the allowed rate of return. Through such an index, a utility company is able to increase its earnings without a full-blown rate case. Theoretically, such an arrangement should reduce the cost of capital by stabilizing earnings and restoring investor confidence.[54]

A final approach involves requirements that certain parties consolidate their briefs and intervene through a single representative. In Massachusetts, for example, the Department of Public Utilities has required citizens' groups to designate one party as spokesperson for all. Thus, the Massachusetts Law Reform Institute intervenes on behalf of a wide variety of citizens' groups. By limiting the number of separate intervenors, the Massachusetts Department of Public Utilities reduces opportunities for citizens' groups to delay proceedings.

In their zeal to achieve administrative efficiency, some commissions may have gone too far. An indexing system, such as the New Mexico system, comes close to providing a guaranteed profit to an industry that is supposed to involve a certain amount of risk. The requirement that citizens' groups consolidate their briefs assumes that citizens' groups are of one mind on most issues—an assumption that is questionable at best. Nevertheless, it is clear that public utility commissions have aggressively dealt with the problem of regulatory lag. The supposition that regulatory lag worsens as public intervention increases is simply incorrect.

Judicial Review

Even if a public utility commission acts expeditiously, it may not act conclusively. With so much at stake, there is a very real possibility that public utility commission decisions will spill over into the courts. If so, one or several courts may become involved. In some states (such as California and Massachusetts), a public utility commission decision is directly reviewable by the state supreme court. This approach recognizes the importance of utility cases and speeds up judicial review, but it does impose a substantial burden on the state supreme court, which has many other cases to hear. In other states, a public utility commission decision must be challenged in one or more lower courts before it can be appealed to the state supreme court. An Illinois Commerce Commission decision, for example, is reviewable by one of several circuit courts. A party dissatisfied with a circuit court's decision can appeal to the appellate courts, and then to the state supreme court. This arrangement protects the state supreme court from insignificant cases, but it can lead to a protracted period of judicial review.

The state courts, like the federal courts, appear to have loosened their standing requirements in recent years. As a result, citizens' groups are generally eligible to contest a public utility commission decision in court if they intervened before the commission. According to some observers, citizens' groups have abused their legal rights by contesting an inordinate number of administrative agency decisions. Tucker is especially critical of environmental groups which, in his view, have waged long "wars of attrition" in the courts.[55] Stewart, though more sympathetic to citizens' groups, nevertheless concedes that judicial review has become a serious problem as citizens' groups have invaded the administrative arena and the courts. In particular, Stewart fears that attorneys for citizens' groups have too many incentives to seek judicial review:

> "Public interest" lawyers representing unorganized interests may have a marked personal preference for formal processes of decision, including judicial review, because a considerable portion of the psychological reward which they receive for their work may depend on the high visibility of their efforts, and because dramatic court victories may assist fund-raising efforts.[56]

If these arguments are correct, judicial review of public utility commission decisions should be increasing as a response to growing challenges by grassroots advocacy groups. To test this hypothesis, each of the 246 major rate cases was examined in greater detail, beyond the commission decision date. To determine the judicial history of each case, public utility commissions and/or utility companies were provided with a list of docket numbers. Staff in the records department or legal department were asked to indicate which cases were appealed to the courts, who filed the appeals, and how each case was resolved by the courts.

As table 15 indicates, the percentage of major rate decisions appealed to the courts increased between 1974 and 1979. Early in this period, three out of every ten decisions were appealed to the courts. Later, four out of every ten decisions were appealed. Some of these cases were never heard by the courts, either because the court found the petition for review wanting or because the parties reached a settlement prior to a hearing. Nevertheless, these findings suggest the possibility of a growing burden on the courts (and on commissions, which must defend themselves in court) as a result of growing dissatisfaction with public utility commission decisions in major rate cases.

Who are the appellants in these cases? In descending order, they are: (1) utility companies, which appealed 14.6 percent of the decisions; (2) other business groups, which appealed 11.4 percent of the decisions; (3) proxy advocacy groups, which appealed 9.3 percent of the decisions; and (4) grassroots advocacy groups, which appealed 7.7 percent of the decisions. Other appellants included city governments, county governments, and individual citizens. It would be a mistake to infer from this that utility companies and business customers are more dissatisfied

Table 15
Judicial Review: Frequency of Appeals
(Major Rate Cases)

	1974	1975	1976	1977	1978	1979
PUC decisions	35	59	44	36	44	28
Decisions appealed	10	17	23	13	16	13
Appeals/decisions	28.6%	28.9%	52.3%	36.1%	36.4%	46.4%

Note: A petition for review submitted to a court was treated as an appeal, whether or not the court eventually heard the case. Cases are grouped according to PUC decision date.

with public utility commission decisions than proxy advocates and grassroots advocates. In fact, attempts to secure judicial review probably reflect the presence of resources as much as the absence of satisfaction.

Who wins cases appealed to the courts? To answer that question, each appealed case was placed in one of three categories. If the public utility commission was reversed in whole or in part, this was treated as a reversal. If the commission was upheld, through either a positive verdict or the dismissal of a petition for review, this was treated as an affirmation. Unresolved cases and moot cases were placed in neither category. As table 16 indicates, there is no clear trend over time with respect to the likelihood of reversal. However, one fact is clear: public utility commissions are much more likely to be affirmed than reversed. Indeed, this study finds greater judicial deference to public utility commissions than an earlier study of judicial review in four states.[57]

Public utility commissions do experience some defeats in the courts. Overall, 23 of 246 decisions were remanded to commissions by the courts. Sometimes the courts return a case to a commission because the commission was unduly modest in exercising its authority. For example, the New York Supreme Court rejected the New York Public Service Commission's claim that it lacked authority to evaluate Consolidated Edison's proposed construction of a controversial power plant on Storm King Mountain.[58] Occasionally the courts also overrule commission decisions that establish revenue requirements without due regard to evidence in the record. For example, the Mississippi Supreme Court reversed a Mississippi Public Service Commis-

Table 16
Judicial Review: Disposition by Courts
(Major Rate Cases)

	1974 (N = 10)	1975 (N = 17)	1976 (N = 23)	1977 (N = 13)	1978 (N = 16)	1979 (N = 13)
PUC affirmed	70.0%	52.9%	56.5%	61.5%	56.3%	53.8%
PUC reversed	20.0	35.3	26.1	38.5	6.3	23.1
Pending or moot	10.0	11.8	17.4	0.0	37.4	23.1

Note: The date is that of the public utility commission decision, not the court decision.

sion order awarding the Mississippi Valley Gas Company a rate hike considerably lower than requested on the grounds that "the commission's order was contrary to the overwhelming weight of the evidence."[59] Even in Mississippi, judicial activism rears its head from time to time. Usually, though, the courts defer to public utility commissions and their expertise.

Although public utility commissions sometimes lose in court, they seldom lose to a citizens' group. Of twenty-three court defeats, only three came at the hands of a citizens' group. Wisconsin's Environmental Decade, a hardy perennial in the courtroom, won two of these cases;[60] the Chicago Area Recycling Group, now defunct, won the third.[61] Citizens' groups have used the federal courts to defeat administrative agencies in a number of key cases, especially environmental cases.[62] However, state courts provide fewer opportunities for such stunning victories. In the state courts, citizens' groups opposed to public utility commission decisions have caused little more than a tremor on the Richter scale.

In contrast, utility companies have proven to be more formidable adversaries. Of the twenty-three defeats sustained by public utility commissions, twelve came at the hands of a utility company. With millions of dollars at stake and with the ability to pass along legal costs to ratepayers, utility companies are prepared to lay siege in court when necessary. Thus, if judicial review poses a threat to the authority of public utility commissions, that threat comes more from utility companies than from citizens' groups. Utility companies are more likely than citizens' groups to challenge public utility commission decisions, and they are also more likely to win in court. The argument that growing public intervention undermines the ability of public utility commissions to govern simply does not hold up.

CONCLUSION

Several years ago, public utility commissions faced a potential crisis of governance. The Arab oil embargo and worsening inflation presaged a sharp upward spiral in fuel and capital costs. Utility companies filed rate hike requests in rapid succession, and public advocacy groups responded with protests, in-

terventions, and court challenges. Governors and state legislators suddenly became aware of utilities issues. The scope of
conflict expanded. Overload seemed a very real possibility. A
crisis still looms, but it is more a crisis of confidence than a crisis
of governance. After some initial confusion, public utility commissions have managed to act with authority and alacrity.

Despite the traumas of regulation in a goldfish bowl, many
continue to choose public utility regulation as a vocation. Public
utility regulators include people who differ markedly in their
party affiliation, professional background, and industry experience. Many differ in their attitudes as well. As expected, Democrats differ from Republicans, at least outside the South. Contrary to expectations, lawyers differ from nonlawyers. However,
people with industry experience do not differ from those without
such experience. Utility companies may wield considerable influence over public utility commissions, but the "revolving door"
is not the key to such influence.

Public utility commissions are also more independent of their
gubernatorial and legislative sovereigns than is commonly recognized. Far from being a colossus, the governor often resembles
a Cyclops—intimidating perhaps but vulnerable as well. As for
the legislature, it is considerably less than the sum of its parts.
Despite the fulminations of individual legislators, the legislature as a whole is reluctant to get involved in the substance of
public utility regulation.

Fears that public advocates might swamp public utility commissions also appear to be largely unfounded. During the 1974–
1979 period, the average length of electric, natural gas, and
telephone rate cases actually declined, as commissions found
various ways to reduce regulatory lag. The frequency of court
appeals did increase during this period, but commissions won
the overwhelming majority of cases brought to the courts.

Overall, public utility commissions have survived a variety of
threats to their institutional integrity. They are not manipulated by their gubernatorial or legislative sovereigns, nor are
they paralyzed with indecision. Commissioners suffer from a
certain amount of disaffection, but this could be healthy if it
promotes turnover and generates new ideas. Commissions as a
whole suffer from a certain amount of dissensus, but this too

could be healthy, since diversity within the bureaucracy can promote innovation.

The growing frequency of judicial review is somewhat disquieting because it suggests growing dissatisfaction with the judgment of public utility commissions. With this exception, however, the commissions have managed to survive a very turbulent period with their institutional integrity intact. Perhaps they prefer authoritativeness to responsiveness. Or perhaps they have found it possible to be both authoritative and responsive. If so, the question arises: responsive to whom? It is to this important question that we now turn.

: PART II :
Political Linkage

If public utility regulation is in a state of crisis, that crisis has been poorly defined. Is there a crisis of accountability? Perhaps, but public advocacy groups are active before nearly three-fourths of all state public utility commissions. Thus, the key question is not whether public advocacy occurs but whether it is effective. More precisely, it is unclear that public advocates have sufficient resources to overcome the well-financed presentations of utility companies. It is also unclear that public advocates have sufficient incentives to participate in all issue areas.

Is there a crisis of governance, or at least a crisis of confidence? Perhaps, but it does not arise from gubernatorial interference, legislative control, or the appointment of former industry employees to public utility commissions. Nor is there evidence of an inverse relationship between governance and accountability. Despite an increase in public advocacy, regulatory lag has actually decreased. Judicial review has increased, but public utility commissions win the overwhelming majority of court challenges. Thus, the key questions remain: Who wins at the commission, where relatively conclusive decisions are reached? Utility companies? Other business groups? Public advocacy groups? Commission staffs? To whom are commissioners responding? Does this vary from state to state? Does this vary from issue area to issue area?

These questions transport us into the realm of political linkage, defined here as the connection between those who make policy and those who care about policy. Three alternative methods may be used to analyze political linkage: the concurrence method, the perceptual method, and the behavioral method. The concurrence method, which measures attitudinal agreement, has been widely used in studies of responsiveness by leaders to citizens, especially at the national level. The perceptual method, which measures reputed influence, has been widely used in studies of decision-making at the local level. The behavioral method, which measures policy impacts, has been widely used in studies of political and economic variables at the state level.

Because multiple methods can cross-validate findings, there is much to be said for using all three. If different methods yield identical or at least complementary results, confidence is justified. If, on the other hand, they yield inconsistent findings, caution is warranted. Moreover, different methods are better suited to addressing different questions. For example, the behavioral method is appropriate only when there is sufficient variation in the independent variable. Though the level of public advocacy activity varies from state to state, the level of activity by public utility commission staffs does not. (They are active everywhere.) To assess staff influence, therefore, it is necessary to use alternative methods, such as the perceptual method or the concurrence method.

The advantage of the concurrence method is that it reveals lines of cleavage over substantive and procedural controversies. Chapter 4 uses the concurrence method to answer the question: Who agrees most with public utility commissioners? It also addresses the related question of whether agreement varies by type of attitude. The chapter looks at three types of attitudes: issue priorities, value priorities, and policy preferences. Its central purpose is to identify patterns of consensus and dissensus.

The advantage of the perceptual method is that it provides a comprehensive measure of political influence in diverse policy domains that need not be specified or weighted in advance. Chapter 5 uses the perceptual method to answer the question: Which model of the policy-making process best describes the public utility regulatory process? It also addresses the related question of whether influence varies by type of state. Chapter 5 looks at four models (the capture model, the interest group model, the organizational model, and a surrogate representation model) and four types of states (acquiescent states, grassroots advocacy states, proxy advocacy states, and dual advocacy states). Its central purpose is to determine who governs in the domain of utility regulatory policy.

The advantage of the behavioral method is that it requires tangible evidence of a relationship between political variables and public policy outputs. Chapter 6 uses the behavioral method to answer the question: What are the policy impacts of those who represent the public? It also addresses the related question of whether policy impacts vary by type of issue area. Chapter 6 looks at four types of issues: those high in complexity, low in conflict; those low in complexity, high in conflict; those low in complexity, low in conflict; and those high in complexity, high in conflict. Its central purpose is to explore the relationship between politics and policy.

Chapters 4 and 5 rely primarily on interviews with 284 public utility regulators, public advocates, and utility company executives in twelve states. Chapter 6, in contrast, relies primarily on the questionnaire survey of public utility commissioners in all fifty states, as well as data on public policy outputs from the same jurisdictions. Chapter 6 also utilizes case study material derived from the interviews to illustrate broader findings. The use of multiple methods, multiple measures, and multiple data bases provides an unusually kaleidoscopic view of political linkage.

: 4 :
Political Attitudes: The Concurrence Method

Political scientists have long been fascinated by the relationship between mass attitudes and elite attitudes. That relationship is sometimes referred to as "concurrence." To Pitkin, concurrence is a particular kind of representation, which she calls "descriptive representation."[1] Pitkin readily concedes that there is a difference between descriptive representation (opinion mirroring) and political representation (acting for a constituency). Nevertheless, the study of concurrence rests on the assumption that political attitudes have demonstrable effects on political behavior. If that assumption is correct, descriptive representation is likely to lead to political representation.

Although the concept of concurrence has been widely used by political scientists, it has been defined too narrowly. As commonly employed, concurrence refers to the extent of agreement between citizens and political leaders.[2] This definition is unduly restrictive. By focusing exclusively on the linkage between citizens and leaders, it ignores others who attempt to influence policy—business groups and agency staffs, for example. Agreement between citizens and public policy makers cannot be properly gauged unless it is measured against some yardstick, such as agreement between business groups and policy makers. For this reason, concurrence will be defined here as the extent of agreement between those who attempt to influence policy and those who make policy.

Before examining concurrence between public utility commissioners and other participants in the public utility regulatory process, it is important to note three caveats. First, concurrence may or may not signify responsiveness by policy makers to participants in the policy-making process. Policy makers recognize the importance of consensus, and they attempt to generate support for policies they wish to pursue. Thus, if agreement suggests responsiveness, it is not absolutely clear who is responding to whom.

Second, concurrence may be the product of long-term political socialization rather than short-term political pressure. Agreement is not necessarily the culmination of a deliberate pursuasive process. Instead, it may attest to the more subtle effects of family, schooling, and peers.

Third, concurrence may or may not have policy consequences. Though highly suggestive, concurrence is neither a necessary nor a sufficient condition for policy impacts. Policy makers may take action despite personal opposition, just as they may fail to take action despite personal support.

Why, then, study concurrence? Despite its murky implications, it provides valuable insights into who disagrees with whom, how intensely they disagree, and over what. It identifies allies and opponents, kindred spirits and implacable foes. It illuminates the battleground. By directing our attention to the substance of public policy disputes, it also helps to clarify what is at stake. Finally, it complements more direct studies of political influence. We need to know who influences whom and with what results, but we also need to know how those results compare with initial hopes and expectations. Without such measures, it is difficult to estimate levels of satisfaction with public policy results.

THE DYADIC APPROACH

In studying concurrence, one must choose between two alternative levels of analysis: (1) the individual level, where comparisons are made between respondents within a given state; and (2) the aggregate level, where comparisons are made between types of respondents across all states. Weissberg refers to these alternatives as the "dyadic" approach and the "collective" approach, respectively.[3] The first has been used by Miller and Stokes, Verba and Nie, Hansen, and Ingram et al.[4] The second has been used by Weissberg and Hansen.[5] In general, the collective approach is less appropriate to public utility regulation than the dyadic approach, because public utility regulatory decisions are made at the state level. In short, the disadvantage of the collective approach is that it ignores state boundaries. Nevertheless, the results of both approaches will be reported here, because the collective approach does a better job of capturing the policy content of belief systems in one revealing snapshot.

Whether they have opted for the dyadic approach or the collective approach, political scientists have measured concurrence in one of two ways. Some have measured it by comparing the political attitudes and policy preferences of citizens and leaders on preselected issues.[6] This procedure has the advantage of providing comparable attitudinal data with explicit policy implications. However, it has the disadvantage of imposing a set of issues on respondents. As a result, respondents may express opinions on issues to which they have given little thought while failing to express opinions on issues about which they care deeply.

Concerned about these drawbacks, others have measured concurrence by comparing the issue priorities or "agendas" of citizens and leaders through open-ended questions.[7] This procedure has the advantage of allowing respondents to identify the key issues facing their community, state, or nation. It also properly recognizes the importance of what Cobb and Elder call "the systemic agenda," or the set of issues generally regarded as requiring government attention.[8] However, as Verba and Nie concede, citizens and leaders may agree on which issues are most important without agreeing on how those issues should be resolved.[9]

To overcome the deficiencies of these alternative measures of concurrence, both were used in this study. Respondents were asked an open-ended question about their issue priorities: What are the three most important issues your state public utility commission ought to be confronting today? Respondents were also asked a battery of twenty closed-ended questions about their attitudes toward public utility commissions, utility companies, public participants, and specific public policies.

A third measure of concurrence, based on value priorities, was also introduced. For this measure, respondents were asked to rank-order eight values widely regarded as desirable elements of a public utility commission decision: clean air, economic development, energy conservation, energy supply sufficient for demand, fair return for utility company investors, low rates for business consumers, low rates for residential consumers, and special protection for the very poor. This particular measure of concurrence simultaneously taps both priorities and preferences, since it requires respondents to rank-order concepts with clear normative implications.

To obtain these measures of concurrence (as well as other data), interviews were conducted in twelve states with 284 participants in the public utility regulatory process. Respondents included public utility commissioners and members of four groups that might be thought to influence them: public utility commission staff members, utility company executives, grassroots advocates, and proxy advocates. Although different types of respondents were asked different questions, all were asked identical questions about issue priorities, value priorities, and policy preferences.

Issue Priorities

The issue priorities of decision makers are enormously important. Owing to limitations of time and resources, policy makers can focus their attention on only a fraction of the total range of issues they might address. There is nothing neutral or antiseptic about the choice of issue priorities. As Schattschneider puts it, "Political conflict is not like an intercollegiate debate in which the opponents agree in advance on a definition of the issues. As a matter of fact, the definition of the alternatives is the supreme instrument of power; the antagonists can rarely agree on what the issues are because power is involved in the definition. He who determines what politics is about runs the country, because the definition of the alternatives is the choice of conflicts and the choice of conflicts allocates power."[10] In public utility regulatory policy, the struggle over issue priorities is the struggle over the public utility commission's agenda. Unless an issue is placed on that agenda, it is doomed to oblivion. Bachrach and Baratz refer to this phenomenon as non-decision making.[11] Ultimately, issue priorities determine which issues will be addressed through decision-making, which issues will be suppressed through non-decision making.

To measure issue priorities, respondents were asked the following open-ended question: "What, in your opinion, are the three most important substantive issues your state public utility commission ought to be confronting today?" Responses were coded and subsequently grouped into nineteen categories, which proved adequate for over 90 percent of all responses.[12] The categories were designed to be sufficiently broad to encompass responses with similar themes under the same heading. Thus, a comment about the untapped potential of solar power is sufficiently similar to a comment about the need to reduce reliance on fossil fuels that the two should be grouped together under the heading "Alternative Energy Sources." To cite another example, a comment about utility companies' expenses for fuel is sufficiently similar to a comment about utility companies' expenses for advertising that the two should be grouped together under the heading "Revenue Requirements." To differentiate further would be to exaggerate differences between respondents, who can hardly be expected to cite identical examples for similar concerns.

It is important to note that the absolute level of concurrence on issue priorities depends on the number of issue categories and the breadth of each category.[13] The greater the number of issue categories and the narrower each category, the lower concurrence will be for all parties. Thus, a coding scheme based on nineteen issue categories yields lower concurrence scores than one based on ten categories. For this reason, it is best to ignore absolute levels of concurrence on issue priorities, focusing exclusively on relative levels of concurrence instead.

To measure concurrence on issue priorities, I have computed separate concurrence scores within each state—a procedure analogous to that employed by Verba and Nie at the community level.[14] Thus, grassroots advocates in California are compared with commissioners in California, grassroots advocates in New York are compared with commissioners in New York, and so forth. This approach makes sense because the politics of public utility regulation takes place almost exclusively within state boundaries.

Like Verba and Nie, I have treated the outsider, rather than the policy maker, as the unit of analysis. However, contrary to Verba and Nie, I have excluded from analysis individuals who declined to mention one or more issues. The assumption that such individuals concur less with policy makers because they are less outspoken seems less tenable than the assumption that even outspoken people have difficulty responding to certain questions in an interview.

The process of determining concurrence scores may be illustrated by considering concurrence between utility company executives and commissioners in a state with four utility company executives and two commissioners. The concurrence score for each utility executive is determined by comparing his issue priorities with those of the two commissioners. Suppose that the first utility executive mentions issues A, B, and C, whereas the first commissioner mentions issues C, E, and F. Of three possible agreements, the two agree on one, for a concurrence score of .33 (1/3). Suppose that the second commissioner mentions issues C and E. Of two possible agreements, the first utility executive and the second commissioner agree on one, for a concurrence score of .50 (½). The average of these two scores is the first utility executive's concurrence score.[15] This process yields a total of four concurrence scores for utility executives in this particular state. These four concurrence scores are merged with concurrence scores in the remaining eleven states to arrive at a national concurrence score for utility executives, with each utility executive receiving equal weight. Concurrence scores may range from 0 (no agreement) to 1 (perfect agreement). The same procedure is followed in calculating concurrence scores for staff members, grassroots advocates, and proxy advocates.

The concurrence scores of these four groups may then be compared through a difference of means test to determine which differences are statistically significant. As table 17 indicates, concurrence between public utility commission staff members

Table 17
Concurrence with Commissioners:
Issue Priorities

	N	Concurrence Score
A. PUC staff	61	.272
B. Grassroots advocates	83	.271
C. Utility executives	51	.234
D. Proxy advocates	33	.158

Note: Concurrence scores in this instance are averages of agreement scores, which may range from 0 to 1.
Difference of Means: A-D, p. < .05; B-D, p < .05.

and commissioners is greater than concurrence between proxy advocates and commissioners. Concurrence between grassroots advocates and commissioners is also greater than concurrence between proxy advocates and commissioners. Other differences, however, are not statistically significant at an acceptable level.[16]

That commissioners agree more with staff members than with proxy advocates is hardly surprising. Given their proximity to commissioners, staff members are in an unusually advantageous position to shape the commissioners' issue priorities. For similar reasons, the commissioners are in an unusually advantageous position to shape the staff's issue priorities. In contrast, proxy advocates come into contact with commissioners much less frequently (and usually in an adversarial setting). This makes it difficult for proxy advocates to persuade commissioners, or vice versa.

Other results are more surprising. For example, concurrence between commissioners and utility company executives is lower than concurrence between commissioners and grassroots advocates. This casts some doubt on the argument that citizens have long been thwarted in their efforts to influence industry-controlled agendas. Commissioners may respond to outside pressure, but there is no evidence to suggest that grassroots advocates are generally less effective than utility executives in placing issues on the public utility commission's agenda. On issue priorities, at least, commissioners and grassroots advocates are no further apart than commissioners and utility company executives.

Value Priorities

Political values receive less scholarly attention than they deserve. Perhaps this is because we seldom think about policy problems in abstract evaluative terms. Perhaps it is because we must devise separate value systems for separate policy areas, thus reducing our inclination to think clearly about the implications of values for public policies. Or perhaps it is because we eschew an open discussion of value conflicts for fear of shattering the myth of a consensual society. Whatever the explanation, this neglect of values is regrettable, because values appear to structure more specific beliefs and patterns of behavior. As Rokeach has noted, "While attitude and value are both widely assumed to be determinants of social behavior, value is a determinant of attitude as well as of behavior."[17] Values are more fundamental and more parsimonious constructs than attitudes. They are also more enduring. Clearly, they warrant our careful attention.

To measure value priorities, respondents were asked to rank eight values on the basis of their desirability as elements of a public utility commission decision. The eight values were: clean air, economic development, energy conservation, energy supply sufficient for demand, fair return for utility company investors, low rates for business consumers, low rates for residential consumers, and special protection for the very poor. The question was phrased as follows:

> I have a list of goals or values that are widely regarded as being desirable elements of a public service commission decision. You may regard all of these as being desirable, but if you had to rank them on the basis of your own system of values, from extremely desirable to just very desirable, how would you rank them, from 1 to 8, with 1 being the most desirable value?

Political elites often refuse to participate in a value-ranking exercise. In interviews with members of the British House of Commons, Searing encountered a 16 percent refusal rate in response to a value-ranking question.[18] In this study, only 6 percent of all respondents refused to answer this question. Cultural differences could account for the greater responsiveness of American political elites. It is also possible that question wording encouraged cooperation.[19]

To measure concurrence on value priorities, I have computed concurrence scores for grassroots advocates, proxy advocates, utility executives, and public utility commission staff members. Concurrence in each instance means the extent of agreement with public utility commissioners in the same state. Since rank-orderings are being compared, an appropriate measure of agreement is the Spearman's rho coefficient.[20] Thus, concurrence scores are averages of Spearman's rho coefficients. For example, suppose that six commission staff members and three commissioners are interviewed in a particular state. The value priorities of the first staff member are compared with the value priorities of commissioners X, Y, and Z. This process yields three Spearman's rho coefficients, which are averaged to produce the first staff member's concurrence score. Each of the other five staff members also receives a concurrence score. The same routine, repeated in the other eleven states, yields concurrence scores for public utility commission staff members in all twelve states, with each staff member receiving equal weight. Because Spearman's rho coefficients may range from −1 to 1, concurrence scores based on such coefficients may also range from −1 (perfect disagreement) to 1 (perfect agreement).

Concurrence scores on value priorities, derived in this fashion, are then compared through a difference of means test. As table 18 indicates, commissioners are more likely to concur with staff members than with grassroots advocates. Commissioners are also more likely to concur with utility executives than with grassroots advocates. Other differences are not statistically significant at an acceptable level, though two come very close.[21]

These findings underscore the importance of moving beyond a measure of concurrence based on issue priorities alone. An analysis of issue priorities indicates that the concurrence of grassroots advocates with commissioners is relatively high. An analysis of value priorities indicates that the concurrence of grassroots advocates with commissioners is relatively low.

Table 18
Concurrence with Commissioners:
Value Priorities

	N	Concurrence Score
A. PUC staff	48	.341
B. Utility executives	41	.318
C. Proxy advocates	35	.218
D. Grassroots advocates	68	.106

Note: Concurrence scores in this instance are averages of Spearman's r coefficients, which may range from −1 to 1.
Difference of Means: A-D, p < .001; B-D, p < .001.

Clearly, respondents may agree on the relative importance of various issues without agreeing on the relative importance of various values. Thus, it is dangerous to draw inferences about value priorities from data on issue priorities. Perhaps it is also dangerous to draw inferences about policy preferences from data on issue priorities.

Policy Preferences

Although values are very important, policy makers resolve value conflicts not in abstract terms but in the context of particular decisions. These decisions may be either "allocative" (substantive) or "structural" (procedural). In the former instance, decisions concern tangible benefits or costs. In the latter instance, decisions concern rules of the game, which will structure future allocative decisions.[22]

To determine concurrence on policy preferences, a list of twenty statements was prepared. The statements, concerning both substantive and procedural policies, covered a wide range of controversies over revenue requirements, rate design, public accountability, private power, and other issues. On revenue requirements, statements concerned the adequacy of current rates of return on utility investments, the advisability of including construction work in progress in the utility's rate base, and the desirability of a fuel adjustment clause. On rate design, statements concerned the merits of inverted rates, time-of-day rates, seasonal rates, and rates for interruptible service. On public accountability, statements concerned the level of citizen involvement, the desirability of reimbursing public participants for the costs of intervention in public utility commission proceedings, and the sensibility of choosing commissioners through popular elections. On private autonomy, statements concerned the extent to which utilities should be free to design rates, estimate demand, and determine the mix of energy sources as they please.

Each statement was read to respondents, who were instructed to answer by using a seven-point Likert scale with the following categories: strongly disagree, disagree, somewhat disagree, not sure, somewhat agree, agree, and strongly agree. Respondents were also given the option of expressing no opinion. In practice, many respondents chose to ignore the Likert scale and responded instead with an unvarnished "agree" or "disagree." Some relied on the interviewer to interpret their response, as in the following exchange:

Q: Citizens' groups should be reimbursed for the costs of their participation in public utility commission proceedings.

A: You bet your sweet bippie!

Other respondents had trouble differentiating between the "not sure" and "no opinion" categories. In view of these complications, responses were collapsed into three categories: agree, disagree, and missing data.

The computation of concurrence scores for policy preferences is relatively straightforward. For any individual, concurrence with a commissioner is defined as the number of policy statements on which both concur divided by the number of policy statements on which both express an opinion. Each individual's concurrence score is the percentage thus calculated, averaged over all commissioners in the same state. Thus, suppose that Grassroots Advocate A expresses an opinion on all twenty statements. Further suppose that Grassroots Advocate A agrees with Commissioner X on five of twenty statements (25 percent), Commissioner Y on eight of sixteen statements (50 percent), and Commissioner Z on nine of twelve statements (75 percent). Grassroots Advocate A receives a concurrence score of 50 percent. The national concurrence score for grassroots advocates is the average of all such concurrence scores, with each grassroots advocate receiving equal weight. Concurrence scores, whether individual or national, may range from 0 (no agreement) to 1 (perfect agreement).

As with issue priorities and value priorities, concurrence scores are compared through a difference of means test. As table 19 indicates, commissioners concur more with public utility commission staff members than with grassroots advocates or proxy advocates. Commissioners also concur more with utility executives than with grassroots advocates or proxy advocates. Other differences, however, are not statistically significant at an acceptable level.

Although commissioners are more likely to concur with utility executives than with grassroots advocates, this difference is not terribly striking. However, if we distinguish between substantive and procedural issues, a clearer picture emerges. On procedural issues, commissioners concur about equally with utility executives and grassroots advocates. On substantive issues, though, commissioners are much more likely to agree with utility executives than with grassroots advocates. These findings suggest the possibility of "symbolic politics." Utilities get tangible benefits (support for substantive policies they favor), whereas grassroots advocates get symbolic benefits (support for certain rules of the game).[23] This arrangement, if tolerated,

Table 19
Concurrence with Commissioners: Policy Preferences

		Concurrence Scores		
	N	*All Issues*	*Procedural Issues*	*Substantive Issues*
A. PUC staff	62	.643	.622	.669
B. Utility executives	51	.621	.574	.661
C. Grassroots advocates	83	.551	.603	.512
D. Proxy advocates	34	.541	.524	.562

Note: Concurrence scores in this instance are averages of agreement scores, which may range from 0 to 1.

Difference of Means:

(All)　　　　A-C, p < .001; A-D, p < .001; B-C, p < .001; B-D, p < .001.

(Procedural)　A-D, p < .01; C-D, p < .05.

(Substantive)　A-C, p < .01; A-D, p < .001; B-C, p < .001; B-D, p < .001.

could legitimize regulation even after the so-called marasmus of the regulatory process has set in.[24]

The Collective Approach

Although the dyadic approach is very useful, it does not illuminate the substance of controversies over issue priorities, value priorities, and policy preferences. A collective approach is more useful in this respect, because it reveals the issues on which respondents disagree and how they disagree. The advantage of the dyadic approach is that it illuminates levels of friction. The advantage of the collective approach is that it illuminates sources of friction. If our purpose is to determine how much people disagree, a dyadic approach is more appropriate. If, on the other hand, our purpose is to discern over what people disagree, a collective approach is more appropriate.

Issue Priorities

To identify particular issues whose importance is disputed, I have calculated the total number of times each issue was mentioned by each type of respondent. From these raw scores, I have derived an aggregate rank-ordering of issues for each type of respondent. This rank-ordering, reproduced in table 20, indicates which issues are ranked highly by which respondents. A closer look may help us to pinpoint similarities and differences in issue priorities.

1. *Public utility commission staff members,* like commissioners, consider rate design, alternative energy sources, an adequate energy supply, and the consumers' rate burden to be especially important issues. Like commissioners, staff members also regard the quality of regulatory personnel, the scope of the commission's jurisdiction, utility company ownership, and utility company competition as relatively unimportant issues.

There are, however, modest disagreements. For example, the staff places more emphasis than commissioners on power plant problems and utility management problems. In the opinion of many staff members, public utility commissions cannot adequately control energy policy if they are locked into power plant decisions made by utility managers and federal officials.

Table 20
Issue Priorities

	Proxy Advocates (N = 33)	Utility Executives (N = 51)	Grassroots Advocates (N = 83)	PUC Staff (N = 62)	PUC Commissioners (N = 38)
Rate design	2	2.5	1	1	1
Adequate energy supply	17	4.5	12	4.5	2
Alternative energy sources	7	8.5	2	2	3
Consumer rate burden	5	6	4	4.5	4
Value trade-offs	17	7	9	6	5
Energy forecasting	7	11	6	13.5	6
Power plant problems	3.5	11	5	3	8.5
Customer service regulations	7	13.5	7.5	7	8.5
Utility co. financing	3.5	2.5	18	13.5	8.5
Efficiency of reg. process	11	4.5	18	19	8.5
Revenue requirements	1	1	7.5	9	11
Federal requirements	17	18	18	9	13
Public understanding	19	18	13.5	11	13
Public accountability	11	11	3	17	13
Utility co. management	11	15.5	15	9	17
Utility co. competition	14.5	8.5	16	13.5	17
Scope of PUC jurisdiction	11	15.5	10.5	13.5	17
Utility co. ownership	11	18	13.5	17	17
Quality of PUC personnel	14.5	13.5	10.5	17	17

Note: Lower numbers reflect higher issue priorities.

The staff also places less emphasis than commissioners on energy forecasting, utility financing, and the efficiency of the regulatory process.

2. *Grassroots advocates,* like commissioners, believe that rate design, alternative energy sources, and the consumers' rate burden are especially important issues. Like commissioners, grassroots advocates also believe that utility company competition and management are relatively unimportant. Grassroots advocates care less about the internal operations of utilities or relationships between utilities than the implications of utility decisions for residential consumers.

As table 20 indicates, however, grassroots advocates differ sharply from commissioners on procedural issues. Despite the fact that they were asked to cite substantive issues only, grassroots advocates place heavy emphasis on the procedural issue of public accountability. Unless public utility commissions and utility companies are more accountable to the public, grassroots advocates argue, substantive decisions will continue to be decided in favor of utility companies. To remedy this problem, grassroots advocates urge that public utility commissions and utility companies open themselves up to greater public input through procedural reform and greater receptivity to public demands. One grassroots advocate puts it this way: "I think that the public utility commission, instead of trying to stifle consumer interest and consumer interest groups by blocking them in every direction, should be throwing open their offices in cooperation with them."

In contrast to commissioners, who rank public accountability thirteenth on their list of priorities, grassroots advocates rank it third. Grassroots advocates also place greater emphasis than commissioners on the scope of the commission's jurisdiction and the quality of public utility commission personnel. In broader terms, grassroots advocates stress the importance of reforming the regulatory process itself. On the other hand, grassroots advocates place less emphasis than commissioners on such issues as an adequate energy supply and utility company financing. They are less troubled than commissioners by the financial problems utilities face in trying to maintain a given level of supply. If utilities have difficulty raising capital, they reason, maybe this will prevent them from building unnecessary power plants.

3. *Utility executives* believe that the most important issues of all are revenue requirements issues. The following observation is typical: "One [important issue] is the cost of capital. Permitting the utilities to earn a sufficient amount so that they can raise capital in today's money market. This is absolutely essential because if the utilities cannot raise the capital . . . they will not be able to provide the service." Utility executives also emphasize the related issue of utility company financing. For example:

[Issue] number one is the financial integrity of the company and by that I mean the company should have at all times the ability to finance its construction program when needed and the amount needed and in the desirable manner. For a utility to become unable to finance at any given time is certainly not in the best interest of either the ratepayers or the utility and in the long run will cost the ratepayer more.

Commissioners are not persuaded that these are the most pressing issues they face. Nor are they persuaded that utility company competition is as crucial an issue as some telephone company executives seem to think. For their part, utility executives are not persuaded that certain issues are as important as commissioners think. For example, they are less inclined to emphasize alternative energy sources, either because they are satisfied with the current mix of power sources or because they believe public utility commissions should not assert themselves in this area. Utility executives also place less emphasis than commissioners on energy forecasting, probably for similar reasons.

Nevertheless, there is some agreement between utility executives and public utility commissioners. Like commissioners, utility executives believe that rate design and energy supply issues are very important. Like commissioners, utility executives believe that utility ownership, utility management, and the scope of jurisdiction are relatively unimportant.

4. *Proxy advocates,* unlike commissioners, regard revenue requirements issues as most important. One proxy advocate puts it this way:

> The first issue is . . . the determination of rate of return, cost of capital. That's the area that I'm most interested in. I also think that it has substantial impact on the revenue determination by the regulatory agency . . . the question whether or not just the entire idea of a rate base/rate of return traditional regulatory model is the most effective. There are some problems, there are some pluses.

Proxy advocates also place relatively greater emphasis than commissioners on such issues as power plant problems, utility financing, management, and ownership. When they elaborate on their concerns, it is clear that they see high rates, inept management, and unnecessary power plants as interrelated prob-

lems urgently demanding attention. In contrast to commissioners, proxy advocates place relatively little emphasis on value
trade-offs or public understanding. To them, problems are clear,
and solutions are equally clear. Thus, they are more interested
in immediate action than in balancing or consensus-building
acts.

Even proxy advocates agree with commissioners on the relative importance of some issues. Like commissioners, proxy advocates regard rate design and the consumers' rate burden as
important. Like commissioners, they also regard utility competition and the quality of commission personnel as relatively
unimportant.

According to Bachrach and Baratz, non-decision making occurs when an issue of importance to a powerless group is denied
agenda status.[25] If commissioners refuse to acknowledge the
importance of an issue deemed important by grassroots advocates (who are most removed from the power structure), this
might be evidence of non-decision making. Public accountability, ranked third by grassroots advocates but thirteenth by
commissioners, could be such an issue. Despite the entreaties
of grassroots advocacy groups, public utility commissioners
continue to regard public accountability as a relatively unimportant problem or one for others to address. This places in
perspective the relatively high level of agreement between
commissioners and grassroots advocates on procedural issues
noted earlier. If procedural issues are denied agenda status,
commissioners lose little by agreeing with grassroots advocates
on how such issues should be resolved.

Value Priorities

To capture the substance of value conflicts, where they exist,
table 21 contains the mean or average ranking of each of eight
values by each of the five types of participants. It should be
recalled that respondents were asked to rank-order values from
1 to 8, with 1 being the most desirable element of a public utility
commission decision. Thus, a lower mean rating signifies a more
desirable value. To explore the substance of value controversies,
we may compare the value priorities of public utility commissioners with those of the other participants.

Table 21

Value Priorities

	Grassroots Advocates (N = 68)	Proxy Advocates (N = 35)	Utility Executives (N = 41)	PUC Staff (N = 48)	PUC Commissioners (N = 32)
1. Energy supply sufficient for demand	4.32	3.00	2.06	1.71	2.06
2. Energy conservation	2.33	2.54	3.77	2.75	3.22
3. Economic development	5.35	4.90	3.88	4.70	4.56
4. Fair return for investors	6.69	5.10	2.21	4.55	4.63
5. Low rates for residential consumers	3.79	4.25	5.58	4.50	4.71
6. Clean air	3.85	5.11	5.54	5.54	5.29
7. Special protection for the very poor	2.88	4.63	6.23	6.04	5.59
8. Low rates for business consumers	6.68	6.32	6.44	5.84	5.76

Note: Lower numbers reflect higher value priorities.

1. *Public utility commission staff members* and commissioners both rank an adequate energy supply and energy conservation high. Both rank low rates for business consumers, special protection for the very poor, and clean air low. Both rank economic development, a fair return for investors, and low rates for residential consumers in between.

Like commissioners, staff members believe that no value is more desirable than an energy supply sufficient for demand. As one staff members puts it, "If you don't have a supply and it's not reliable, price becomes a secondary concern." Like commissioners, staff members tend to view the commission's role in relatively narrow terms. They are especially vocal on the subject of special protection for the very poor, which they regard as a legislative, not an administrative, responsibility. The following comment is typical: "It's my personal belief that social objectives should not be achieved through the regulatory process. I think we have other vehicles of government intended, designed, and set up to establish that goal. I don't think it should be a consideration of the regulatory process."

2. *Utility executives,* like commissioners, are strongly committed to an adequate energy supply. One utility company executive puts it this way:

I think the Commission has to recognize, and I think they do, that to attract industry . . . to keep people getting up at eight o'clock in the morning and having a place to go to work, they have to have energy, because the factories don't run without it. So I think it's extremely important that the energy is there.

Like commissioners, utility executives regard clean air and special protection for the very poor as relatively low priorities. As they see it, clean air is already adequately protected by the federal Environmental Protection Agency and its state counterparts. As for special protection for the very poor, they see that as a legislative matter:

Special protection for the very poor is something that I certainly think is a job for our legislative bodies, but I don't see it as a job for the public service commission. In fact, under their particular statutory scheme, it's not something that I think they are legally empowered to do except in a very ephemeral kind of way.

Although utility executives and commissioners agree on many values, they disagree on the relative desirability of low rates for residential consumers and a fair return for utility investors. Commissioners regard these two values as equally desirable, but utility executives believe a fair return for investors is much more desirable than low rates for residential consumers. Utility executives justify their emphasis on a fair return by arguing that an adequate energy supply is impossible without higher rates of return. As one utility executive comments: "Unless you have that fair return for utility company investors, you would find yourself in a position very soon of not having the energy to meet your demand." There are, of course, other ways to ensure an adequate energy supply—by reducing demand through energy conservation, for instance. With this in mind, it is important to note that utility executives are somewhat less enthusiastic about energy conservation than commissioners. Nevertheless, the fact that commissioners and utility company executives agree that an adequate energy supply is more desirable than energy conservation places them both in a position to

justify higher rates of return to forestall blackouts and brownouts in the future.

3. *Proxy advocates,* like commissioners, regard an adequate
energy supply and energy conservation as the most desirable
values. Unlike commissioners, proxy advocates regard energy
conservation as more desirable than an adequate energy supply.
The distinction surfaces in the choice between building more
and using less. To achieve an equilibrium between supply and
demand, proxy advocates prefer energy conservation to power
plant construction. One proxy advocate places the goal of an
energy supply sufficient for demand in context:

> Energy supply sufficient for what demand? You can deter-
> mine demand depending on how you establish rates . . . I
> don't think there should be energy supply sufficient for any
> level of demand. There should be energy supply sufficient
> for an economic level of demand, and those who make the
> expensive demands should get price signals so that they are
> perfectly free to make those energy demands if they're will-
> ing to pay the real costs of those energy demands.

At a superficial level, proxy advocates and commissioners
agree on revenue requirements matters. Both rank a fair return
for investors and low rates for residential consumers as more
desirable than some values, less desirable than others. However, although commissioners regard these two values as relatively equal in desirability, proxy advocates see lower rates for
residential consumers as more desirable than a fair return for
investors. Here is one proxy advocate's rationale:

> I'm personally not hostile to investors. I mean, I think this
> office has to work within the way society is created. . . . It's
> just that I think that in the past there's been so much atten-
> tion paid to investors and so little paid to ratepayers and
> energy conservation and other problems of our current
> energy environment that I think we need a more balanced
> perspective.

4. *Grassroots advocates* disagree with commissioners on the
relative importance of a number of values. In contrast to com-

missioners, who regard an adequate energy supply as most desirable, grassroots advocates care much more about other values. In contrast to commissioners, who regard a fair return for investors and low rates for residential consumers as relatively equal in desirability, grassroots advocates are far less enthusiastic about a fair return. These disagreements have important implications for rate hikes. In effect, grassroots advocates are rejecting both direct and indirect rationales for rate increases—the argument that utility company investors are entitled to a fair rate of return and the argument that a higher return is necessary to avert power outages. Grassroots advocates also provide little support for low rates for business consumers. One grassroots advocate explains her value priorities:

The reason I put low rates for business consumers fairly down toward the bottom is that they are able to pass their costs along to the customer, so they don't really suffer. As long as all of them are treated equally, it doesn't erode their competitive position so, you know, it's not the hardship on them that it is to the residential customer where the buck stops there, you know. And fair return for utility company investors—well, there again, they have a choice of where they can put their money. The residential consumer has no choice in where he's going to get his power, so he's locked in with whatever he has to pay.

A final difference between grassroots advocates and commissioners is that grassroots advocates have a much more expansive role in mind for the public utility commission. As they see it, the commission should not hesitate to address important societal goals, such as environmental and redistributive goals. Grassroots advocates and commissioners disagree most sharply on the question of special protection for the very poor. To grassroots advocates, such protection is highly desirable and second only to energy conservation. In contrast, commissioners strongly reject the contention that special protection for the very poor should take precedence over other values. Indeed, some commissioners argue that it has no place whatsoever in the calculus of public utility regulation. To the extent that dissimilar value priorities impede political persuasion, grassroots advocates appear to have a long, uphill battle ahead.

The preceding analysis suggests a tendency for public utility commissioners to tilt in the direction of utility companies when key values come into conflict. Despite frequent references to public utility regulation as a "balancing act," public utility commissioners do more leaning than balancing. Even where they disagree with utility executives, as on the relative desirability of a fair rate of return, there is less to this disagreement than meets the eye. Once the central importance of an adequate energy supply is acknowledged, a case can be made for a higher rate of return in order to attract capital necessary for plant expansion. Thus, the fact that commissioners and utility executives agree on a critical "terminal" value makes it possible for them to agree on certain "instrumental" values whose intrinsic importance may be disputed.[26]

Policy Preferences

To clarify lines of cleavage on policy preferences, I have computed the mean agreement score of each type of respondent with each of twenty policy statements, averaged across all twelve states. For the sake of convenience, substantive and procedural issues have been grouped separately, although they were deliberately intermixed in the interview schedule. The mean agreement scores, reproduced in table 22, permit us to differentiate between consensual and conflictual issues.

1. *Public utility commission staff members* agree with commissioners on many specific policies. Yet even staff members disagree with commissioners some of the time. As a general rule, the staff expresses stronger support for utility companies than commissioners do. Although staff members express sympathy for consumers, they often accept the utilities' perspective on where consumer interests lie. For example, the staff is more supportive than commissioners of putting construction work in progress in the utility's rate base, as the following comment illustrates: "If we have a company that is relatively efficient and is not running into . . . cost overruns, then they should be allowed CWIP. The consumer is better off with CWIP. It will lead

Table 22
Policy Preferences

	Proxy Advocates (N = 34)	Grassroots Advocates (N = 83)	Utility Executives (N = 51)	PUC Staff (N = 62)	PUC Commissioners (N = 38)
Substantive Issues					
1. Investor-owned utilities are generally more efficient than publicly owned utilities.	36.0%	15.1%	96.0%	92.3%	79.2%
2. Construction work in progress should not be included in the rate base of utility companies.	92.6	94.8	0.0	37.5	51.9
3. Utility companies are allowed excessive rates of return on common stock equity.	50.0	68.1	0.0	1.9	0.0
4. Some environmental damage must be tolerated for the sake of economic prosperity.	78.8	32.1	86.0	85.7	71.4
5. Residential ratepayers pay less than their fair share the costs of service.	10.7	5.2	91.5	63.0	48.5
6. Public utility commissioners should promote greater competition in the sale of electric power to large industrial customers and to retail distribution systems.	88.5	80.0	19.2	43.5	52.2
7. An inverted rate structure, with residential customers paying more per kilowatt hour as they consume more, is a good idea.	78.1	87.2	24.4	44.9	45.5
8. Mandatory time-of-day rates for residential customers should not be implemented at the present time.	43.3	55.6	76.3	54.9	72.4
9. Electric and gas companies should not be allowed to shut off service during the winter to apartment buildings whose landlords refuse to pay their bills.	93.5	93.8	48.6	64.8	57.6

10. Rates for interruptible service are impractical for residential customers.	40.7	39.7	60.0	62.0	75.0
11. A fuel adjustment clause is a good idea.	58.1	28.2	100.0	91.1	87.5
12. Seasonal rates should be adopted for both residential and business customers.	92.0	64.8	69.4	76.6	73.3
Procedural Issues					
13. There is already enough citizen involvement in public utility commission decisions.	3.0	6.1	64.0	43.3	28.6
14. Investor-owned utilities have a tendency to provide misleading information to regulators.	79.4	92.8	2.0	38.6	32.4
15. Utility companies should be allowed flexibility to design rates, provided that they are not discriminatory.	28.1	25.0	91.8	59.0	57.1
16. Popular election of public utility commissioners is not a good idea.	44.8	34.4	90.7	78.2	77.8
17. Citizens' groups that participate in public utility commission proceedings ought to be reimbursed for the costs of their participation.	82.4	93.9	14.9	40.4	36.4
18. Public utility commissioners move too slowly in making decisions.	43.3	59.4	90.0	66.7	60.0
19. Public utility commissioners should not rely on utility company estimates of future energy demand.	90.6	97.6	27.3	66.1	88.2
20. The desirability of alternative modes of electricity generation is best determined by utility company management.	12.5	1.2	81.0	37.0	31.4

Note: The percentages here refer to the proportion of respondents in each category who agree with each statement.

to lower rates in the long run, and we've done studies that demonstrate this."

The staff is also more willing than commissioners to endorse the argument that residential consumers pay less than their fair share of the costs of service.

2. *Utility company executives* and commissioners are especially likely to argue on substantive issues. They are more likely to disagree on procedural issues, such as public accountability and the proper balance between private autonomy and government authority. For example, utility company executives are much less likely than commissioners to support citizen involvement. As utility executives see it, the public is already adequately represented by the commission itself. Moreover, they argue, citizens are congenitally incapable of addressing complex issues in a calm, deliberate manner. One utility executive puts it this way:

> My experience has been, at least in our rate proceedings, and I've been to some electric proceedings, that . . . the public has screamed and raved and ranted with arguments such as, "The rates are too high! We're being ripped off!" And there is no consideration of whether the utility has done an excellent job and needs rate relief in the face of rising costs and I think, in my experience, they're strictly emotional.

Utility company executives are also very jealous of their autonomy. They bristle at suggestions that their demand forecasts are unreliable. The following comment is typical: "It's in the utility's best interest to forecast future demands as accurately as possible, because ideally . . . [the utility] should neither overbuild nor underbuild. . . . Overbuilding creates expensive reserves. Underbuilding adversely affects the economy of the region."

Utility executives and commissioners also disagree on certain substantive issues. Utility executives are less supportive of inverted rates and competition between utilities. Utility executives are more supportive of CWIP in the rate base and rate designs favorable to business customers.

3. *Grassroots advocates* and commissioners are especially

likely to disagree on substantive issues. There are, for example, sharp disagreements between grassroots advocates and commissioners on revenue requirements issues. Though grassroots advocates regard other issues as more important, their views on revenue requirements issues are often extreme. Consider, as a case in point, one grassroots advocate's observations on the allowed rate of return:

> I believe that there's got to be a redefinition of the term "investor" to take account of the fact that private utilities in this country are allowed not only to get a fair return on investment but are allowed . . . [to] get back their investment completely once it's approved by the Commission. . . . So-called investors . . . are in effect no more than term depositors. . . . In other words, we should be talking in terms of a rate of return equivalent to a term deposit in the bank, for example, or government bonds.

Grassroots advocates are also more skeptical than commissioners of arrangements that preserve the utility companies' autonomy. The following comment is illustrative:

> Companies, if they're stock companies, want to make money. You can translate this out to a five-letter word which is called GREED. Many times their greed for making a buck will cause them to tailor their impact, their demands on the public, and their way of delivering service to the public in a certain way. . . . They shouldn't be the sole ones to decide.

Thus, there are differences between grassroots advocates and commissioners on procedural issues as well.

4. *Proxy advocates* and commissioners agree somewhat more on substance than on procedure. Though proxy advocates disagree with commissioners on a number of substantive issues, they are generally more cautious in their assessments than grassroots advocates. Proxy advocates are fairly evenly divided, for example, on such questions as whether a fuel adjustment clause is a good idea and whether utilities get an excessive rate of return. One proxy advocate suggests that a fuel adjustment clause "may be a good idea if in fact there is some regulatory

oversight and if in fact there are some incentives for the utility to bargain for the lowest-cost fuel." Another proxy advocate supports the idea of a ban on electric and gas shutoffs in the winter but also supports "some kind of expedited procedures" so that utilities can collect unpaid bills.

Proxy advocates are less equivocal on certain procedural issues—for example, those concerning the role of utilities in determining our energy future. On the subject of utility forecasts, one proxy advocate suggests that utilities tend to look at the future "through rose-colored glasses." Another puts it this way:

> Electric utilities . . . are run by engineers, and they're like kids with erector sets. And if you give them the money, they'll buy the biggest doggone erector set that you ever saw. . . . If you give an electric utility manager who is an engineer the money, he'll take it and he'll build something with it, and then you're gonna pay on it for thirty years.

In reviewing these findings, it is tempting to suggest that public utility commissioners are less conservative than utility company executives and commission staff members, more conservative than grassroots advocates and proxy advocates. If conservatism means support for the views of regulated industries, then this assessment is reasonably accurate. On most issues, utilities are more likely to be supported by the staff than by the commissioners, more likely to be supported by the commissioners than by public advocates.

Yet if conservatism means support for the status quo, such an assessment may be premature. For example, on the question of allocating the costs of service between classes of customers, public advocates are more content with the status quo than commission staff members and utility executives, who would like to reduce the business community's share of the rate burden. On the question of regulatory efficiency, public advocates are less interested than staff members and utility executives in expediting the regulatory process.

In reality, the politics of public utility regulation is more complex than either definition suggests. There are lines of cleavage not merely between those who favor change and those who oppose it but also between those who favor a better break for utilities and those who favor a better break for consumers, between those who favor relief for residential consumers and those who favor relief for business consumers, between those who seek to help the middle class and those who seek to help the poor, between those who favor lower rates even if it means higher consumption and those who favor lower consumption even if it means higher rates. In short, the politics of public utility regulation may be viewed in liberal-conservative terms, but other lines of cleavage are also important.

CONCLUSION

In contrast to previous studies of concurrence, this study utilizes data on issue priorities, value priorities, and policy preferences. It also uses both a dyadic and a collective approach. The former, based on individual-level data, makes comparisons within states for the purpose of discovering levels of agreement and disagreement. The latter, based on aggregate-level data, makes comparisons across states for the purpose of discovering sources of agreement and disagreement.

Whether one looks at issue priorities, value priorities, or policy preferences, one finds that public utility commissioners concur more with public utility commission staff members than with other participants in the regulatory process. One also finds that commissioners concur more with staff members than with utility company executives and more with executives than with proxy advocates. However, the position of grassroots advocates fluctuates. On issue priorities, commissioners concur more with grassroots advocates than with utility company executives. On value priorities and policy preferences, commissioners concur more with utility company executives than with grassroots advocates. These findings suggest that data on issue priorities should not be used to draw inferences about value priorities or policy preferences.

Although levels of agreement and disagreement are important, sources of agreement and disagreement are equally important. A focus on the content of belief systems reveals several interesting patterns. First of all, commissioners, staff members, and utility executives are alike in emphasizing energy supply issues, which grassroots advocates and proxy advocates deemphasize. Utility executives and proxy advocates are alike in emphasizing revenue requirements issues, which commissioners and staff members deemphasize. On at least one issue, there appears to be some evidence of non-decision making. Despite strong emphasis on public accountability issues, grassroots advocates have been unsuccessful in placing these issues on commission agendas. If this persists, commissions could eventually face a serious crisis of authority, with large numbers of ratepayers refusing to pay their bills. Indeed, this is already a troublesome problem.

Second, commissioners, staff members, and utility executives attach greater weight to a sufficient energy supply than to energy conservation, whereas grassroots and proxy advocates attach greater weight to conservation. On revenue requirements issues, utility executives value a fair return for investors more highly than low rates for residential consumers, whereas grassroots and proxy advocates value low rates more highly. Commissioners strike a balance here. On other issues, however, commissioners tilt toward the utilities. For example, although grassroots advocates believe that the commission should pursue redistributive and environmental values, commissioners agree with utility executives that such matters are beyond the scope of the commission's jurisdiction. Commissioners occupy the middle ground between grassroots advocates and utility executives, but they do not occupy the middle of that middle ground.

Third, commissioners concur more with utility executives than with grassroots advocates on a variety of specific policy controversies. The gap between commissioners and grassroots advocates is considerably wider on substantive than on procedural issues. This is consistent with a "symbolic politics" interpretation. When the allocation of tangible benefits is at stake, commissioners tend to side with utilities; when the allocation of symbolic benefits is at stake, commissioners are more willing to side with grassroots advocates.

Although concurrence is a useful concept, it falls short of revealing the relative influence of various participants in the public utility regulatory process. It also fails to reveal the specific policy impacts of various participants. Concurrence between participant A and policy maker B could mean that A has persuaded B, or that B has persuaded A, or that both A and B shared similar beliefs in the first place. Thus, the meaning of concurrence is ambiguous. Furthermore, concurrence is neither a necessary nor a sufficient condition for influence. An intervenor may persuade public utility commissioners of the desirability of a particular policy, but the public utility commission may still do nothing if commissioners believe they lack authority to act. Conversely, an intervenor may have an impact without persuading commissioners that a particular policy is desirable, by applying enough political pressure to induce commissioners to adopt a policy they do not fully support. In short, concurrence is not an acceptable indicator of behavioral change. To assess political influence and policy impacts, it is necessary to utilize alternative approaches.

: 5 :
Political Influence: The Perceptual Method

For years, students of regulatory politics have been preoccupied with the question of business influence over regulatory decisions. Social scientists who wrote in the 1950s and '60s concluded that regulatory agencies tend to be dominated by the industries they are supposed to regulate. Some even went so far as to suggest that regulatory agencies become "captives" of regulated industries over time.[1] Others, carefully eschewing the word *capture*, nevertheless argued that regulatory agencies are overly responsive to regulated industries,[2] that they confer tangible benefits on regulated industries while placating the general public with symbols,[3] and that they will continue to behave this way unless the legislative branch curbs their authority.[4]

More recent analysts have reached remarkably different conclusions. According to them, regulatory agencies have become impervious to the costs of regulation, which can be enormous.[5] These critics contend that regulatory agencies are not too lenient but too strict. More modest claims are made by scholars who see a mixture of pro-producer and pro-consumer policies emerging from fierce competition among conflicting interest groups. These observers argue that regulatory agencies will adopt pro-cosumer policies if an organized constituency presses consumer claims,[6] if economic conditions are expansionary,[7] or if policies under consideration involve widely distributed benefits.[8] This chapter tests these conflicting perspectives by using "perceptual" measures of the influence of

: 132 :

business groups and other participants in the public utility regulatory process.

MODELS OF THE REGULATORY PROCESS

The two leading models of the regulatory policy-making process are the capture model and the interest group model. Both share a common emphasis on nongovernmental participants in the regulatory process. However, the capture model stresses the special importance of regulated industries, which are thought to dominate the regulatory process. In contrast, the interest group model emphasizes the presence of competing pressure groups, with conflicting objectives and demands. These models have so dominated our thinking that they have blinded us to equally plausible alternatives.

One such alternative is an organizational model, which highlights the role of regulatory agency staff members. Several recent works treat the regulatory staff as a discrete entity worthy of separate analysis.[9] Nevertheless, most studies of regulatory policy-making do not ask the question: Who influences the commissioners? Rather, they ask: Who influences the commission? This approach relegates the staff to an insignificant role. It assumes that the staff is a mere extension of regulatory commissioners or a regulatory administrator. It contributes to the belief that faceless bureaucrats are also powerless bureaucrats.

Another model worthy of consideration may be described as a surrogate representation model. As noted in chapter 2, it is now common for public officials to intervene in state agency proceedings as surrogates for consumers. These "proxy advocates" include the attorney general in some states, a consumer counsel in others. Because proxy advocacy offices are government organizations, they cannot be subsumed under the "interest group" category. Thus, we need to consider not two but four competing models of the regulatory policy-making process: the capture model, the interest group model, the organizational model, and the surrogate representation model.

The capture model views regulatory agencies as the captives of the industries they are supposed to regulate. It portrays administrative decisions as responses to external pressure, exerted primarily and sometimes exclusively by regulated industries. It does not deny the importance of regulatory agency staff members, but it regards them as conveyor belts for industry sentiments. It does not deny the existence of other pressure groups, but it views them as uninterested or ineffectual.[10]

According to capture theorists, capture is a direct result of the independence of regulatory commissions. Because the chief executive lacks authority over regulatory commissions, he quickly loses interest in them. Without his leadership, the legislative branch also loses interest, and public awareness wanes. In contrast, the attentiveness of regulated industries increases, as they respond to the potential threat of vigorous regulation. Besieged by regulated industries and lacking political support, regulatory commissions must come to terms with regulated industries or be overwhelmed by the litigation they can spawn. Thus, as a regulatory commission ages, regulation yields to accommodation, and public interest goals are displaced by the preferences of private interests.[11]

The interest group model, in contrast, views regulatory agencies as the targets of competing pressure groups. It characterizes administrative decisions as compromises designed to balance competing interests and values. It stresses the mixed incentives of regulatory agency officials, who profit from close ties to regulated industries but who must reckon with other groups as well. It does not deny the power of regulated industries, but it views them as supplicants who often experience defeats.[12]

Group theorists concede that some interests remain latent for long periods of time. If certain interests are slow to organize, though, sympathetic administrative elites may help to organize them. Alternatively, a crisis may precipitate mobilization and participation. The result is a pattern that Freeman describes as "creeping pluralism."[13] Eventually, it is argued, important interests receive the attention they deserve.

The organizational model suggests a different perspective. In contrast to the interest group and capture models, which stress forces external to regulatory commissions, the organizational model views regulatory agencies as organizations that produce policy outputs in accordance with standard operating procedures or routines. It portrays administrative decisions as efforts by agency officials to maximize personal or professional values, subject to limited time, skill, and knowledge. It stresses the primacy of specialization and a division of labor, as opposed to unity of command and centralized authority. It does not deny the presence of outside pressure but sees administrative expertise as a shield that reduces susceptibility to such pressure.[14]

According to organization theorists, the regulatory staff is extremely influential. Staff members identify issues, define problems, and suggest alternatives. They gather, organize, and interpret information. Inevitably, their reporting of information is selective. Indeed, they may deliberately package or suppress information to promote a particular point of view or to prevent a policy proposal from receiving serious consideration.

The surrogate representation model, like the organizational model, focuses on government officials. However, the surrogate representation model views regulatory agencies as the targets of professional reformers (proxy advocates) who champion underrepresented interests from a governmental niche outside the regulatory agency. Since they are not employees of the regulatory agency, proxy advocates cannot be viewed as fitting the organizational model, which focuses on internal influence. Since they are government employees, proxy advocates cannot be viewed as fitting the interest group or the capture model, both of which focus on private-sector influence. Which of these competing models best describes the public utility regulatory process? Perceptual measures of influence may be used to answer that question.

The Perceptual Method

The perceptual method is based on the premise that perceptions of complex social phenomena are no less valid than other measures of "reality." Weber argued, for example, that events have no cultural meaning until they are linked to value judgments: "The quality of an event as a 'social-economic' event is not something which it possesses 'objectively.' It is rather conditioned by the orientation of our cognitive interest, as it arises from the specific cultural significance which we attribute to the particular event in a given case."[15] In a similar vein, Campbell and Converse have stressed the need to focus on "the human meaning which human beings attribute to the complex and multifarious social environment in which they find themselves enmeshed."[16]

As employed here, the perceptual method relies on interviews with knowledgeable people to discern which participants in the policy-making process are perceived to be more influential than others.[17] It has been widely used by social scientists in community power studies as a means of testing "pluralist" and "elitist" hypotheses concerning the concentration of power in local decision-making.[18] It has also been used as a means of assessing the relative influence of consumers and regulated industries on the Food and Drug Administration's decisions.[19] Finally, it has been used in numerous evaluations of citizen participation programs, which rely on perceptions of learning, satisfaction, or change as measures of program success.[20]

The advantage of the perceptual approach is that it can provide a comprehensive overview of influence. In contrast to the concurrence approach, it does not assume that attitudinal congruence on issues is a necessary or sufficient condition for influence. In contrast to the behavioral approach, it does not assume that a representative cross-section of decisions (or nondecisions) can be assembled for analysis.

The perceptual approach also has its flaws. More than other methods, it depends on the judgment of people who may not be well informed or objective. More than other methods, it also depends on unambiguous questions and a manageable coding scheme. Fortunately, these problems can be partially overcome through the careful selection of respondents and through the use of closed-ended questions. The former helps to curb institutional biases; the latter helps to eliminate coding errors.

One of the weaknesses of perceptual studies is that they often rely exclusively on interviews with policy makers. A superior method involves interviews with policy makers and people who attempt to influence them. This approach was used by Friedman, who conducted a questionnaire survey of 302 members of FDA advisory committees, including scientists, consumers, and businessmen. In Friedman's survey, respondents were asked to assess the extent to which consumer and industry interests are listened to by FDA advisory committees and by the FDA itself. Most questions were closed-ended, with four-point Likert scale response categories—a great deal, some, a little, not at all. To supplement the survey, Friedman conducted approximately twenty-five interviews with FDA staff members and spokespersons for industrial and consumer organizations.[21]

The approach taken here is similar to Friedman's, although it is based on personal interviews with 284 people in twelve states, including public utility commissioners, public utility commission staff members, grassroots advocates, proxy advocates, and utility company executives. All respondents were asked to assess the influence of eight actors who openly participate in public utility commission proceedings in many states: the attorney general (or consumer counsel), business groups other than utility companies, citizens' groups, individual citizens, labor groups, municipalities, public utility commission staff, and utility companies.

In each of the twelve states, respondents were asked to assess the influence of each type of participant on a scale of 1 to 10, with 1 representing very low influence and 10 representing very high influence. To minimize recall problems but provide a consistent frame of reference, respondents were asked to assess influence on public utility commission proceedings "over the past year." Thus, this approach resembles Friedman's except that it asks about a wider variety of participants, examines a wider variety of regulatory agencies, uses a ten-point scale rather than four response categories, and relies on extensive interviews rather than the combination of an extensive survey and less extensive interviews.

The influence of each type of participant on public utility commission decisions can be measured by pooling influence estimates within each state, weighting each respondent's estimate equally in computing a mean or average.[22] This procedure yields a separate influence estimate for each type of participant in each of the twelve states (with the exception of proxy advocates, who are inactive in six states). The reliability of each estimate can be measured by computing the standard deviation, which reflects the extent of disagreement among respondents (the larger the standard deviation, the less reliable the estimate).

For the sake of convenience, an influence estimate between 1 and 4 will be described as low; an estimate between 4 and 7 will be described as moderate; an estimate between 7 and 10 will be described as high.

AN OVERALL ASSESSMENT

Which of the conflicting models provides an accurate description of the public utility regulatory process? One way to answer that question is through an overall assessment of influence in all twelve states. Table 23, which summarizes the estimated influence of all eight types of participants in all twelve states, may be used for this purpose.[23]

The Organizational Model

As predicted by the organizational model, the role of the regulatory staff is extremely important. In fact, aside from public utility commissioners, regulatory staff members are the most influential participants in the public utility regulatory process. In eight of twelve states, the staff is more influential than any outside participant. The staff plays many important roles in the public utility regulatory process. The staff educates commissioners and explains bewildering concepts from the fields of economics, engineering, accounting, and law. As an extension of its educational role, the staff analyzes proposals submitted by utility companies, public advocates, and others. In addition, the staff develops its own policy proposals and offers recommendations to the commissioners. Although much staff activity is behind the scenes, the staff actively participates in public hearings on which the record of each case is based. After these hearings, the staff interprets the positions of other parties to the commissioners, who lack the time to read every transcript and every brief. Finally, the staff writes the opinions rendered by commissioners, choosing the precise words that will constitute the commission's point of view.

A commissioner from a large state sums up the staff's influence:

We make the decisions. However, we have a very large staff. The staff is rather competent, and so the commission looks

Table 23

Estimated Influence of Participants in Public Utility Commission Proceedings

	Calif. (N = 32)	Fla. (N = 23)	Ga. (N = 17)	Ill. (N = 30)	Mass. (N = 23)	Mich. (N = 20)	Miss. (N = 11)	N.J. (N = 23)	N.Y. (N = 42)	N.D. (N = 9)	Wis. (N = 27)	Wyo. (N = 13)	Average Score
PUC staff	7.62 (2.55)	8.78 (1.06)	8.00 (1.91)	7.48 (2.20)	7.39 (1.80)	8.25 (1.59)	7.68 (1.82)	7.89 (1.93)	8.83 (1.04)	9.00 (1.06)	8.43 (1.04)	8.45 (1.59)	8.15
Utility companies	8.10 (1.56)	7.57 (1.50)	7.06 (2.49)	7.48 (1.84)	7.78 (1.69)	7.40 (1.67)	5.80 (2.49)	7.61 (1.82)	8.31 (1.52)	7.44 (2.36)	7.33 (1.79)	7.27 (2.79)	7.43
Proxy advocacy groups	—	7.28 (1.74)	7.00 (1.63)	—	8.41 (1.68)	5.38 (1.83)	—	8.93 (1.33)	5.20 (2.39)	—	—	—	7.03
Business groups other than utility companies	5.56 (2.39)	4.67 (2.06)	5.29 (2.26)	4.95 (2.50)	3.85 (2.10)	4.58 (2.01)	5.73 (2.52)	4.70 (2.34)	4.38 (2.18)	3.13 (1.38)	4.81 (2.11)	4.14 (2.98)	4.65
Grassroots advocacy groups	5.55 (2.38)	4.67 (1.59)	3.81 (1.48)	5.95 (2.17)	5.07 (1.71)	3.98 (1.56)	—	3.43 (1.64)	3.89 (2.01)	3.06 (1.55)	4.89 (1.68)	3.68 (2.43)	4.36
Municipalities	5.10 (2.38)	4.21 (2.00)	2.65 (1.87)	3.68 (2.08)	2.90 (2.02)	3.06 (2.13)	4.91 (2.91)	3.67 (1.89)	3.49 (2.23)	3.78 (2.32)	4.06 (2.26)	2.91 (2.27)	3.70
Labor groups	3.66 (1.98)	2.10 (1.83)	2.18 (1.81)	4.67 (2.31)	2.25 (2.20)	3.68 (2.04)	3.91 (2.33)	2.57 (1.73)	2.39 (1.70)	3.31 (2.05)	3.57 (1.59)	2.27 (1.57)	3.05
Individual citizens	2.40 (1.30)	2.54 (1.49)	2.78 (2.65)	2.33 (1.87)	2.52 (1.45)	1.63 (0.90)	6.50 (1.99)	1.76 (1.27)	1.67 (1.19)	3.00 (2.00)	3.04 (2.03)	3.50 (2.52)	2.81

Note: Entries are mean estimates of impact on public utility commission decisions, with standard deviations in parentheses. A dash indicates a total absence of activity by a particular group during the time period under investigation. A rating of 1 signifies a very low impact; a rating of 10 signifies a very high impact.

to the staff, particularly the senior staff, quite heavily for information and opinions with respect to matters that come before us. Since we have such a variety and large number of things which we can't always investigate ourselves, we are very often, you know, dependent on the staff.

It is certainly possible to exaggerate staff influence on public utility regulatory policy. In contrast to other participants in the regulatory process, staff members can be silenced by commissioners if they become too outspoken. Also, staff members may appear to be more influential than they actually are, simply because their issue priorities, value priorities, and policy preferences are most likely to coincide with those of commissioners. Finally, it is doubtful that staff members are influential when they are pressured by only one side in a potentially bipolar or multipolar dispute. The ability of staff members to influence commissioners in any meaningful way may depend on the presence of alternative suppliers of information. Without such outside competition the staff can easily become an extension of a dominant outside interest. Thus, a key empirical question is whether outside influence is balanced or lopsided.

The Capture Model

As predicted by the capture model, utility companies wield more power than any other outside participants in the public utility regulatory process. In nine of twelve states, utility companies are the most influential outside participants in public utility commission proceedings. There are several reasons for their substantial influence. First, utility companies determine the timing of major rate cases. When a utility company files a rate hike request, a public utility commission must begin a proceeding, ready or not. In many states, the commission is required to render a decision within a specified time; otherwise, requested rate hikes automatically go into effect. Thus, utility companies determine the tempo of regulatory decisions. Second, utility companies control the flow of information to public utility commissions. By virtue of their intimate familiarity with customers, investors, and fuel suppliers, the companies are in an excellent position to predict demand, the cost of capital, and the cost of fuel. Unfortunately, they are also likely to base their predictions on questionable assumptions, to justify their requests for more money. This would be less of a problem if assumptions, data, and conclusions were easily disentangled, but they are not. In practice, public utility regulators must rely heavily on the analyses and prognoses of utility company officials. Third, utility companies, as monopolies, are very difficult to evaluate on the basis of acceptable performance criteria. Since the companies generally do not compete with one another, the marketplace provides no barometer of managerial efficiency. Although audits sometimes reveal glaring instances of mismanagement, it is difficult to know whether another utility company might do better. Finally, utility companies have abundant financial resources they can use to present a strong case before the public utility commission. Because utility companies can pass along their costs to ratepayers, they are able to respond effectively to obstreperous intervenors, aggressive regulators, or both. Furthermore, public utility regulators know that if they fail to satisfy a utility company, the company will meet them in court—a prospect that disheartens and sometimes intimidates already overburdened regulatory officials.

Public advocates are also intimidated by the utilities, although they try not to wilt under pressure. One public advocate describes the frustrations of jousting with utility companies:

> The utility companies over the years ... have attained greater weight in terms of agency consideration of their points of view than anybody else has. . . . My God, we walk into these cases, we're facing seventy years of legal precedents where they have been able to outspend us, and in many cases, simply outthink us. Okay? That aggregated weight should not be dismissed. They have shaped the assumptions, they have shaped the rationale, and they certainly have the resources to come in and outspend any of us.

Another public advocate expresses similar sentiments:

> You're always outgunned in resources by enormous odds. There's always two or three or four lawyers on the other side. There is an unlimited number of dollars to do what

they need to do. There is a ton of vice-presidents.... They're waiting to order up whatever is needed on their side. There's a study to support anything.... They can go out and hire anybody. And if they want to appeal a case and they don't have enough lawyers, they go hire a new law firm. It's happened several times.

The influence of regulated industries, like that of the regulatory staff, should not be exaggerated. Though utility companies are influential participants in the public utility regulatory process, other groups are also influential. The strongest outside challenge to utility companies comes from proxy advocates. In New Jersey, Massachusetts, and Georgia, proxy advocates are either more influential than utility companies or nearly so. Also active to varying degrees are other business groups, grassroots advocacy groups, labor groups, municipalities, and individual citizens. Whatever the individual impact of each, the cumulative weight of these groups may be considerable. In short, we need to take a closer look at the combined influence of outside groups besides utility companies.

The Interest Group Model

As predicted by the interest group model, a number of competing pressure groups play a significant role in the public utility regulatory process. In most states, industrial and commercial customers of utility companies are active participants. Indeed, in ten of twelve states, business groups other than utilities are moderately influential participants in public utility commission proceedings.[24] Although industrial and commercial customers sometimes join utility companies in opposing new rate structures, they often oppose utility companies on revenue requirements issues. Thus, those who believe that corporations run America should keep in mind that corporations do not always agree. Detroit Edison is a powerful company, but it sometimes finds itself at odds with General Motors and Dow Chemical.

Nor are business groups the only interest groups of any consequence. In six of twelve states, grassroots advocacy groups are moderately influential participants in the public utility regulatory process. Although grassroots advocacy groups are less influential elsewhere, they are almost always more influential than individual citizens. The sole exception is Mississippi, where no citizens' group participated in the public utility regulatory process during the period under investigation. In contrast, individual citizens communicated frequently with Mississippi's elected public utility commissioners, who dutifully listened to complaints by their constituents. Despite the anomalous case of Mississippi, these findings underscore the importance of grassroots advocacy organizations as vehicles for citizen participation. As Checkoway and Van Til have argued, "Organization is a central factor for citizens seeking to participate. . . . Organizational involvement can stimulate awareness of common problems, increase levels of citizen efficacy and activity, and provide a context in which to reach agreement and build a sense of collective identity around which a program can be developed."[25]

Despite the influence of various business groups and grassroots advocacy groups, the interest group model has its limitations. Labor groups, encompassed by the interest group model, are seldom effective participants in the public utility regulatory process.[26] Municipalities, not encompassed by the interest group model, are moderately effective participants in four of twelve states.[27] Furthermore, the interest group model cannot account for the role played by proxy advocates. Indeed, proxy advocacy may be viewed as a response to the failures of interest group politics. In some states, it is a response to the absence of active grassroots advocacy groups; in other states, it is a response to their weakness. In either situation, proxy advocates attempt to remedy the deficiencies of existing interest groups by serving as surrogates for underrepresented interests, such as those of consumers. This suggests the need to look beyond an interest group model of politics.

The Surrogate Representation Model

As predicted by the surrogate representation model, proxy advocates are influential participants in the public utility regulatory process. In all six states where they have participated in public utility commission proceedings, proxy advocates are either moderately influential or very influential. Proxy advocates generally receive high marks, even from their foes at utility companies and the public utility commission. Consider the comments of a commission staff member who frequently disagrees with his state's attorney general:

> A lot of people can't stand the attorney general's guts. I can't either, as far as that goes, but his people are helpful. . . . One of them is a particularly good cross-examiner. He can turn over rocks like nobody I've seen that's in practice here. . . . The attorney general is a pain in the fanny, to put it politely, a burr in the saddle and so forth, and he makes life miserable sometimes. But in those facets, he's helpful.

The surrogate representation model has been overlooked for too long. Yet even the surrogate representation model has its flaws. In particular, proxy advocates are inactive in approximately half of the states. The central problem with proxy advocates is not that they don't participate or that they don't participate effectively, but that they often don't exist. The decision to establish a proxy advocacy office requires a frank acknowledgment by public officials that other public officials have failed to protect the public interest. In many states, public officials are unwilling to make that admission.

To sum up, the evidence suggests that there is some truth to each of the four models but full truth to none. As Wilson has argued,[28] regulatory politics is so complex and variable that it often defies generalizations. However, we may be able to generalize about political influence if we shift our focus from public utility commissions as a whole to public utility commissions in certain kinds of states.

A COMPARATIVE ASSESSMENT

No single model of the policy-making process adequately explains the behavior of state public utility commissions, but perhaps it is unrealistic to expect such uniformity. In view of the fact that public advocacy activity levels vary from state to state, perhaps models of the policy-making process are not equally applicable to all states. To test this hypothesis, the twelve states may be grouped into four categories: (1) grassroots advocacy states, where grassroots advocates are very active participants in public utility commission proceedings but proxy advocates are not (California, Illinois, Wisconsin); (2) proxy advocacy states, where proxy advocates are very active participants but grassroots advocates are not (Florida, Georgia, New Jersey); (3) dual advocacy states, where both grassroots and proxy advocates are very active participants (Massachusetts, Michigan, New York); and (4) acquiescent states, where neither grassroots nor proxy advocates are very active (Mississippi, North Dakota, Wyoming). The survey of public utility commissioners in all fifty states, discussed in chapter 2, indicates that approximately 20 percent of all states are grassroots advocacy states, 20 percent are proxy advocacy states, 30 percent are dual advocacy states, and 30 percent are acquiescent states.

Do different models of the policy-making process fit different types of states? Before addressing that question, it is necessary to specify certain relationships between alternative models of the policy-making process. First, the capture model, as defined here, is incompatible with the interest group model and the surrogate representation model.[29] The capture model states that regulated industries capture the agency that is supposed to regulate them. If pressure groups other than utility companies are at least moderately influential participants in public utility commission proceedings, then capture has not occurred.

Second, the capture model is usually incompatible with the organizational model. The capture model postulates that regulated industries are the only formidable interest groups in the regulatory agency's environment. Without access to alternative sources of information and alternative points of view, most staffs will become mere conduits for the demands of regulated industries. However, highly professional staffs may be able to generate their own information and ideas, thus resisting capture.[30]

Third, the interest group model and surrogate representation model are compatible with one another. There is no reason why strong interest groups cannot complement the activities of a strong proxy advocacy office. In particular, there is no reason why strong grassroots advocates and strong proxy advocates cannot coexist. Grassroots advocacy groups often unite against a common foe by forming coalitions, whether temporary or permanent.[31] Alliances between grassroots advocacy groups and proxy advocacy groups are equally likely, if not more so.

Fourth, the organizational model is compatible with the interest group model and the surrogate representation model. Regulatory staff influence is diminished by lopsided outside pressure, but it is not diminished by outside pressure per se. In fact, the presence of competing pressure groups, with conflicting objectives, may actually enhance the influence of the regulatory staff.

These propositions help to clarify relationships between alternative models of the policy-making process, but they do not disclose which states are characterized by which models. That requires an inquiry into how patterns of influence vary from state to state.

Acquiescent States

In Mississippi, North Dakota, and Wyoming, neither grassroots advocates nor proxy advocates are very active participants in the public utility regulatory process. Not surprisingly, grassroots advocates and proxy advocates are ineffective in all three states. Labor groups are ineffective in all three states, and business groups other than utility companies are moderately effective only in Mississippi. In short, neither the interest group model nor the surrogate representation model applies to acquiescent states.

The capture model fares better. Utility companies are very influential in two of the three states, moderately influential in the third (Mississippi). Regulatory agency staff members are described as very influential in all three states, but such a description must be viewed with skepticism in this instance. If public utility commission staffs in these states were large, well trained, and well paid, they might be able to challenge utility companies. However, public utility commission staffs in Mississippi, North Dakota, and Wyoming are decidedly ill equipped to pose such a challenge.[32] Thus, acquiescent states fit the capture model but not the organizational model. This is not to suggest that utility companies win every battle in acquiescent states. In Mississippi, for example, allowed rates of return on equity tend to be rather low. However, public utility commissions in acquiescent states do tend to reject changes that pose a potential threat to utility companies, such as rate structure reforms that would encourage energy conservation.

Grassroots Advocacy States

In California, Illinois, and Wisconsin, grassroots advocates are very active participants in public utility commission proceedings but proxy advocates are not.[33] Since proxy advocates are inactive in all three states, the surrogate representation model does not apply. However, in all three states, grassroots advocacy groups are moderately influential. In all three states, business groups other than utility companies are moderately influential. In one of the states (Illinois), even labor groups are moderately influential. Thus, the interest group model aptly describes grassroots advocacy states.

Given the influence of competing interest groups in grassroots advocacy states, the capture model offers a poor explanation for regulatory agency behavior. Utility companies are very influential in all three states, but they must fend off opposition from grassroots advocacy groups and various business groups as well. These diverse pressures help to liberate the regulatory staff. In all three states, the regulatory staff is very influential. Public utility commission staff members may or may not adopt pro-utility positions in these states.

Proxy Advocacy States

In Florida, Georgia, and New Jersey, proxy advocates participate very actively in the public utility regulatory process, but grassroots advocates do not. In all three states, proxy advocates are either moderately effective or very effective. In contrast, grassroots advocates are moderately effective only in Florida.[34] Business groups other than utility companies are moderately effective in all three states, but labor groups are moderately effective in none. Clearly, the surrogate representation model applies to proxy advocacy states. In contrast, the interest group model fares poorly. Although the interest groups model fits proxy advocacy states better than acquiescent states, it is difficult to describe states with largely ineffective grassroots advocacy groups as fulfilling the conditions of the interest group model.

Because proxy advocacy states fit the surrogate representation model, they cannot be described as fitting the capture model. Whatever else may be said about proxy advocates, they consistently oppose utility companies on revenue requirements issues. This is not to deny that utility companies are very influential in proxy advocacy states. Rather, it is to suggest that they are challenged by formidable adversaries, including proxy advocates and other business groups. Regulatory agency staff members are also very influential in these states. Here, as in grassroots advocacy states, the presence of conflicting outside pressures enhances the discretion of the regulatory staff.

Dual Advocacy States

In Massachusetts, Michigan, and New York, both grassroots advocates and proxy advocates are very active participants in public utility commission proceedings. In all three states, proxy advocates are either moderately influential or very influential. Thus, the surrogate representation model applies. However, grassroots advocates are moderately influential only in Massachusetts.[35] Business groups other than utilities are moderately influential in two of the three states (Michigan and New York), but labor groups are moderately influential in none. In dual advocacy states, as in proxy advocacy states and acquiescent states, the interest group model does not offer a satisfactory explanation for political behavior.

Because the surrogate representation model applies to dual advocacy states, the capture model does not apply. Utility companies are very influential in these states, but they must cope with aggressive proxy advocates and business groups. Here, as in other states, conflicting pressures work to the advantage of the regulatory agency staff. Because utility companies are not the only influential pressure groups in these states, regulatory staff members are free to promote policies contrary to those endorsed by the utilities, if they choose to do so.

Table 24 summarizes the results of the preceding analysis and notes the states in each category. The capture model applies only to acquiescent states, the interest group model only to grassroots advocacy states. The surrogate representation model applies to proxy advocacy states and dual advocacy states. The organizational model applies to grassroots advocacy states, proxy advocacy states, and dual advocacy states.

These findings contradict the conventional wisdom concerning regulatory politics. The two leading models of the regulatory policy-making process are the capture model (popular in the fifties and sixties) and the interest group model (popular in the sixties and seventies). Ironically, these two models do a poorer job of explaining the behavior of state public utility commissions than the organizational and surrogate representation models.

The interest group model errs by blurring the distinction between activity and influence. Grassroots advocates, it turns out, are more active than effective, more vocal than influential. Thus, the interest group model breaks down, though not for the reasons cited by Olson.[36] In public utility regulatory policy, the central problem facing grassroots advocates is not a lack of incentives but a lack of resources. Grassroots advocates have found it easier to organize and participate than to participate effectively.

The capture model, in contrast, errs by blurring the distinction between influence and control. Utility companies are very influential, but they do not control the public utility regulatory process. The failure of the capture model is due not so much to

Table 24

Alternative Models of the Policy-Making Process by Type of State

| | | Proxy Advocacy Activity | |
		Low	High
Grassroots Advocacy Activity	High	Interest group model, organizational model (Calif., Ill., Wis.)	Surrogate representation model, organizational model (Mass., Mich., N.Y.)
	Low	Capture model (Miss., N. Dak., Wyo.)	Surrogate representation model, organizational model (Fla., Ga., N.J.)

competing interest groups as to the new phenomenon of proxy advocacy. Whether the surrogate representation model applies to federal regulatory policy depends on one's definition of surrogate representation.[37] However, public utility regulatory policy cannot be understood without taking institutionalized public advocates into account.

Finally, both the interest group model and the capture model understate the importance of the regulatory agency staff. Instead of asking, Who influences regulatory commissions? social scientists need to ask, Who influences regulatory commissioners? In most states, one answer must certainly be: the staff. The direction taken by the staff, of course, is problematic. If the staff is free to oppose utility companies in most states, it is also free to support them. Thus, it is also important to ask, Who influences the regulatory staff? As suggested in chapter 3, the professions (law, economics, engineering, and so forth) are important sources of regulatory policy preferences. As suggested in this chapter, regulated industries are often important, too. However, it is unreasonable to assume that the staff will invariably be a mouthpiece for regulated industries. Where outside political competition is strong, staff members need not be shills for utility companies.

Conclusion

One way to study political influence is to ask knowledgeable observers for estimates of the effectiveness of different participants in the policy-making process. This method, which may be described as a perceptual method, permits an inquiry into influence in diverse policy domains that need not be specified or weighted. If applied to a carefully drawn sample of states and a carefully drawn sample of respondents, it can be a useful tool for identifying patterns of political influence in state public utility commission proceedings.

Interviews with 284 respondents in twelve states yield the following conclusions: (1) public utility commission staff members and utility companies are very effective participants in the public utility regulatory process; (2) proxy advocates, though inactive in half of the states, are moderately effective or very effective when they do participate; (3) grassroots advocates and business groups other than utilities tend to be moderately effective; and (4) municipalities, labor groups, and individual citizens tend to be ineffective.

From a national perspective, these findings suggest that there is some truth to the capture model, the interest group model, and the organizational model. They also suggest the need for a fourth model, described here as a surrogate representation model. This model accounts for the emergence of proxy advocates as a response to the weaknesses of interest group politics.

From a state perspective, though, alternative models of the policy-making process are sometimes incompatible. Nor is there a simple relationship between activity and influence. State-by-state comparisons reveal that the two leading models of the policy-making process (the capture model and the interest group model) are less satisfactory than other models. They also reveal that the politics of public utility regulation varies from state to state.

If public utility regulatory politics varies from state to state, it may also vary from issue area to issue area. As Lowi has argued, regulatory politics differs from distributive politics and redistributive politics, because each involves a different set of prospective winners and losers.[38] Since public utility regulation involves a wide variety of conflicts, the effectiveness of different participants in public utility commission proceedings may vary from issue area to issue area. That possibility is the subject of chapter 6.

: **6** :
Policy Impacts:
The Behavioral Method

The proposition that politics determines public policy is a fundamental tenet of political science. The outcome of a political dispute depends in large measure on who is opposing whom, on where lines of cleavage are drawn. In Schattschneider's words, "Every shift of the line of cleavage affects the nature of the conflict, produces a new set of winners and losers and a new kind of result. Thus a change in the direction and location of the line of cleavage will determine the place of each individual in the political system, what side he is on, who else is on his side, who is opposed to him, how large the opposing sides are, what the conflict is about and who wins."[1]

Yet the relationship between politics and policy is not unidirectional. In recent years, political scientists have suggested that the political process varies from issue area to issue area—in short, that policy determines politics. Lowi argues that there are four types of policies—distributive, regulatory, redistributive, and constituent—and that each triggers a distinctive configuration of political alignments.[2] Wilson argues that there are four types of policies—involving concentrated benefits, concentrated costs; distributed benefits, distributed costs; concentrated benefits, distributed costs; and distributed benefits, concentrated costs—and that each produces a peculiar kind of organizational combat.[3] Salisbury and Heinz, Sabatier, Hayes, and Price have also introduced typologies of policies or policy processes.[4]

If these arguments are correct, the politics of public utility regulation should vary from issue area to issue area, with important policy consequences. Such variations will occur if participants in the public utility regulatory process are either more active in some issue areas than others, or more effective in some issue areas than others. These two possibilities are, of course, interrelated. Participants may be more effective in issue areas where they are more active, and participants may be more active in issue areas where they expect to be more effective. In either case, politics will vary from issue area to issue area, and so too will public policy.

A behavioral approach may be used to test the hypothesis that there is a relationship between political activity and governmental behavior. For example, if public advocacy really makes a difference, states that differ in their level of public advocacy should also differ in their public policies, after controlling for other variables. This approach has been widely used by students of comparative state politics.[5] Its advantage is that it requires tangible evidence of a relationship between political variations and policy variations across all fifty states.

A behavioral approach is especially appropriate for an analysis of political institutions with similar jurisdictions but dissimilar political environments. For the most part, this is an apt description of state public utility commissions. However, the behavioral approach must be limited to the study of political variables that vary from state to state. Unfortunately for research purposes, some political variables do not vary from state to state. For example, activity by public utility commission staffs and utility companies is almost always high, whereas activity by individual citizens and labor groups is almost always low. Nevertheless, there are important interstate differences in levels of activity by both grassroots advocates and proxy advocates. Are such differences associated with different public policies in some issue areas but not others? This question will be addressed by utilizing a new typology of public policies, based on a theory of public advocacy.

A THEORY OF PUBLIC ADVOCACY

Role Differentiation

At first glance, grassroots advocates and proxy advocates appear to play very similar roles in the public utility regulatory process. Both are relatively new participants in public utility commission proceedings. Both represent or at least claim to represent underrepresented interests. Both oppose utility companies and public utility commissions on a wide variety of issues. Yet interviews with eighty-one grassroots advocates and thirty-eight proxy advocates in twelve states reveal that grassroots advocates and proxy advocates differ in certain crucial respects. As noted in chapter 2, proxy advocates are much better funded than grassroots advocates, because they receive substantial financial support from the government. The two types of public advocates also differ in their technical expertise, strategic preferences, statutory requirements, and conceptions of accountability. These differences, discussed next, lead grassroots advocates and proxy advocates to specialize in different issue areas.

1. *Technical expertise.* Some regulatory issues (concerning legal rights, social equity, and so on) are not exclusively or primarily technical. In such issue areas, expertise is not a prerequisite to successful participation. However, many regulatory issues (especially those concerning new technologies or the financial requirements of regulated industries) are highly technical. In such issue areas, Sabatier is probably correct in arguing that unless a citizens' group provides technical information, the regulated industry is likely to triumph.[6] Nelkin and Pollak put it this way: "Expertise is a crucial political resource, and if parties in conflict are to have any sense of political efficacy, they must have access to technical advice."[7]

A number of organizations provide special training programs in the utilities area. These organizations include the National Association of Regulatory Utility Commissioners, the National Regulatory Research Institute, the National Consumer Law Center, the National Association of State Utility Consumer Advocates, and Michigan State University's Institute of Public Utilities. As a measure of expertise, public advocates were asked if they had had special training in the utilities area. Of thirty-five proxy advocates, 85.7 percent had special training. In contrast, of seventy-five grassroots advocates, only 44 percent had special training. Clearly, the expertise of proxy advocates exceeds that of grassroots advocates.

2. *Strategic preferences.* Like economic interest groups, public advocacy groups choose strategies designed to capitalize on their organization's strengths. These strategies may be viewed as part of the lobbying process. According to Zeigler, lobbying strategies tend to fit a communications model (which views lobbying as an informing process), or a mechanistic model (which views lobbying as an exercise in persuasion), or some combination of the two.[8] No strategy is always best. A group with limited financial resources but a powerful constituency may wisely pursue a persuasion strategy, whereas a group with substantial resources but a weak constituency may sensibly pursue an informing strategy.

To determine strategic preferences, public advocates were asked the following closed-ended question:

> As you assess the contribution of your organization to your public utility commission's decisions, what single factor would you say best summarizes your organization's ability to shape the course of public policy?
> ——Organization applies political pressure.
> ——Organization provides useful information.
> ——Organization provides a different point of view.

Some respondents were unable to identify a primary strategic preference, but most were. Of eighty-four grassroots advocates, 36.9 percent primarily apply political pressure, 26.2 percent primarily provide a different point of view, and 19 percent primarily provide useful information. Of thirty-six proxy advocates, 5.6 percent primarily apply political pressure, 33.3 percent primarily provide a different point of view, and 30.6 percent primarily provide useful information. Clearly, grassroots advocates place much more emphasis on the application of political pressure (which requires no expertise), and proxy advocates place more emphasis on useful information and an alternative viewpoint.

3. *Statutory requirements.* Although the legislative branch generally eschews substantive regulatory issues, it often imposes procedural requirements on organizations that participate in regulatory agency proceedings. The legislature may require a government organization to represent a certain consti-

tuency; it may require a nongovernmental organization to represent a certain constituency if it wishes to receive government funds. Such statutory language circumscribes behavior, for a public advocacy group that ignores strong legislative signals runs the risk of losing government funds, whether state or federal. Indeed, in at least one instance, a proxy advocacy office has been limited by a state legislature in its use of federal funds.[9]

The statutory responsibilities of grassroots advocacy groups are easily determined, since only legal aid societies are required by law to represent a certain constituency.[10] The statutory responsibilities of proxy advocacy groups may be determined by inspecting the enabling legislation of the six in our sample. Of seventy-two grassroots advocacy organizations, only 19.4 percent are legal aid societies, required by law to represent the poor.[11] Of six proxy advocacy organizations, four are required by law to represent all consumers or the general public as a whole.[12] The fifth, the Massachusetts Attorney General, may represent any group of consumers.[13] The sixth, the Georgia Consumers' Utility Counsel, is required to represent residential and small business consumers.[14] Thus, proxy advocates are much more circumscribed by statutory requirements than grassroots advocates.

4. *Conception of accountability.* A public advocacy group may or may not be accountable to the people it claims to represent, but it is almost always accountable to someone. Accountability may flow downward (to constituents) or upward (to sovereigns). If it flows downward, public advocates may be accountable to all consumers, all residential consumers, middle-class consumers, or poor consumers. If it flows upward, public advocates may be accountable to the legislature, the governor, the courts, or the federal government.

To identify conceptions of accountability, grassroots advocates and proxy advocates were asked, "To whom is your organization accountable?" Although some respondents offered more than one answer to this question, only the first responses will be reported here. Of eighty-one grassroots advocates, 43.2 percent are accountable to members or member groups, 23.5 percent are accountable to an executive board, 9.9 percent are accountable to the citizenry as a whole, 3.7 percent are accountable to their "leadership," and 3.7 percent are accountable to government officials. Of thirty-three proxy advocates, none is accountable to members, member groups, or an executive board, 33.3 percent are accountable to the citizenry as a whole, 21.1 percent are accountable to their "leadership," and 45.5 percent are accountable to government officials. Proxy advocates are particularly likely to mention accountability to the state legislature. In short, although grassroots advocates view themselves as accountable to identifiable constituency groups, especially members, and to an executive board, often elected by the membership, proxy advocates see themselves as accountable to other government officials, especially the state legislature, and to the citizenry as a whole.

The role differentiation process is ultimately traceable to different funding levels and different funding sources. Because grassroots advocates and proxy advocates differ in their funding levels, they also differ in their technical expertise and strategic preferences. Proxy advocates, who are better funded and better trained, attempt to influence public utility regulators by supplying information, whereas grassroots advocates prefer to apply political pressure. Because grassroots advocates and proxy advocates differ in their funding sources, they also differ in their statutory requirements and their conception of accountability. Grassroots advocates, who are less circumscribed by law, are free to represent one class of consumers against another. Indeed, some grassroots advocacy groups (legal aid societies) are required to do so. Proxy advocates, in contrast, are usually bound to represent all consumers or the general public as a whole.

Role differences lead grassroots advocates and proxy advocates to allocate their budgetary resources in different ways, as table 25 indicates. Proxy advocates, with ample resources but circumscribed authority, focus on revenue requirements issues, which do not pit one segment of consumers against another. Although revenue requirements issues are highly complex, that is not a major obstacle for proxy advocates. Grassroots advocates, with fewer resources but more flexible authority, focus on rate design, customer service regulations, power plant construc-

Table 25
Budget Allocations of Public Advocates

Mean Estimate of Budget Allocation	Grassroots Advocacy Organizations (N = 70)	Proxy Advocacy Organizations (N = 6)
Revenue requirements issues	22.6%	69.2%
Rate design issues	28.0	19.3
Other issues	49.4	11.5

tion, and other issues that are less complex. Although these issues frequently pit one segment of consumers against another, that is not a legal or political hurdle for grassroots advocates.

A Typology of Public Policies

These findings indicate that grassroots advocates will lack the resources to participate effectively in certain issue areas, and proxy advocates will lack the incentives to participate effectively in certain issue areas. When issues are highly complex, grassroots advocates will be unable to participate effectively. When issues are highly divisive with respect to the citizenry as a whole, proxy advocates will be unwilling to participate effectively. These observations suggest a fourfold typology of public policies, built around the two concepts of technical complexity and consumer conflict (see table 26).

It may also be useful to consider a fifth category—transitional policies, characterized by changing levels of issue complexity or consumer conflict.

Underlying this typology is the proposition that the relationship between public advocacy and policy responsiveness varies from issue area to issue area. To test this hypothesis, it is appropriate to focus on decisions in electric rate cases, where public advocacy activity is most likely to take place. Public advocacy is defined as the level of intervention by grassroots advocates and proxy advocates in PUC proceedings during the 1974–1978 period, as estimated by PUC commissioners in each state. Both grassroots advocacy and proxy advocacy are measured by a scale ranging from 1 (very low activity) to 10 (very high activity). As noted in chapter 2, it is assumed that this is an interval-level scale. This assumption seems warranted because of extremely

Table 26
A Typology of Public Policies

Technical Complexity

		Low	High
Consumer Conflict	High	Effective grassroots advocacy	Neither
	Low	Both	Effective proxy advocacy

high correlations between actual activity levels (clearly an interval scale) and estimated activity levels.

Policy responsiveness is defined as the adoption of policies that benefit consumers as a whole or a particular segment of consumers. Since the public advocacy data span the 1974–1978 period, the policy responsiveness data reflect decisions at the end of this period. Measures of policy responsiveness include: (1) high complexity, low conflict policies—a lower ratio of the rate hike granted to the rate hike requested by a utility company; (2) low complexity, high conflict policies—the adoption of lifeline rates, which help the poor to meet minimal energy needs; (3) low complexity, low conflict policies—a ban on late payment penalties for residential consumers and a longer "grace period" between notification of intent to disconnect service and disconnection; (4) high complexity, high conflict policies—a lower ratio of residential rates to business rates; and (5) transitional policies—the adoption of rate structure reforms that promote energy conservation. These dependent variables are interval-level in some instances, dichotomous in others. The unit of analysis is the state, except for policies high in complexity and low in conflict, where the unit of analysis is the firm. Data on policy outputs are derived from a variety of sources, including the National Association of Regulatory Utility Commissioners, the Electric Power Research Institute, and the Department of Energy.

Methodology

Model Specification

To estimate the effects of public advocacy on policy responsiveness, it is necessary to specify a multivariate model with appropriate control variables. The criterion for inclusion used here is the likelihood that a given variable is related to both public advocacy and policy responsiveness. A study aimed at explaining a high percentage of the variance in policy responsiveness might use a different criterion, such as the overall explanatory power of a given variable. Based on the chosen criterion, however, only three control variables are needed: political culture, the method of selecting PUC commissioners, and regulatory resources.

Political culture. Elazar has classified states as traditionalistic, individualistic, and moralistic.[15] The traditionalistic states, he argues, are less supportive of citizen participation. Sigelman and Smith have found that traditionalistic states are also less likely to adopt pro-consumer policies.[16] For these reasons, it is advisable to control for political culture. As recommended by Sharkansky,[17] political culture has been operationalized as a nine-point scale, with 1 representing an extremely moralistic state and 9 representing an extremely traditionalistic state. Following Sharkansky, it is assumed that political culture is an interval-level variable. In view of the findings by Sigelman and Smith, it is expected that more traditionalistic states will be less responsive than other states.

Regulatory resources. In his classic study of independent regulatory commissions, Bernstein argued that a reduction in regulatory resources contributes to "capture" by regulated industries.[18] More recently, William Berry has found that PUCs with relatively large regulatory resources encourage a relationship between public salience and public policy that benefits residential consumers.[19] Thus, it seems appropriate to control for regulatory resources. One way to do so is through an index that measures commission staff size, commission budget size, commissioners' salary levels, and the commission's data processing capacity. Following Bernstein and Berry, it is expected that commissions with more substantial resources will be more responsive than commissions in other states.

Method of selection. Lineberry and Fowler have demonstrated that elected local governments are more responsive to socioeconomic cleavages than appointed local governments.[20] Although the relationship between method of selecting commissioners and PUC policies is unclear,[21] there is clearly less citizen participation in states with elected commissioners, apparently because citizens' groups assume that elected commissioners will be more responsive to their interests. In view of these findings, it is advisable to include method of selection as a control variable. Method of selection has been operationalized as a dichotomous variable with 0 representing an appointed commission and 1 representing an elected commission. Following Lineberry and Fowler, it is generally expected that elected public officials will be more responsive than appointed officials.

Other control variables, such as interparty competition and region, were considered but rejected. Political scientists have generally found weak or nonexistent relationships between interparty competition and policy outputs at the state level.[22] Moreover, the inclusion of interparty competition in the model could create a multicollinearity problem since interparty competition is intercorrelated with both political culture and method of selection. The inclusion of a region variable in the model would create a certain multicollinearity problem, since there is an extremely high correlation between region and political culture. As suggested by Tufte, region has been excluded from the model because it is intercorrelated with another variable of greater theoretical interest.[23]

Estimating Techniques

To assess the effects of grassroots advocacy, proxy advocacy, and the three control variables on policy responsiveness, it is necessary to use estimating techniques that vary with the dependent variable under investigation. If the dependent variable is an interval-level variable, ordinary least squares multiple regression analysis is appropriate. Standardized b's or beta weights measure the strength of each relationship, and p values, derived from F scores, measure statistical significance. If the dependent variable is dichotomous, however, multiple regression analysis is inappropriate.[24] Probit analysis, in contrast, yields consistent, efficient estimates of the effects of independent variables on a dichotomous dependent variable.[25] Maximum likelihood coefficients provide estimates of population parameters and maximum likelihood coefficient/standard error ratios provide indicators of statistical significance. The use of standardized maximum likelihood estimates facilitates comparisons of independent variables with different means and standard deviations. Because direction has been predicted for all five independent variables, a one-tailed statistical significance test is warranted.

Findings

1. *High complexity, low conflict policies.* Some issues are very complex technically but not very devisive with respect to consumers as a whole. They are technically formidable but politically attractive. One measure of policy responsiveness in this issue area is the percentage of a utility company's rate hike request actually granted by PUC commissioners.[26] This variable encompasses a multitude of more specific issues concerning the utility company's total revenue requirements, including rate base determination, calculation of a fair rate of return, and the determination of allowable expenses.

Because data on rate hike requests are not available for every firm in every state, the unit of analysis must be the firm, not the state. Yet state-specific effects could distort relationships between public advocacy and public policy decisions concerning particular firms. To control for state effects, a dummy variable has been assigned to each state included two or more times in the sample of firms. The data base includes all privately owned electric companies serving 5 percent or more of the state's residential customers for which recent data were available.[27]

As table 27 indicates, two variables are especially helpful in predicting the percentage of a utility company's requested rate hike actually granted by the PUC: proxy advocacy and regulatory resources. When proxy advocacy is high, an electric utility gets a smaller percentage of the rate hike it requests.[28] In contrast, a utility company gets a larger percentage of what it asks for in states with ample regulatory resources. Far from promot-

Table 27
Effects of Public Advocacy:
High Complexity, Low Conflict Policies
(N = 89)

Variable	Rate Granted/Rate Requested	
	Standardized b	p
Grassroots advocacy	.220	.133
Proxy advocacy	−.342	.068
Political culture	−.042	.398
Regulatory resources	.441	.041
Method of selection	.098	.265
R^2 = .421 (includes nineteen state dummy variables)		F = 1.94

Note: To avoid an unnecessary loss of degrees of freedom, state dummy variables with F scores lower than .1 were omitted. This procedure resulted in the omission of six state dummy variables from this equation.

ing responsiveness, regulatory resources seem to promote capture! This finding, discussed more fully later in this chapter, suggests that regulatory resources are indeed important, though their consequences are often surprising. Other relationships are weaker. Indeed, the overall explanatory power of the model in this issue area is not high. This could be because the rate hike requested and the rate hike granted both depend on a wide variety of controversial assumptions, for example, concerning how the cost of capital ought to be measured.

Despite the complexity of revenue requirements issues, proxy advocates excel at them. Armed with alternative accounting procedures, tax computation methods, and cost of capital estimates, proxy advocates challenge the overall rate hikes requested by utility companies. A Massachusetts regulator discusses the impact of the state attorney general in a 1979 Boston Edison rate case:

> Boston Edison requested a $46 million rate increase. And the attorney general in his brief, in his case, advocated a position which indicated that there was not only not a revenue deficiency of $46 million, but in fact a revenue surplus. Now while the commission didn't agree with him in the end, we did cut Edison's rate request back to about $19 million and certainly the constant arguments of the attorney gen-

eral that there should be no increase at all were weighing heavily on the commission's mind when they were considering this case.

In some states, proxy advocates have an impact on rate levels by settling or "stipulating" an agreement with a utility company. In New Jersey, for example, the Department of Public Advocate's Division of Rate Counsel settles approximately half of the state's major rate cases. A New Jersey regulator explains how this works:

Rate Counsel has a major impact in virtually every case that we hear. For example, they participate actively in the stiuplation process, which we have relied upon heavily in order to meet the growing case load, and in that process, I think, have a major impact. Rate Counsel has gotten from a number of companies commitments, for example, that they will not institute any higher rates for a certain period of time, and that has been part of stipulations that have come to us. So Rate Counsel has a major impact on cases.

Grassroots advocates also care about revenue requirements issues, but they usually lack the resources to offer cogent testimony on such issues. The grassroots advocates who do have resources are typically environmental activists, who care more about enery conservation and alternative energy sources than rate levels. Some of these environmental activists have aligned themselves with regulators who prefer short-term rate hikes to a dreaded cycle of underpriced energy, excessive consumption, and painful choices between power failures and new power plants. This could help to explain why grassroots advocacy and regulatory resources are both positively related to the rate hike granted/rate hike requested ratio. Grassroots advocates seldom support higher rates, but they strongly endorse energy conservation, and many regulators see higher rates as an excellent way to promote conservation. Regulatory resources permit commissioners to pursue this route, despite utility company opposition to conservation and proxy advocacy opposition to higher rates. Thus, what appears at first glance to be "capture" could in fact be a sign of independence. In other issue areas, however, different forces are at work.

2. *Low complexity, high conflict policies.* Some issues, though not very complex, tend to fragment the consumer class. They are technically manageable but politically controversial. One indicator of policy responsiveness in this issue area is the adoption of lifeline rates, operationalized as a dichotomous variable (0 = no, 1 = yes). Lifeline rates, which apply to residential consumers, are designed to help the poor meet minimal energy needs. They do so by charging less per kilowatt-hour for the consumption of small amounts of energy (for example, 300 kilowatt-hours per month) or by providing poor people with a stipend that helps them pay their utility bills. As of 1979, 13.6 percent of the states supplying data had lifeline rates.[29]

As table 28 indicates, grassroots advocacy and political culture have discernible effects on lifeline rates. PUCs are more likely to adopt lifeline rates when grassroots advocacy activity is high, and less likely to do so when the political culture is highly traditionalistic. Other relationships, though generally in the expected direction, are weaker.

The positive, though weak, relationship between proxy advocacy and lifeline rates is somewhat surprising, in view of the controversy surrounding lifeline rates. However, the efforts of proxy advocates on behalf of all consumers may permit grassroots advocacy groups to concentrate on redistributive and environmental goals. The principal result of consumer conflict, it seems, is not open disagreement but greater specialization of function and purpose.

Table 28
Effects of Public Advocacy:
Low Complexity, High Conflict Policies
(N = 44)

Variable	Lifeline Rates	
	MLE[a]	p
Grassroots advocacy	.543	.051
Proxy advocacy	.485	.115
Political culture	− .814	.029
Regulatory resources	.153	.283
Method of selection	−1.447	.460

Estimated R^2 = .836 −2 × Log Likelihood Ratio = 13.36

a. MLE = Maximum Likelihood Estimate (Standardized).

Although intervention in PUC proceedings is important, lifeline rates receive an additional boost if pressure is applied to state legislators as well. Two citizens' groups used these tactics to secure approval of lifeline rates in California several years ago. The Citizens' Action League (CAL) and Toward Utility Rate Normalization (TURN) urged the California Public Utility Commission to adopt lifeline rates in a Pacific Gas and Electric rate case. Simultaneously, CAL urged the state legislature to require lifeline rates. Although initially skeptical of lifeline rates, the California Public Utility Commission decided to act when it became apparent that the state legislature would act in any event. In September 1975, the commission approved lifeline rates for Pacific Gas and Electric. Several weeks later, Governor Jerry Brown signed a lifeline bill into law.[30]

In general, proxy advocates lack grassroots advocates' enthusiasm for the lifeline concept. One proxy advocate, referring to lifeline as "a big bone of contention," recalls that the issue arose recently in his state but got nowhere. "I think we were a little skeptical," he recalls. The nub of the problem is that lifeline rates are too redistributive for proxy advocates, who see themselves as representing consumers, not the poor. Proxy advocates will support policies that offer special benefits to the poor, but only if such policies can be portrayed as part of a pro-consumer package.

3. *Low complexity, low conflict policies.* Some issues are neither complex nor conflictual. They do not require expertise, and they appear to benefit or protect all consumers. One measure of policy responsiveness in this issue area is a ban on late penalty payments for residential consumers. A second measure is the requirement that a number of days elapse between notification of intent to disconnect service and disconnection. The first variable is dichotomous (0 = no ban, 1 = a ban). The second is an interval-level variable, ranging from 0 to 15 days. As of 1979, 37.3 percent of the states supplying data banned late payment penalties for residential customers,[31] and 27.7 percent required that at least 10 days elapse before disconnection.[32]

As table 29 indicates, there are clear relationships between several variables and the imposition of a ban on late payment penalties for residential consumers. Such a ban is less common

Table 29
Effects of Public Advocacy:
Low Complexity, Low Conflict Policies

Variable	Late Payment Penalty Ban (N = 51)		Grace Period Before Disconnection (N = 47)	
	MLE[a]	p	Standardized b	p
Grassroots advocacy	1.071	.002	.101	.250
Proxy advocacy	.510	.035	.425	.003
Political culture	−.680	.007	−.294	.030
Regulatory resources	.324	.098	−.128	.180
Method of selection	.500	.044	.081	.315
Estimated R^2 = .627	−2 × Log Likelihood Ratio = 24.46		R^2 = .241	F = 2.60

a. MLE = Maximum Likelihood Estimate (standardized).

in traditionalistic states, more common in states with high grassroots advocacy activity, high proxy advocacy activity, and elected commissioners. States with high grassroots advocacy activity are especially likely to prohibit late payment penalties. There are also clear relationships between two variables and the number of days that must elapse before service is disconnected. Consumers have more time to avert termination of service in states with high proxy advocacy, less time in traditionalistic states. The absence of a significant relationship between grassroots advocacy and the length of the grace period before disconnection could be due to greater emphasis by grassroots advocates on other related issues, such as the critical question of whether disconnection may occur during the winter.

Grassroots advocates and proxy advocates often cooperate in support of pro-consumer service regulations. In Georgia, for example, citizens' groups worked together with the Consumers' Utility Counsel to secure approval of a consumer bill of rights. Georgia Action, a senior citizens' group, took the lead by providing public testimony in support of more lenient disconnection policies. In conjunction with Georgia Action, Georgia Legal Services drafted an interim rule banning disconnection in exceptionally harsh winter weather or in the event of a medical emergency. The Georgia Public Service Commission adopted such an interim rule. Subsequently, the Consumers' Utility

Counsel urged approval of a final rule. The commission adopted a final rule similar to that proposed by the Consumers' Utility Counsel. Thus, although proxy advocates do not support policies that offer special benefits to the poor (lifeline rates), they do support policies that benefit the poor along with other consumers (a consumer bill of rights). As this example indicates, the support of proxy advocates can be important.

4. *High complexity, high conflict policies.* Some issues, unlike a consumer bill of rights, are very complex and very conflictual. They are intimidating, both technically and politically. One indicator of policy responsiveness in this issue area is the disparity between residential prices and industrial prices, as measured by two ratios: first, the price per kilowatt-hour for residential customers of 500 kilowatt-hours divided by the price per kilowatt-hour for industrial customers of 200,000 kilowatt-hours; and, second, the price per kilowatt-hour for residential customers of 250 kilowatt-hours divided by the price per kilowatt-hour for industrial customers of 200,000 kilowatt-hours. These ratios vary from state to state because PUCs use widely different methods for allocating costs among classes of customers.

As table 30 indicates, there are noteworthy relationships between regulatory resources and both ratios, with residential consumers faring better when regulatory resources are relatively high (lower ratios are more favorable to residential cus-

Table 30
Effects of Public Advocacy:
High Complexity, High Conflict Policies
(N = 51)

	Residential Price: 500 KWH/ Industrial Price: 200,000 KWH		Residential Price: 250 KWH/ Industrial Price: 200,000 KWH	
Variable	*Standardized b*	*p*	*Standardized b*	*p*
Grassroots advocacy	−.173	.138	−.174	.133
Proxy advocacy	.019	.444	.009	.500
Political culture	−.133	.190	−.092	.268
Regulatory resources	−.249	.047	−.309	.019
Method of selection	−.090	.300	−.098	.279
	$R^2 = .096$	$F = 0.95$	$R^2 = .120$	$F = 1.22$

tomers). Thus, the same resource-rich PUCs that approve relatively large rate increases for all consumers also approve rate designs that benefit residential consumers at the expense of industrial consumers. If this combination of policies has mixed implications for responsiveness, that is because regulatory resources provide insulation from political pressure when issues are complex enough to enhance the stature of those who possess vital expertise. During the period under investigation, resource-rich PUCs attracted economists as commissioners and key staff members. Economic theory led many of these professionals to favor higher prices overall but especially for industrial customers, who are usually responsible for a disproportionate share of peak-load demand, which is more costly to satisfy than off-peak demand. Perhaps this helps to explain why scholars have reached such different conclusions about the relationship between regulatory resources and policy responsiveness. When technical complexity is high, regulatory resources permit the pursuit of certain principles without requiring the cultivation of certain constituencies. Thus, the effects of regulatory resources on policy responsiveness, though real, are more or less accidental.

In contrast to the relationship between regulatory resources and cost allocation decisions, none of the other relationships is even moderately strong. Indeed, the overall explanatory power of the model in this issue area is weak. As Williams[33] discovered in a study of privately owned electric utilities, variations in "rate discrimination" are not easily explained. Perhaps such variations depend not merely on PUC resource levels but also on the precise mix of accountants, engineers, and economists in different job categories.

In any event, grassroots advocates and proxy advocates have negligible impacts on the allocation of costs between residential and business customers. Grassroots advocates openly favor a reduction in the proportionate rate burden borne by residential consumers, but they seldom offer a persuasive rationale for such a reduction. A Wyoming regulatory staff member puts it this way: "All they know is the end result. They don't know how to get there." A Georgia regulatory staff member is more caustic: "You cannot, as most of these citizens' groups do, go in and just cause a lot of heat and no light, talk a lot about the great inequities and how nobody can afford to pay high rates. That's baloney! You've got to be specific, you've got to do it in a manner which creates a good record."

Proxy advocates, in contrast, have sufficient expertise to influence cost allocation decisions but have few incentives to do so. From a legal point of view, proxy advocates are usually required by law to represent all consumers, not just residential consumers. From a political point of view, proxy advocates tend to think twice before squaring off against business groups, which have substantial influence in the state legislature. If proxy advocates antagonize the business community, they may also antagonize key state legislators who control their agency's purse strings. Under such circumstances, proxy advocates prefer to avoid rate design controversies altogether.

5. *Transitional policies.* Many of the most important issues that public utility commissions face are high in complexity, high in conflict. Yet issue characteristics are not immutable. Although it is very difficult to simplify a highly complex issue, it is sometimes possible to reduce conflict over a conflictual issue. As conflict reduction efforts ensue, certain policies enter a state of flux. Their fate depends on how issues are perceived and how problems are defined. Transitional policies today include those that promote energy conservation through rate structure reform. Energy conservation, a new and unsettling concept not so long ago, is increasingly becoming a consensual value.[34] Rate structure reforms that promote conservation, alarming to many several years ago, are increasingly gaining acceptance.

Three indicators of policy responsiveness in this issue area are decisions to adopt time-of-day rates, seasonal rates, or rates for interruptible service. Time-of-day rates, which usually apply to business customers, charge more per kilowatt-hour for consumption during peak hours, when inefficient supplemental generating equipment must be used, than during off-peak hours, when electricity can be provided more efficiently. Seasonal rates, which may apply to either residential or business customers, charge more per kilowatt-hour for consumption during peak months when demand is greatest (usually summer) than during off-peak months. Rates for interruptible service, which usually apply to business customers, charge less per kilowatt-hour to customers who allow their service to be shut off temporarily during emergencies or when aggregate demand for electricity exceeds certain levels. All three variables are dichotomous (0 = no, 1 = yes). As of 1979, 37 percent of the states supplying data had time-of-day rates, 63.6 percent had seasonal rates, and 58.7 percent had rates for interruptible service.[35]

As table 31 indicates, there are only two unequivocal relationships between variables in the model and the adoption of rate structure reforms that promote energy conservation. States with more substantial regulatory resources are more likely to adopt time-of-day rates, and traditionalistic states are less likely to do so. Several other tendencies are apparent. Seasonal rates tend to be rejected in traditionalistic states, adopted in states with high regulatory resources. Rates for interruptible service tend to be rejected in traditionalistic states, adopted in states with high proxy advocacy activity. However, there is no sustained relationship between public advocacy activity and the adoption of policies that promote energy conservation.

If energy conservation policies are transitional, the transition is far from complete. In particular, there is no evidence that

Table 31
Effects of Public Advocacy:
Transitional Policies

Variable	Time-of-Day Rates (N = 46)		Seasonal Rates (N = 44)		Rates for Interruptible Service (N = 46)	
	MLE[a]	p	MLE[a]	p	MLE[a]	p
Grassroots advocacy	.061	.402	.040	.433	.113	.303
Proxy advocacy	.323	.111	.117	.307	.325	.067
Political culture	−.647	.011	−.312	.088	−.303	.080
Regulatory resources	.746	.010	.405	.066	.123	.276
Method of selection	−.235	.232	−.234	.169	.188	.217

Estimated R^2 = .581
−2 × Log Likelihood Ratio = 19.69

Estimated R^2 = .306
−2 × Log Likelihood Ratio = 9.10

Estimated R^2 = .145
−2 × Log Likelihood Ratio = 4.33

a. MLE = Maximum Likelihood Estimate (standardized).

either grassroots or proxy advocates have had a major impact on the adoption of rate structure reforms that promote energy conservation. Nevertheless, proxy advocates do appear to have contributed in a modest way to the adoption of rates for interruptible service. Also, there seems to be a growing recognition by proxy advocates that energy conservation benefits all consumers by reducing the need for expensive new power plants. As this perception becomes widespread, proxy advocates may find it politically acceptable to play a more active role in promoting energy conservation.

The role of proxy advocates may be changing already, if the case of the Michigan Attorney General is illustrative. In 1974, when the Michigan Public Service Commission first considered time-of-day rates, the attorney general remained largely on the sidelines, while citizens' groups led the charge in favor of time-of-day rates. By 1978, however, the attorney general was in the thick of the fight for interruptible service rates. In a Detroit Edison case, the attorney general proposed that all central air-conditioning customers switch to interruptible air-conditioning rates within three years. When the administrative law judge rejected that recommendation, the attorney general filed extensive exceptions to the ALJ's proposal for decision. Specifically, the attorney general argued that interruptible air-conditioning service is essential to avoid construction of nuclear power plants, since virtually all of Detroit Edison's projected load growth over the next decade is due to projected increases in central air-conditioning demand. Whether proxy advocates embrace energy conservation as a high priority remains to be seen. However, as energy conservation issues become more consensual, old barriers to effective advocacy by proxy advocates may crumble.

Discussion

These findings tend to confirm the theory of public advocacy advanced earlier. The policy impacts of public advocates vary from issue area to issue area, depending on the technical complexity of an issue and the extent to which the issue fragments the consumer class. When an issue is highly complex, grassroots advocates will lack the resources to participate effectively.

When an issue is highly conflictual with respect to consumers, proxy advocates will lack incentives to participate effectively. Yet these findings need to be qualified in several respects.

First of all, some grassroots advocacy groups possess sufficient resources and expertise to participate effectively in a highly complex issue area. In contrast to their local counterparts, a number of national citizens' groups, such as the Environmental Defense Fund, the Natural Resources Defense Council, and the Sierra Club, are well funded and well staffed. These national citizens' groups have successfully addressed highly complex issues in key public utility commission cases across the country. The Environmental Defense Fund (EDF), with an annual budget of $2 million, a staff of sixty, and offices in four cities, provides a good example of how a well-funded and well-staffed citizens' group can make a major contribution, even when an issue is highly complex.

Beginning in 1973, the Environmental Defense Fund presented expert testimony in favor of marginal cost pricing principles before a number of state public utility commissions.[36] Although the EDF concentrated its attention on Wisconsin, New York, and California, it also provided testimony in Michigan, Colorado, North Carolina, Pennsylvania, and Arkansas. Despite the complexity of the issue area, the EDF helped to convince these commissions to adopt marginal cost pricing principles.[37] More precisely, the EDF's expert testimony, supplemented by excellent legal representation, put evidence in the record that enabled favorably disposed commissions to adopt marginal cost pricing principles. Indeed, it is important to note that the EDF deliberately intervened in states with public utility commissions likely to be responsive to its efforts. Such commissions tended to be highly professional, with large budgets and large staffs. Joskow puts it this way:

> Many regulatory commissions simply do not have the staff expertise to evaluate properly the issues associated with rate structure reform or to supervise properly the calculation of the relevant marginal costs and the establishment of associated rate structures. It is therefore not too surprising that most progress has been made in states like New York,

Wisconsin, and California, where commissions have larger, more qualified staffs and the commissioners themselves are better trained to evaluate the issues carefully.[38]

This helps to explain why the level of regulatory resources is a better predictor of time-of-day rate decisions than the level of grassroots advocacy. The level of grassroots advocacy in this instance was partly determined by the level of regulatory resources.

Second, grassroots advocacy groups can have an indirect impact on public utility commission decisions without setting foot in a state, through effective testimony in bellwether states. If a citizens' group persuades a leading public utility commission to adopt an innovative policy, such as a rate structure reform, that commission may in turn persuade others to adopt the policy. As Walker has argued, policy innovations are diffused from state to state by public administrators who take cues from their counterparts in key states.[39] Extending Walker's research, Light has found that pacesetters in nonfiscal regulatory policy are California, New York, Michigan, Wisconsin, and New Hampshire.[40]

Interestingly enough, the EDF presented testimony on marginal cost pricing in four of these five states. That testimony appears to have had a multiplier effect. By offering the California, New York, Michigan, and Wisconsin commissions a rationale for adopting marginal cost pricing principles, the EDF helped to bring marginal cost pricing to other states which look to these states for ideas. Thus, the EDF's choice of target states was fortunate. The EDF wisely concentrated its efforts on public utility commissions widely regarded as cuegivers in the regulatory policy.

Third, proxy advocates are not altogether unwilling to speak out on conflictual issues that divide consumers. There is, of course, a vast difference between paying lip service to a goal and actively promoting that goal through persuasive research and testimony. Nevertheless, there are instances where proxy advocates have plunged into the thicket of an ostensibly conflictual issue.

The New York Consumer Protection Board (CPB), for example, has actively promoted the extension of marginal cost pricing principles to all classes of customers, despite the fact that marginal cost pricing tends to benefit some more than others. Since 1976, when the New York Public Service Commission ordered New York utilities to draw up rates based on marginal costs, the CPB has urged the speedy implementation of that order. In rate cases involving the Long Island Lighting Company, New York State Electric & Gas, and Niagara Mohawk, the CPB has persuaded the Public Service Commission to extend marginal cost pricing principles to both residential and business customers. A New York regulator puts it this way:

> The Consumer Protection Board has . . . had an effect on rate structure throughout many of the electric cases, I think, in the direction of marginal cost pricing. So they have helped along in the direction of time-of-use rates and seasonals, and things of that sort. I think they did particularly well in the gas cases. Really put some things in the record that staff was not putting in the record, and it was helpful.

Although proxy advocates did not make a significant contribution to the adoption of rate structure reforms in the first place, they could play an important role in extending those reforms. The distinction is important. In general, it is safer to recommend a policy's implementation than to recommend its adoption. The formal adoption of a policy does not solve the underlying problem, but it does reduce conflict somewhat. In doing so, it may reduce disincentives to participation by proxy advocates.

CONCLUSION

The behavioral method draws inferences from observed differences or changes in governmental behavior, not from attitudes or perceptions. In comparative state politics, it compares differences among states in political conditions with differences among states in public policy outputs, while controlling for other variables. If variations in public advocacy are associated with variations in public policy decisions, then politics determines policy. If the roles of public advocates vary from issue area to issue area, then policy also determines politics.

The behavioral approach confirms a theory of public advocacy based upon a fourfold policy typology: (1) when issues are high in technical complexity, low in consumer conflict, proxy advocates will be effective, grassroots advocates will not be effective; (2) when issues are low in technical complexity, high in consumer conflict, grassroots advocates will be effective, proxy advocates will not be effective; (3) when issues are low in technical complexity, low in consumer conflict, proxy advocates and grassroots advocates will both be effective; and (4) when issues are high in technical complexity, high in consumer conflict, neither proxy advocates nor grassroots advocates will be effective.

These differences in policy impacts are due to differences in the roles that grassroots advocates and proxy advocates play. Proxy advocates, who are better funded and better trained, prefer strategies based on information to strategies based on political pressure. In contrast to grassroots advocates, they are able to address highly complex issues, and they shape their budgetary priorities accordingly. Grassroots advocates, who are less dependent on government funds and less circumscribed by statutes, view themselves as accountable to specific constituencies rather than to government officials or consumers as a whole. In contrast to proxy advocates, they are willing to address highly conflictual issues that divide consumers, and they allocate funds accordingly.

It would be a mistake to suggest that these are iron laws. Some grassroots advocacy groups possess sufficient resources and expertise to address highly complex issues effectively. Some proxy advocacy groups take strong public positions on issues that divide consumers, especially when some consensus has already been achieved. Also, issue characteristics do change over time; as issues are redefined, new lines of cleavage emerge.

Nevertheless, the politics of public utility regulation varies from issue area to issue area in fairly predictable ways. The interest group model, which sees grassroots advocacy groups as playing a significant role, breaks down when issues are highly complex. Conversely, the surrogate representation model, which sees proxy advocacy groups as playing a significant role, breaks down when issues are highly conflictual with respect to consumers as a whole. Thus, although it may be useful to classify agencies in different states, such a classification must be provisional and tentative. If an agency deals with different types of issues, it will be subjected to different types of external pressures. In short, the politics of public utility regulation will vary not only from agency to agency but from issue area to issue area as well.

: PART III :
Reconstruction

The state politics literature is filled with references to the governor and the state legislature, widely regarded as the focal points of public policy-making at the state level. This study does not challenge their supremacy in many issue areas. In public utility regulation, however, politicians are very much like airplane pilots: they act in an emergency, but the real work is normally left to others. A decade ago, one might have pointed to a lack of awareness or understanding as the reason for such inactivity. Today, though, it is clear that politicians lack incentives to get involved. This leaves a wide variety of enormously important decisions in the hands of public utility commissioners.

Although commissioners bear ultimate responsibility for commission decisions, they often hear from parties with diverse issue priorities, value priorities, and policy preferences. These parties include: (1) the regulatory staff, whose professionalism (resources, expertise) varies from state to state; (2) utility companies, whose ability to control the flow of information varies from state to state; (3) proxy advocates, whose influence is largely confined to issue areas low in consumer conflict; and (4) grassroots advocates, whose influence is largely confined to issue areas low in technical complexity. Other interested parties include industrial and commercial customers, labor groups, municipalities, and individual citizens.

Over the past decade, the public utility regulatory process has improved in many respects. Nevertheless, there is widespread dissatisfaction with the status quo. Some argue that public participants are severely handicapped because they lack the resources to advance their interests in commission proceedings.

Others point to weak regulatory staffs and poorly educated commissioners as evidence that commissions are ill equipped to deal with technical problems. Still others object to uncertainties in the rate-making process, which impair the ability of utility companies to plan for the future. Finally, some express dismay at the willingness of governors and legislators to remain largely on the sidelines, while our energy future is determined by others.

These diverse perspectives suggest a wide variety of reform proposals and some difficult questions. Should new forms of public representation be encouraged? Should commissioners be elected by the people? Should commissions be abolished? Should the civil service system be reformed? Should litigation be discouraged? Should political parties be reinvigorated? Answers to these questions depend on the values one seeks to maximize. The purpose of chapter 7 is not to advance a particular hierarchy of values but to identify reforms most likely to promote several values: democratization, professionalism, administrative efficiency, and leadership. In a nutshell, chapter 7 is an exercise in institutional reconstruction.

If normative theories suggest that our practices are wanting, regulatory practices suggest that our empirical theories are wanting. Is "capture theory" tenable when regulated industries find themselves challenged by formidable adversaries, both inside and outside regulatory commissions? Is "interest group pluralism" tenable when important interests remain underrepresented? Is the concept of the "iron triangle" viable when the legislature delegates substantial authority to the bureaucracy? The purpose of chapter 8 is not to debunk popular theories but to develop an alternative approach, based on the concepts of complexity and conflict. It is, in short, an exercise in theoretical reconstruction. Overall, part III seeks to improve both the politics of public utility regulation and our understanding of it.

: 7 :
Regulatory Reform

It is impossible to discuss regulatory reform without first specifying values worthy of consideration and pursuit. The specification of values is both a difficult and a controversial enterprise. Yet it is a prerequisite to policy analysis, whether the policies to be analyzed concern the allocation of resources or the design of institutions that will allocate resources. Policy analysis always proceeds from normative premises, whether latent or manifest. Clarity and honesty are served by making such premises manifest.[1]

Nevertheless, there is a crucial distinction between discussions of substantive and procedural reforms. In the former case, it is altogether appropriate to specify certain substantive criteria, such as equity (social justice) or efficiency (Pareto optimality). Indeed, the evaluation of substantive policy options commonly proceeds along these lines.[2] In discussing procedural reforms, however, it is appropriate to begin with procedural, not substantive criteria.

This is not to suggest that substantive policy consequences are irrelevant to a discussion of procedural reforms. Power to the people is a procedural value but a rather hollow one if it leads to ineffectual participation. Technical expertise is a procedural value but a rather hollow one if it leads to more elaborate and less comprehensible justifications of policies that would have been adopted in any event. Policy entrepreneurship is a procedural value but a rather hollow one if it publicizes entrepreneurs without publicizing policies. Procedural change without substantive significance does little to promote procedural fairness. However, the role of substantive considerations in procedural choices must be limited. The key is not whether the ultimate policy consequences of procedural reforms are desirable but whether it is desirable that a particular group—the people, the experts, the politicians—have a greater impact on public policy.

According to Kaufman, three procedural values have commanded the attention of students of public administration over the years: representativeness (often equated with legislative control), neutral competence, and executive leadership.[3] This typology is a useful starting point, despite its unfortunate assumption that "neutral" competence is actually attainable.[4] However, it exaggerates the distinctiveness of gubernatorial and legislative control, both of which involve administrative accountability to elected sovereigns. It also neglects two crucial values of growing importance: public participation (or democratization) and managerial soundness (or administrative efficiency). Thus, in evaluating administrative decision-making, four procedural values need to be considered: (1) democratization—responsiveness to the full range of interests in society; (2) professionalism—substantive expertise to deal with complex, technical problems; (3) administrative efficiency—the ability to reach decisions with minimal delay and duplication; and (4) leadership—creative entrepreneurial activity by authoritative decision makers, such as the governor or the state legislature.

DEMOCRATIZATION

Few would deny that public utility commissions deal with complex, technical issues. Yet choices between normalized and flow-through accounting methods or declining block rates and inverted rates involve competing values and interests as well. Science, ethics, and politics are extremely difficult to disentangle. For this reason, faith in scientific expertise must be tempered by the recognition that technical analysis is seldom value-free. For example, marginal cost pricing is rooted in a normative premise—namely, that the public interest is served by Pareto optimal solutions.

Citizens have a right to participate in public utility commission decisions because their vital interests are at stake. However, the right to participate does not guarantee that participation will occur or that it will be effective. Despite the growth of public advocacy activity in public utility commission proceedings, grassroots advocacy groups are not very active in approximately half of the states. When active, they are often ineffective, especially when issues are complex. These conditions are by no means unique but apply to other regulatory agencies as well. This has led to pleas for better public representation in regulatory agency proceedings,[5] including public utility commission proceedings.[6] Democratization, it is argued, is necessary to improve and legitimize public utility commission decisions and to afford diverse interests a full opportunity to be heard.

Popularly Elected Commissioners

One route to democratization would be the direct popular election of public utility commissioners, whether statewide or at the district level. At the present time, eleven states have popularly elected public utility commissioners.[7] The number of states with popularly elected commissioners has remained stable over the years. Florida recently switched from elected to appointed commissioners, but no states have moved in the opposite direction for some time. However, direct election is currently under consideration by legislatures in Illinois, Oregon, Wisconsin, and other states. In several other states, initiative drives on direct election of public utility commissioners are under way.[8]

Proponents of direct election believe it would result in the election of consumer-oriented commissioners who would help to arrest the upward spiral in utility rates. There is no credible evidence to support this proposition. As we have seen, the ratio of the rate granted to the rate requested is no lower in states with elected commissioners. Nor is this an isolated finding. Other studies, using different data bases and models, have found that direct election is not associated with either lower rates[9] or a lower allowed rate of return on equity.[10]

It would be unwise to infer from these studies that method of selection has no impact on rates. In states where utilities issues are high in salience (such as Georgia), direct election may result in the election of pro-consumer commissioners who fight strenuously to keep rates down. In states where utilities issues are low in salience (such as North Dakota), direct election may result in the election of pro-utility commissioners who are very receptive to rate hike requests. Expressed a bit differently, direct election may result in the election of candidates who take extreme positions on the balance to be struck between utility and consumer interests. In the short run, direct election could result in either lower or higher rates, depending on the level of public salience in a given state.

In the long run, though, direct election may do more to undermine democratization than to promote it. Where commissioners are elected, citizen participation in public utility commission proceedings tends to be low, even after controlling for political culture. With elected representatives in power, citizens may be lulled into a false sense of security. Alternatively, they may participate, only to find themselves snubbed by commissioners who claim to have a clear "mandate" from the people. Thus, direct election may foreclose opportunities for the attentive public to participate effectively in public utility commission proceedings.

To oppose direct election may appear to be undemocratic. However, it is worth recalling that Robert LaFollette, the "father" of the direct primary and a staunch supporter of popular control, opposed the direct election of public utility commissioners on the grounds that a long ballot does little to promote popular control.[11] To oppose direct election is not to oppose democratization but to oppose the long ballot as a means of achieving it. If democratization is our goal, there are other ways to achieve that.

Proxy Advocacy

One alternative to direct popular election of commissioners is the creation of a proxy advocacy office, whether as a separate state agency or as a special consumer protection unit within the attorney general's office. Either approach institutionalizes public representation in public utility commission proceedings without turning decision-making responsibility over to elected commissioners. Many states established proxy advocacy offices in the 1970s as a response to rising utility rates. Other states are considering this option today.

In contrast to grassroots advocacy groups, proxy advocacy offices tend to be well funded and well staffed. In addition, proxy advocates are well trained, as lawyers, economists, or engineers. According to knowledgeable observers, proxy advocates are moderately effective or very effective in those states where they participate in public utility commission proceedings. Proxy advocates are especially good at addressing revenue requirements issues, despite their high complexity. In fact, the evidence suggests that proxy advocates have helped to trim utility company rate hikes.

Nevertheless, proxy advocacy is flawed in one crucial respect. Intrepid though they may be in opposing utilities on revenue requirements issues, proxy advocates are reluctant to address issues that pit one segment of consumers against another. By and large, they remain on the sidelines when issues involve conflicts between residential and business customers, large and small users, the rich and the poor. Unwilling to ruffle the feathers of powerful constituents or legislators on whom they depend for funding, proxy advocates prefer a "lowest common denominator" approach to consumer representation: they focus their attention overwhelmingly on rate hike requests, at the expense of other issues.

The structural weaknesses of proxy advocacy are compounded by more specific problems associated with representation by an office of consumer counsel or the attorney general. One problem is accountability. Offices of consumer counsel are headed by appointed public officials who are free to choose priorities as they see fit. By and large, such officials are not accountable to the people they claim to represent, except indirectly, through legislative oversight. Thus, the expertise of an office of consumer counsel is harnessed to purposes defined by the consumer counsel alone.

In contrast, the state attorney general is usually elected by the people. However, the representation of utility consumers by the attorney general poses a special problem in many states, where the attorney general also serves as legal counsel to the public utility commission. This arrangement creates potential conflicts of interest, as the attorney general may be tempted to represent one side better than the other. Also, the attorney general, like the consumer counsel, will tend to define consumer interests in relatively noncontroversial terms.

Citizens' Utilities Board

Dissatisfaction with grassroots advocacy and proxy advocacy has led to a search for hybrid alternatives that provide effective public representation through intervenors who are accountable to their constituents.[12] One such alternative is the Citizens Utilities Board (CUB), created by the Wisconsin State Legislature in 1979. CUB, a nonprofit organization, has the authority to intervene before state and federal government agencies, including administrative, legislative, and judicial bodies. CUB is headed by a board of directors, elected by members in each congressional district. CUB members are adults who contribute $3 or more to the organization. Under the law that created CUB, membership solicitations are occasionally inserted in utility bills, with CUB paying any additional postage charges that result. Like grassroots advocacy groups, CUB is a nongovernmental organization, dependent for its survival on voluntary contributions. Like proxy advocacy groups, CUB is a well-funded organization, with sufficient resources to address complex, technical issues. At the present time, CUB has a membership of 55,000 and an annual budget of $300,000.[13]

In at least two respects, CUB is an attractive alternative to proxy advocacy. First, it improves consumer representation in public utility commission proceedings without imposing additional financial burdens on ratepayers or taxpayers. CUB needs money to survive, but contributions are strictly voluntary. Second, CUB provides a high degree of accountability, since its leaders are chosen by members through periodic elections. The potential for membership influence is enormous.

Nevertheless, CUB is flawed for the same reason that proxy advocacy is flawed: by providing for consumer representation through a single organization charged with representing all consumers, it reduces the likelihood that diverse values and preferences will be effectively represented. Like proxy advocacy organizations, CUB is unlikely to plunge into the thicket of issues that pit one segment of consumers against another. Indeed, this is precisely what has happened. As expected, Wisconsin's CUB has directed its attention almost exclusively to revenue requirements issues or the level of rates. In rate case after rate case, CUB has challenged the utility's rate hike request, while neglecting other important issues.

Reliance on a single organization to represent the public assumes that underrepresented public interests are monolithic. In fact, the existence of consumer groups, low-income groups, environmental groups, and antinuclear groups across the country underscores the fact that underrepresented public interests are diverse in the utilities area. No single organization can faithfully reflect these varied interests in debates over conflictual issues such as lifeline rates, utility financing of conservation efforts, cogeneration, and public power.

Intervenor Funding

One way to promote the representation of diverse interests is through intervenor funding for grassroots advocacy groups that participate in public utility commission proceedings. Colorado's intervenor funding program offers one example. In Colorado, the Public Utilities Commission selectively and retrospectively reimburses expenses incurred by participants in commission proceedings, at the discretion of the three commissioners. Any intervenor who makes a substantial contribution to a proceeding is eligible for reimbursement, although reimbursement is by no means guaranteed. Expenses that may be reimbursed include legal and expert witness fees. The funds for reimbursement in a rate case are provided by the utility company that initiated the case (and ultimately by that company's ratepayers).

The Colorado reimbursement program is a good faith effort to deal with a serious problem, but it is flawed in several respects. By allowing the regulatory agency to make funding decisions, it encourages favoritism by regulators partial to certain viewpoints and conformity by intervenors eager to meet the expectations of the regulators. By providing for retrospective reimbursement rather than prior funding, it erodes the ability of severely underfunded groups, unable to risk the possibility of not being funded, to participate in agency proceedings. Also, the Colorado program fails to provide accountability to consumers.

An alternative program, approved by the Michigan State Legislature in October 1982, does not suffer from these drawbacks. This program creates a Utility Consumer Representation Fund, administered by a five-person Utility Consumer Protection Board,[14] to facilitate and improve consumer representation in fuel purchase and power purchase proceedings. One-half of the money is allocated automatically to the attorney general; the remainder is distributed on a competitive basis to nonprofit organizations and local governments that promote the interests of residential consumers. Recipients can use these funds to defray the costs of participation in administrative or judicial proceedings at the state or federal level. Allowable expenses include those for staff support, legal fees, expert witness fees, and related purposes. The Utility Consumer Representation Fund is financed by electric and gas utilities, which pass the expenses along to ratepayers.

The Michigan intervenor funding program has much to commend it. By funding various groups with diverse values and goals, it improves representation for a variety of underrepresented interests. By requiring groups to compete for funds, it provides for quality control and encourages the submission of superior proposals. Although the program is currently limited in scope, it could easily be extended to all utilities issues.

There is a danger that some organizations might become excessively dependent on a Utility Consumer Representation Fund. Such dependence would be particularly unfortunate if it were to weaken bonds between grassroots advocacy groups and their constituents, on whom they currently depend for substantial financial support. To avoid this possibility, one might place a limit on the amount of funds any one group could receive in a given year (for example, 20 percent of the discretionary amount allocated). One might also specify that a citizens' group's ability to raise funds from other sources shall not jeopardize its application for a grant from the fund. With these stronger accountability provisions and a broader scope, the Michigan program could be an outstanding solution to the problem of public underrepresentation.

PROFESSIONALISM

Efforts to democratize public utility regulation assume that regulatory problems are due to conflicts over competing values and interests. However, one could argue that there are correct answers to certain regulatory problems. If so, the solution is not more pluralism but more expertise. This is the premise behind efforts to professionalize public utility regulation. In a setting characterized by conflicting claims and disputed facts, professional training and technical expertise can transform bargaining into problem-solving. Professionals cannot pluck rabbits out of hats, but they can reduce areas of disagreement.

Public utility commissions are much more professional today than they were a decade ago. Commissions are larger and better funded. Commissioners are better educated. Key staff members are better trained and better paid. Yet these improvements may be deceiving. Commission resources are greater than a decade ago, but are they sufficient to cope with the huge quantities of data furnished by utility companies in closely interspersed rate cases? Commissioners are more knowledgeable than a decade ago, but do they know enough to see through the mysterious vapors of the financial markets? Commission staffs are better trained than a decade ago, but are they capable of responding to deregulation, competition, and the uncertainty they entail? If the answer to these questions is no, then perhaps it is necessary to professionalize public utility commissions still further.[15]

Better Commissioners

If a better commissioner is a better-educated commissioner, then public utility commissioners are better today than a decade ago.[16] On the other hand, a surprisingly large number of commissioners are not particularly well educated. In fact, one out of every four commissioners does not even have a college degree.[17] Two conclusions are inescapable: first, many commissioners are not chosen on the basis of their professional credentials (expertise in law, economics, engineering, and so forth); and second, many commissioners are chosen on the basis of other criteria (such as political connections with the governor, the state legislature, or the people). If better-educated commissioners are needed, then either professionalization or depoliticization might achieve that result.

One solution would be longer terms, to encourage the selection and retention of professionals rather than professional politicians. Geller has suggested, for example, a fifteen-year nonrenewable term for certain regulatory commissioners.[18] Only the Pennsylvania Public Utility Commission, with ten-year terms, approaches that goal; most public utility commissioners have four-year or six-year terms. However, commissioners with longer terms are not better educated than other commissioners.[19] Furthermore, longer terms could reduce accountability and contribute to a hardening of the administrative arteries. This could be tragic in a period of rapid change. As Robinson puts it, "I cannot think of anything worse for the regulatory process than creating a class of regulators who want to die with their regulatory boots on."[20]

A more promising solution would be to eliminate elected commissions in favor of appointed commissions. This would almost certainly upgrade the technical expertise of commissioners, since appointed commissioners are better educated than elected ones. Although 82.7 percent of commissioners appointed by the governor have college degrees, only 56.4 percent of commissioners elected by the people do.[21] Nor does gubernatorial appointment pose a threat to accountability. In fact, appointed commissioners are more enthusiastic about citizen participation in public utility commission proceedings than elected commissioners.[22]

Admittedly, though, gubernatorial appointment does not guarantee the selection of competent individuals. A more affirmative approach would be to try to upgrade the quality of gubernatorial appointments. For example, the governor might create a special screening committee for regulatory appointments. As one of its responsibilities, the committee would submit the names of three to five qualified applicants for each public utility commission vacancy. Such a committee would be similar to the American Bar Association's Standing Committee on the Federal Judiciary, which appraises the credentials of nominees to the federal bench, except that it would suggest nominees in addition to evaluating candidates suggested by the governor.

Also, it would consist not only of lawyers but of other professionals as well.

The abolition of elected commissions and the creation of an outside screening committee for regulatory appointments might well result in better commissioners, or at least better-educated commissioners. However, without a large, capable professional staff, commissioners may still be unable to discharge their responsibilities and function effectively. Thus, an alternative approach would be to hire additional staff members.

Larger Staffs

Some public utility commissions do appear to be understaffed. One wonders, for example, how the North Dakota Public Service Commission, which regulates utilities, motor carriers, railroads, and grain elevators, can cope with a staff of fifty-three people and an annual budget of $1.4 million. One wonders how the Wyoming Public Service Commission, which regulates utilities and motor carriers, can cope with a staff of thirty-seven people and an annual budget of less than $1 million. Many small commissions find themselves on a regulatory treadmill. Under the best of circumstances, they may be able to stand still. When the federal government imposes additional requirements on them, however, as in the case of the Public Utility Regulatory Policies Act (PURPA), they find themselves hopelessly backlogged. In desperation, they may comply halfheartedly with federal requirements. Alternatively, they may challenge federal authority in court.[23]

As a general rule, smaller public utility commission staffs tend to be found in states with smaller populations and, one supposes, smaller problems. Yet staff needs are not merely a function of population size. Staff needs are greater in states where the public utility commission has a broader jurisdiction, as in Virginia and Oklahoma. Staff needs are also greater in states with low electric reserve margins and growing populations, such as California, Florida, Colorado, Nevada, and New Mexico.[24] In these and other Sunbelt states, the clock is ticking. Unless they devise imaginative programs to reduce demand or increase supply, they are likely to face the prospect of blackouts, brownouts, or both. California, a pacesetter in many respects, has met these challenges by promoting conservation through a variety of programs (such as utility company financing of residential conservation efforts) and policies (such as lower allowed rates of return for companies which are slow to promote cogeneration). California has also established a separate body, the Energy Commission, to provide detailed forecasts and projections.

There is something to be said for larger staffs, at least in certain states. However, the principal problem with public utility commission staffs is not their size but their composition. The problem is not how many people they hire but whom they hire; not a lack of expertise but a lack of the kind of expertise needed to face the challenges of the future. The key question, in short, is not *whether* to professionalize but *how* to professionalize. It is the mix of professionals and not the number of professionals that matters most.

Declassification

Professionalism is more than just substantive expertise; it is the right kind of substantive expertise. Expressed a bit differently, professionalism is the expertise needed to address the problems of the future rather than the problems of the past. One way to promote professionalism in this sense would be to declassify key public utility commission staff positions. Under declassification, jobs now classified as "career executive" or civil service positions would become "political executive" or exempt positions. At first glance, this appears a rather odd recommendation. Historically, the classification of administrative positions promoted professionalism by encouraging the transition from a "spoils system" to a "merit system." By requiring job applicants to meet specified criteria for employment, it eliminated payoffs by machine politicians; by protecting administrative officials from arbitrary dismissal, it ensured that capable people could not be fired for partisan reasons. Overall, it promoted such values as honesty, expertise, and stability.[25]

The civil service system has served and will continue to serve a useful purpose, especially at the middle and lower levels of the bureaucracy. However, its continuation at the upper levels could retard the recruitment and promotion of people with valuable skills. The classification of key staff positions makes it difficult to hire outstanding job applicants; by the time testing and certification are complete, applicants have accepted other jobs. Classification also makes it difficult to encourage excellence through salary increases: financial rewards are so dependent on seniority that performance incentives are weak. Finally, classification makes it extremely difficult to fire or reassign people whose performance has slipped or whose skills are obsolete; change occurs but largely through the glacial process of voluntary retirements and transfers.

Public utility commissions differ dramatically in their mix of classified and unclassified positions. In Wisconsin, Michigan, California, and New Jersey, most or all top staff positions are filled by career executives, covered by civil service. In Illinois, Massachusetts, New York, and Florida, many top staff positions are filled by political executives, who serve at the pleasure of the commissioners or the chairperson of the commission. In general, commission practices coincide with broader state practices.[26] As for state practices, they appear to reflect the state's political culture and the history of its political parties. Thus, states with "moralistic" political cultures[27] and "issue-oriented" political parties[28] favor career executives, whereas states with "individualistic" political cultures and "job-oriented" political parties favor political executives. States that have opted for career executives undoubtedly did so in good faith and with the noblest of motives; states that have opted for political executives may have acted in bad faith and with questionable motives. Nevertheless, we cannot judge the civil service system by its high-minded origins or political appointments by the partisan purposes they were once intended to serve.

Ironically, many of the commissions with heavily classified staffs are located in states that are unlikely to need classification as a barrier to corruption, because of a long-standing animus against the spoils system. These commissions—in Wisconsin, Michigan, California, and elsewhere—are needlessly handicapped as they face the future. In these states, the choice between political executives and career executives is not a choice between partisan hacks and skilled professionals but rather a choice between professionals with different skills. Unfortunately, in a period of rapid technological change, skills quickly become outmoded.

In the past, it may have been appropriate to hire electrical engineers who knew how to move electricity from one point to another; in the future, it may be necessary to hire industrial engineers who can do operations research and statistical analysis. In the past, it may have been appropriate to hire economists trained to design rate structures consistent with marginal cost pricing principles; in the future, it may be necessary to hire economists who can develop econometric models suitable for forecasting. In the past, it may have been appropriate to hire attorneys who knew the difference between a natural monopoly and a competitive firm; in the future, it may be necessary to hire antitrust lawyers who can clear a path through the dense underbrush of holding companies, subsidiaries, and partly regulated firms. If they are to address the needs of the future rather than the needs of the past, public utility commissions must be free to alter the mix of professionals. The point is not that a particular mix of professionals is needed but that commissions should be free to define the mix and act upon it.

Declassification is not without its risks. It could be harmful, for example, if it were extended to the lower or middle levels of the bureaucracy, where the promise of job security may be a vital enticement to job applicants. Declassification might also be unwise if staff turnover were abnormally high. However, top-level public utility commission staff members have worked an average of a dozen or so years for their commission. The average is a little lower for political executives than for career executives, but not by much.[29] Thus, declassification could result in a modest increase in turnover, but it is unlikely to result in a serious loss of institutional memory.

On the positive side, declassification offers the opportunity for flexible hiring and rapid adaptations to changing needs. It may not result in fewer lawyers, economists, and engineers, but it could result in lawyers, economists, and engineers with different skills. Alternatively, it could result in the appointment of people with interdisciplinary training, since such individuals are likely to prove most durable in a period of rapid change. Imagine a

Renaissance man or woman—someone capable of planning, analyzing, calculating, and evaluating; someone who does not shiver at the sight of a statistic but who is also capable of addressing questions of social equity; someone trained in both the social sciences and the natural sciences who can also explain commission policies to members of the public. This "bionic" person may be the ideal staff member of the 1980s, but many public utility commissions will be unable to hire such a person, owing to antiquated civil service laws. Declassification could go a long way toward correcting that problem.

ADMINISTRATIVE EFFICIENCY

Efforts to professionalize public utility regulation assume that we need better answers to regulatory problems, whereas efforts to democratize public utility regulation assume that we need fairer answers. In contrast, efforts to streamline public utility regulation assume that we need quicker answers. According to some critics of the administrative process, regulatory agencies move too slowly in making decisions,[30] especially in rate cases.[31] Although rate-making is sometimes considered a quasi-legislative process,[32] it tends to be quasi-judicial in its reliance on trial-type hearings and exclusiveness of record requirements. The ostensible purpose of these quasi-judicial procedures is to strengthen the due process rights of rate case participants. In practice, though, the judicialization of the administrative process may support the status quo by making it difficult to move in new directions in the absence of a strong evidentiary record.[33]

As we have seen, public utility commissions are coping well with the potentially vexing problem of regulatory lag. In fact, the length of electric, natural gas, and telephone rate cases actually declined from 1974 to 1979. Nevertheless, rate cases may still take longer than necessary. Also, appeals to the courts have increased. Even though public utility commissions win most cases that go to court, the entire process is costly and time-consuming. In view of these developments, there is much to be said for greater administrative efficiency. As one observer puts it, "Efficiency is no proof of the inherent worth of an agency but a lack of efficiency is an indictment even of agencies that are valuable."[34]

A Single Administrator

Among proposals to promote administrative efficiency, the most widely discussed is the elimination of regulatory commissions in favor of agencies headed by a single administrator. According to the Ash Council, this reform is likely to speed up and improve regulatory decision-making by eliminating the need for collegial accommodation by agency heads.[35] Unfortunately, there is no empirical evidence to support the Ash Council's assertions. As Cramton notes, "There is a lack of factual basis for the Ash Council's conclusion that single-headed agencies perform better. It is something you have to arrive at by a leap of faith, by an intuitive jump."[36]

Indeed, there are reasons to doubt that a single-headed agency performs better than a multimember commission. The elimination of conflicts among commissioners does not end conflicts elsewhere within the bureaucracy. In fact, conflicts between staff factions at single-headed agencies are often intense, as a recent study of the Environmental Protection Agency illustrates.[37] Nor is there any evidence to suggest that the commission form has peculiar consequences for public policy. According to an assessment based on performance indicators in six program areas, "monocratic" agencies are no more effective than their "collegial" counterparts.[38] In short, the abolition of the commission form offers little hope for improving the performance of public utility commissions.

Settlements

An alternative to abolishing commissions would be to expedite the rate-making process. Although utility rate cases do not take quite as long as they used to, they still last long enough to consume substantial amounts of time and money. Furthermore, many rate decisions are challenged in court. Some of these cases are litigated for years, especially in states where successive appeals to more than one court are possible. One way to dejudicialize the public utility regulatory process would be through greater reliance on settlements.

Settled or "stipulated" cases are common at a number of federal regulatory agencies, including the Federal Trade Commission, the Federal Energy Regulatory Commission, and the National Labor Relations Board. One study of federal settlements has concluded that they often produce "dramatic results" in the form of substantial reductions in regulatory lag.[39] Furthermore, settlements virtually eliminate the prospect of judicial review. If parties agree to a settlement, they are barred from challenging that settlement in court. Other parties may seek judicial review, but the courts are likely to support a settlement approved by the major parties to a case.

Public utility commission rate cases have seldom been settled, but this is beginning to change. In New Jersey, settled rate cases are now more or less routine. The New Jersey Department of Public Advocate and the Board of Public Utilities staff have stipulated agreements with a number of major utilities. In Missouri, the Public Counsel and the Public Service Commission staff have successfully negotiated agreements with a large number of small utilities. In Ohio, the Consumers' Counsel and the Public Utility Commission staff have stipulated agreements with Ohio Bell Telephone, Ohio Edison, and Dayton Power & Light. The common denominator in these states seems to be the presence of a vigorous proxy advocacy office with enough resources to frighten utility companies and enough credibility with consumers to assure them that a settlement is in their best interest. Without the approval of such an office, a "deal" between the public utility commission staff and a major utility might strike ratepayers as a Faustian bargain. In states where utilities issues are highly salient, the active involvement of a proxy advocacy office may be a prerequisite to settlement.

The settlement process is not without its dilemmas. As the number of participants in rate cases increases, consensus will prove more difficult to achieve. Yet the exclusion of certain interests from the settlement process would surely undermine the legitimacy of any agreement. As the negotiating process is opened up to the press, posturing may replace bargaining. However, closed negotiations are unlikely to inspire public confidence. Another problem is that rate decisions must be based on evidence in the record. Since parties to a settlement normally agree on a result without agreeing on the premises underlying such an agreement, this places a major burden on the regulatory staff, which must somehow contrive a rationale to justify the stipulated result.

Despite these problems, there is much to be said for settlement as an alternative to the familiar cycle of rate-making and litigation. It not only saves time and money but also encourages mutual understanding and consensus. As Schuck puts it, "Bargaining may do for us what litigation and law increasingly cannot: it may nourish those impulses toward integration, accommodation, reconciliation, and mutuality of interests which an adversary society tends to stifle, but without which no society can effectively discharge its business."[40] If so, bargaining will have accomplished a great deal indeed.

Rule-making

A still bolder departure from conventional rate-making would be to shift from rate-making to rule-making. Specialists in administrative law have long argued that administrative agencies should rely more on rule-making. Davis has gone so far as to describe rule-making as "one of the greatest inventions of modern government."[41] Rule-making has several advantages over case-by-case decision-making. First, rule-making encourages advance planning by both the agency and the business community. Clear administrative policy facilitates predictable behavior by regulators, regulated firms, and consumers. Second, rule-making promotes consistency and evenhandedness in the application of the law. Rules apply to all firms, without favor or discrimination. Third, rule-making eliminates unnecessary overlap and duplication of effort. In fact, it may be viewed as a means of consolidating individual cases for the sake of administrative efficiency. Finally, rule-making usually offers flexibility in the choice of administrative procedures. In informal rule-making, sometimes known as "notice and comment" rule-making, an agency need not hold a trial-type hearing. So long as it notifies the public of its proposed rule and allows the public to comment on that proposed rule, the agency has fulfilled its legal obligations.

Despite the advantages of rule-making, public utility commissions continue to avoid it. There are several reasons for this. First, rule-making affects many companies and many customers. As a result, it normally arouses more diverse interests, more participation, more conflict, and more dissensus. Second, rule-making requires agencies to formulate policy with precision. This is difficult, both technically and politically. In the long run, policy-making through administrative rules is likely to save time and money. In the short run, however, it may appear more costly and time-consuming than rate-making. Third, rule-making reduces administrative discretion in future cases. It is easier to depart from a loose precedent in a rate case than it is to abandon a rule. Finally, rule-making subjects an agency to more vigorous legislative oversight. This is especially true in states that provide for a legislative veto of administrative rules. In such states, public utility commissions have a legislative Sword of Damocles hanging over rule-making proceedings. By avoiding rule-making, they avoid the possibility of a legislative veto.

The federal courts have often expressed a preference for administrative rule-making, but they have also argued that agencies should be free to choose between rule-making and other alternatives.[42] The position of the state courts is more difficult to discern. Occasionally, state courts have rebuked agencies for making policy without recourse to the rule-making process.[43] Overall, though, the state courts, like the federal courts, will probably continue to allow administrative agencies flexibility in their choice of administrative procedures.

The fact is that public utility commissions are unlikely to shift from rate-making to rule-making unless state legislatures require them to do so. Some state legislatures are considering that possibility. For example, State Senator Joseph Strohl of Wisconsin has introduced bills that would require the Wisconsin Public Service Commission to conduct rule-making inquiries into advertising expenses, conservation-based rates, and the determination of an allowed rate of return. One might also require public utility commissions to hold rule-making proceedings on construction work in progress, the treatment of taxes, and the allocation of costs between residential and business customers.

There is much to be said for rule-making. At the present time, public utility commissions "reinvent the wheel" in rate case after rate case. Greater reliance on rule-making could promote administrative efficiency. There is also much to be said for a legislative requirement that certain issues be addressed through rule-making. Without a requirement, extensive rule-making is unlikely. However, if state legislatures are to instruct public utility commissions to engage in rule-making, the question arises: What kind of rule-making should they require? More specifically, should they require a trial-type hearing (as in formal rule-making), no hearing at all (as in informal rule-making), or something in between (as in "hybrid" rule-making)?

If our goal is administrative efficiency, perhaps nothing more elaborate than informal rule-making should be required. An agency could permit oral testimony, the cross-examination of witnesses, and rebuttal arguments, or some combination of these, but it would not be required to do so. On the other hand, it is certainly possible to strike a balance between administrative efficiency and due process. For example, state legislatures might require public utility commissions to provide at least what Stewart calls a "paper hearing," with all evidence being submitted in writing and being subjected to written criticism.[44] A paper hearing requirement could guarantee opportunities for comment, criticism, and judicial review without the burdens of a trial-type hearing. In conjunction with a rule-making requirement, it could promote administrative efficiency without infringing on due process.

LEADERSHIP

Even if public utility commissions are prompt and efficient, they may be timid and incremental. Dismayed by the sluggish performance of the bureaucracy, some observers have recommended creative leadership by politicians.[45] Yet if politicians are to lead, several conditions are necessary: (1) awareness of a policy problem; (2) authority to deal with the problem; (3) resources to develop a solution; and (4) incentives to pursue a solution. The behavior of governors and state legislatures in the

1970s suggests the absence of one or more of these conditions. Governors have often spoken out on utilities issues, but they have seldom transcended banal declarations of support for energy conservation and an adequate energy supply. State legislatures have occasionally passed utility-related legislation, but they have seldom clarified vague exhortations to public utility commissions to provide a "fair return" to investors, "just and reasonable rates" to consumers. In short, public utility regulation has not been characterized by a great deal of gubernatorial or legislative leadership.

Why has leadership been lacking? One reason is "divided government," where one party controls the governorship, and another party controls one or both legislative houses. Over the past two decades, divided government has spread from sixteen states to twenty-five. As we have seen, there are real differences between Democrats and Republicans on utilities issues, at least outside the South. In view of these differences, successful leadership is hampered by divided government. Greater cooperation between the governor and the state legislature might break this stalemate. Another approach would be independent action by either the governor or the legislature.

Executive Orders

The executive order has long been used by the president as a device for acting swiftly without securing congressional approval.[46] In general, the courts have upheld executive orders at the federal level, unless Congress expressly considered and rejected the delegation of authority to the president in a particular area.[47] Executive orders are less common at the state level, but their use appears to be growing. In Wisconsin, for example, Governor Lee Dreyfus issued a total of twenty-nine executive orders during his first year in office; in contrast, Wisconsin governors had issued fewer than ten executive orders during an earlier eighteen-year period.[48]

There are several circumstances under which a governor could exercise leadership in energy policy by issuing an executive order. First, the governor might issue an executive order in response to an energy crisis or emergency. Thus, during the energy crises of 1973 and 1979, many governors declared an energy emergency, which enabled them to gather valuable data from oil companies and to allocate scarce fuel supplies. Many governors also adopted odd-even gasoline rationing plans in order to ensure that fuel would be available for other purposes, such as home heating.

Second, the governor might create or reorganize government agencies with energy responsibilities. During the mid-1970s, many governors created state energy offices, sometimes through a statute, sometimes through an executive order. In some states, where the governor is authorized to reorganize without explicit legislative approval, the governor might even merge the public utility commission with the state energy office. Less dramatically, the governor could create an energy-related unit within an existing agency—for example, a solar energy or a nuclear operations unit.

Third, the governor might impose energy-related requirements on state agencies. For example, the governor could require state agencies to lower their thermostats during the winter and to raise their thermostats during the summer. Or the governor might instruct state agencies to reduce their use of state cars, as an energy-saving measure.

Finally, the governor might establish task forces to investigate substantive or procedural problems. One possibility would be a special task force to investigate a specific substantive problem, such as the inability of poor people to pay their utility bills. Another possibility would be a special commission to investigate the merits of proposed procedural reforms, such as declassification of top positions in the bureaucracy.

Overall, the executive order has probably been underutilized. In states where the governor and the legislature are barely on speaking terms, the executive order offers considerable potential as a means of effecting a "legislative bypass." Elsewhere, the executive order offers the opportunity for the governor to move quickly on utility-related issues.

However, there are limits to what the governor can accomplish through an executive order. For example, governors may reorganize within agencies, but they often lack authority to merge or consolidate agencies. Even in states where governors have such authority, they may be reluctant to use it, for fear of incurring the wrath of the state legislature.[49] To cite another example, governors may require agencies under their purview to take specific conservation measures, but a number of large state agencies are often independent of the governor (for example, the state university system). Thus, the governor's ability to impose standards on the entire state bureaucracy is frequently limited.

The more fundamental problem is that executive orders are inappropriate for a great deal of policy-making. Executive orders enable a governor to respond to a crisis but seldom to avoid one, to investigate a problem but seldom to solve one, to manage the bureaucracy but seldom to lead the citizenry. Executive orders can point us in the right direction, but they are unlikely to embody bold new policy ventures. Given the limitations of executive orders, it is appropriate to consider other proposed routes to leadership, such as legislative vetoes.

The Legislative Veto

The legislative veto is a mechanism for invalidating a decision by the chief executive or an administrative agency if that decision fails to secure legislative approval. The original legislative veto, adopted by Congress in 1932, authorized the president to reorganize the executive branch unless one house of Congress objected. Since that time, Congress has frequently attached legislative veto provisions to bills ceding authority to particular administrative agencies. Although the constitutionality of the congressional veto has been challenged, the Supreme Court thus far has not invalidated legislative veto provisions aimed at agency rules.[50] Also, the legislative veto is increasingly popular at the state level. At the present time, approximately thirty-four state legislatures have the authority to review and invalidate proposed agency rules.[51]

Because a legislative veto typically does not require the governor's approval, it can be a means of fostering legislative leadership when the legislature and the governor disagree. Indeed, the legislative veto sometimes permits the invalidation of agency rules when a handful of legislators conclude that a given rule is ill conceived. In Connecticut, Michigan, Tennessee, and West Virginia, for example, legislative review committees have the authority to suspend proposed rules indefinitely, unless the legislature acts affirmatively to sustain the agency.[52] Thus, in some states, a consensus among legislative committee members may be sufficient to overturn an agency rule.

The legislative veto facilitates legislative oversight of the bureaucracy, which is a potentially important form of leadership. Nevertheless, it has some serious flaws. First of all, the legislative veto is a very blunt instrument. Although it enables the legislature to register opposition or support, it is far less flexible than lawmaking, with its opportunities for compromise and amendment. Second, the legislative veto lengthens the administrative rule-making process. Although legislative review committees are required to meet specific deadlines in most states, they are free to take as long as they wish in others. Even where deadlines exist, agencies are likely to move with considerable and possibly excessive caution to avoid a "mistake" that could trigger a veto. Third, the legislative veto discourages rule-making. If a public utility commission knows that its proposed rules are subject to legislative reversal, it will avoid rule-making as much as possible. This will perpetuate the tendency of administrative agencies to opt for rate-making rather than rule-making.

The most serious weakness of the legislative veto is that it does not change legislative incentives. Rather, it presupposes that the reason for legislative inaction is a lack of oversight opportunities. This may be true in some policy domains. In public utility regulation, however, the principal reason for legislative inaction is a lack of will. If legislators are unwilling to exercise power in the first place, then additional oversight opportunities are unlikely to generate legislative leadership.

Lawmaking

Although independent action by the governor or the legislature is beguiling in certain respects, neither is an acceptable substitute for lawmaking. Executive orders permit the governor to act in an emergency, but they are of little use outside crisis situations. Legislative vetoes enable the legislature to negate ill-conceived administrative rules, but they are of little use outside rule-making situations. Neither executive orders nor legislative vetoes enable politicians to exercise bold, creative leadership in addressing the long-term problems posed by a diminishing energy supply, rising energy prices, and air pollution.

In an ideal polity, the governor and the state legislature would act together to address these problems. However, governors and legislators often view one another as competitors, rather than partners. This is especially true in states where the governor and the legislature are controlled by different political parties. As Francis has shown, strong legislation is less likely to be approved in states with divided government.[53] For this reason, many political scientists have recommended a "responsible party" system as a solution to the "deadlock of democracy."[54] Thus, it is argued that less ticket-splitting and more cohesive legislative parties will result in stronger leadership.

Certainly, divided government may inhibit leadership. Yet gubernatorial success in the legislature appears to depend more on the governor's popularity within his own party than on the proportion of legislative seats controlled by the governor's party.[55] Furthermore, a chief executive whose party controls both houses of the legislative branch may still lack vital legislative support. When Jimmy Carter proposed a comprehensive energy program in 1977, the Democrats controlled both houses of Congress. Nevertheless, Congress rejected major elements of the Carter program, including a gasoline tax hike, mandatory rate structure reforms, a crude oil tax, and the indefinite continuation of natural gas controls. Finally, and most significantly, there is no indication of a reversal in the trend toward party disaggregation. At the mass level, the public actually views divided government in positive terms. At the elite level, the dispersion of legislative power makes party leadership exceptionally difficult. For better or worse, divided government and irresponsible parties are here to stay.

The more fundamental problem with the responsible parties argument is that it presupposes that politicians want to lead in the first place. In fact, it is doubtful that either the governor or the state legislature wishes to exercise leadership in the public utilities area. As Price has argued, legislative leadership depends on perceptions of salience and conflict. When issues are low in conflict, high in salience, legislators have ample incentives to get involved. When issues are high in conflict, low in salience, legislators have no incentives to get involved. When issues are high in conflict, high in salience, legislators have mixed incentives.[56] If levels of citizen participation are any indication, the salience of utilities issues appears to vary from state to state. It is clear, though, that utilities issues are high in conflict, as they pit consumers against utilities, residential consumers against business consumers, environmental groups against consumer groups, the rich against the poor. These conflicts discourage legislative leadership. This is not to say that legislative leadership will never occur in the utilities area. It may occur, for example, as a response to policy initiatives by the chief executive.[57]

However, the governor, like the legislature, has few incentives to blaze new trails in utility regulation. The modern governor has a very crowded agenda, dominated by fiscal crises which show every sign of worsening as taxpayer resentment increases and federal aid decreases. Under such circumstances, the governor is likely to play a relatively passive role, unless he is compelled to act. Former Wisconsin Governor Martin Schreiber puts it this way: "No governor will be able to develop his own agenda when things are going to hell outside."[58]

Furthermore, the governor, like the legislature, is intimidated by highly conflictual issues. If the governor is interested in reelection, and most governors are, he is likely to avoid zero-sum policy disputes. There may be exceptions to this general rule. A governor who seeks to establish a national reputation, such as California's Governor Jerry Brown, may take a forceful stand on a controversial issue (for example, nuclear power) in order to attract media attention and build a national constituency. By and large, though, governors have few incentives to direct their attention to utilities issues.

Gubernatorial awareness of energy issues has clearly increased over the past decade.[59] Legislative awareness has probably increased as well. However, if awareness is a necessary condition for lawmaking, it is not a sufficient one. Paradoxically, as politicians have become more aware of utilities issues, they have become less willing to address them through legislation.

Unless the incentives of state politicians are changed, they are unlikely to play a leadership role in the 1980s.

Initiatives

It is relatively easy to increase the authority or the resources of the governor or the state legislature; it is much more difficult to alter their incentives. Yet a prerequisite to lawmaking in a highly conflictual issue area is that politicians have incentives to lead. Otherwise, bills may be introduced and speeches may be given, but laws will not be passed. One way to restructure the incentives of politicians might be through increased citizen participation in gubernatorial and legislative campaigns. If the single most important goal of politicians is reelection—a widespread assumption among political scientists—then this could make a difference. Yet gubernatorial campaigns are expensive; state legislative campaigns are much less expensive, but there are many of them. Furthermore, electoral mandates are often ambiguous. Even if utilities issues contribute to the outcome of a state election, politicians might conclude that other issues were decisive. If so, campaign activity by issue-oriented citizens could be largely fruitless.

A more serious threat to politicians would be a frontal assault on their lawmaking authority. By and large, governors and legislators have abdicated their responsibilities in the utilities area. In view of this, the people might reclaim their sovereign power through the use of the initiative, which permits citizens to draft legislation and place it on the ballot by petition. The initiative, currently permitted in twenty-three states, is under consideration in at least ten more.[60] Widely used in western states, it is an issue-specific form of public control.

The initiative is becoming an increasingly important vehicle for making laws when more conventional routes are blocked. During the 1970s, the number of statewide initiatives was twice as high as during the previous decade.[61] Furthermore, reliance on the initiative appears to be increasing. Indeed, there is even talk of a national initiative.[62]

Although taxpayer initiatives have received more attention, many recent initiatives have involved public utility regulation.

A large number of these have concerned power plants in general or nuclear power plants in particular. For example, in 1978, the voters of Montana approved an initiative placing restrictions on nuclear power plant licensing and operations. In 1981, the electorate of the state of Washington voted to require public approval before issuing bonds to construct or acquire power plants with a capacity of 250 megawatts or more. Other initiatives have concerned tax credits for energy conservation, lifeline rates, and direct popular election of public utility commissioners.[63]

In a narrow sense, the success rate for initiatives is not particularly high. Of fifteen initiative drives, only three are placed on the ballot, and only one is approved by the electorate.[64] However, initiatives that "fail" may trigger legislative, gubernatorial, or administrative action. In South Dakota, for example, the Public Utilities Commission approved lifeline rates for the elderly and the poor in 1980, following the defeat of a more comprehensive lifeline rate initiative at the polls two years earlier. In California, the state legislature responded to a 1976 antinuclear initiative while the campaign was still under way. One week before the scheduled election, the legislature approved a milder alternative to the antinuclear initiative, which was subsequently rejected by the electorate.[65]

Thus, the value of the initiative could lie more in its indirect effects on public policy than in its direct effects. An initiative drive that fails may nevertheless convince politicians that they cannot dodge an issue forever. Alternatively, politicians might respond to an abortive petition drive by placing the issue on the ballot themselves, through a referendum. This could provide an authoritative expression of public sentiment on a controversial issue, such as construction work in progress or lifeline rates.

Several objections have been raised to initiatives. First, they are said to attract low voter turnout, permitting a small minority of the electorate to determine the outcome of an important issue election. Second, they are said to be vulnerable to media blitzes by well-financed organizations. If so, special interest groups could use the initiative to private advantage, at the expense of the general public. Third, they are said to undermine the credibility of the legislative branch. Instead of inducing legislative leadership, it is argued, they induce legislative timidity and indecision.[66]

Although these are serious objections, they do not appear to be supported by the facts. First, turnout in initiatives, though lower than turnout in gubernatorial elections, is higher than turnout in other state races.[67] Thus, the proportion of the electorate that participates in initiatives is not abnormally low. Second, it is altogether possible for an initiative drive to succeed despite well-financed opposition. In the recent Washington State initiative, for example, supporters won despite being outspent six to one. Third, there is no evidence to suggest that initiatives weaken legislative leadership. Indeed, according to one study, state legislatures are actually stronger in initiative states.[68] In short, the dangers of initiatives appear to have been greatly exaggerated.

Greater reliance on the initiative is, admittedly, a strong remedy for the absence of political leadership in public utility regulation. Without such a catalyst, however, politicians are unlikely to act. If, on the other hand, the electorate insists that certain issues be addressed through lawmaking, politicians are likely to heed that signal. A key element of leadership is responsiveness to public preferences. In a highly conflictual issue area, the surest way to secure political leadership is for the people to demand it.

CONCLUSION

Regulatory reforms, like other public policies, often fail to accomplish what they were intended to accomplish. Popular election of public utility commissioners brings regulators closer to the people but allows them to hide behind a vague, inconclusive electoral mandate. Thus, it does not get to the root of the democratization problem, which is that the people lack control over policies, not personnel. Larger budgets enable public utility commissions to hire additional staff members. However, they do not get to the root of the professionalism problem, which concerns the quality and not the number of staff members. An end to the commission form eliminates an agency head's dependence on other commissioners but may increase dependence on the staff. Furthermore, it does not get to the root of the efficiency problem, which is the rate-making process itself. A "responsible parties" system eliminates certain obstacles to legislative-gubernatorial cooperation. However, it does not get to the root of the leadership problem, which is that legislators and governors lack incentives to act in highly conflictual issue areas.

In contrast, other regulatory reforms successfully promote important values. Indeed, some promote more than one value simultaneously. Intervenor funding promotes democratization by facilitating the participation of grassroots advocacy groups in public utility commission proceedings. In addition, it encourages professionalism by improving the technical expertise of grassroots advocacy groups. Declassification promotes professionalism by enabling commissioners to hire and promote job applicants whose skills match the challenges of the future rather than the challenges of the past. It also encourages administrative efficiency by expediting hiring and firing decisions. Rule-making promotes administrative efficiency by channeling important controversies into generic proceedings rather than a repetitive series of ad hoc decisions. In addition, it encourages leadership by providing state legislators with more meaningful opportunities for oversight. The initiative promotes leadership by encouraging reluctant governors and legislators to act. It also promotes democratization by affording the electorate an opportunity to make policy through the ballot box.

The most surprising discovery to emerge from this review of regulatory reforms is that trade-offs are less exasperating when one looks at procedural questions than when one looks at substantive questions. It may be necessary to choose between higher and lower rates or between consumer protection and environmental protection, but it is not necessary to choose between democratization and professionalism or between leadership and administrative efficiency. Indeed, in public utility regulation, it would be dangerous to do so. Utilities issues are too conflictual for a retreat from accountability, too complex for a retreat from competence.

Yet choices among reforms can and should be made. In fact, the relative merits of various reforms are much clearer than the relative merits of the values they purport to promote. Surely, a reform that promotes democratization (intervenor funding) or professionalism (declassification) is better than one that promotes neither (direct election of commissioners). Surely, a reform that promotes administrative efficiency (rule-making) or leadership (initiatives) is better than one that promotes neither (the legislative veto). There is also a case to be made for somewhat flawed reforms (proxy advocacy, larger commission staffs), which at least come close to promoting important values.

There is no guarantee that these reforms will have consistent policy consequences. Intervenor funding could promote environmental goals, despite the costs for ratepayers—costs that proxy advocates are trying to contain. More professional commissions could result in higher rates, and proxy advocacy could result in lower rates. Yet the simultaneous pursuit of accountability and competence, in their various forms, is likely to promote policies that offer some hope of achieving consensus— policies such as energy conservation. The more professional commissions and the overwhelming majority of citizens' groups are already strongly supportive of conservation efforts. Proxy advocates and utility companies, though less enthusiastic initially, show signs of coming around.

Debates over rate levels are unlikely to become any less controversial. Indeed, the mobilization of investor groups suggests that these disputes will become even more controversial in the future. Under such circumstances, conservation-based policies will be especially attractive to commissions searching for "correct" but popular solutions to the energy crisis. Those policies are most likely to emerge from a coalition of highly professional commissions and highly skilled citizens' groups. The politics of public utility regulation is likely to be highly complex and highly conflictual for some time to come. However, the emergence of energy conservation as a consensual policy could at least limit the scope of conflict.

: 8 :
Conflict and Complexity

Utilities issues are extremely conflictual. They pit investors against consumers, business groups against residential consumers, consumer groups against environmental groups, low-income consumers against consumers as a whole. They have many of the characteristics of a zero-sum game. Utilities issues have not always been conflictual. During the 1960s, for example, they aroused very little controversy. Over the past decade, however, bitter disputes have arisen. As we have become more aware of the scarcity of our natural resources and the harmful environmental effects of fossil fuel consumption, conflict has increased. As economies of scale have vanished and inflation has worsened and rates have climbed, conflict has increased.

Utilities issues are also extremely complex. As regulators decide whether CWIP should be included in the rate base, whether normalized or flow-through accounting methods should be used, whether average cost pricing or marginal cost pricing is appropriate, and what reserve margins are adequate, they need to muster considerable technical expertise. Although utilities issues have always been somewhat complex, they have become much more so over the past decade. The capital-intensive nature of coal-fired and nuclear plants has made it especially difficult to predict construction costs in a period of inflation. The reliability of nuclear power has become suspect as safety problems have emerged. The behavior of consumers has become less certain as they have begun to conserve energy and switch to renewable energy sources.

The complexity and conflictuality of utilities issues sets them apart from many other regulatory issues. Some issues, such as broadcast regulation and rent control, are highly conflictual but not particularly complex. Others, such as the regulation of securities and the setting of sewer rates, are highly complex but not very conflictual. Still others, such as billboard regulation and motor vehicle inspections, are neither conflictual nor complex. In short, complexity and conflictuality are not inevitable characteristics of regulatory issues. They are, however, important variables, with significant consequences for regulatory politics.

Thus, the complexity and conflictuality of utilities issues intimidates most politicians. The governor, who recognizes an albatross when he sees one, prefers to remain aloof from the fray. Legislators, for similar reasons, prefer rhetoric and occasional committee hearings to significant collective action. Conflictuality discourages politicians from getting involved; complexity provides a welcome excuse. From the vantage point of politicians, the independence of public utility commissions is not a troublesome myth but a useful reality.

Yet independence from politicians does not necessarily mean independence from outside pressure. Indeed, the absence of gubernatorial and legislative involvement emboldens regulated industries, whose support for the regulatory scheme becomes crucial. Under these circumstances, one expects that utility companies will be especially influential, and indeed they are. Some might even go so far as to predict "capture" by utility companies. After all, they have more expertise than anyone else, and expertise is precious in this issue area. However, utilities issues today are too controversial to be relegated to regulated industry officials. Utility companies may be natural monopolies, but they no longer monopolize the politics of public utility regulation. If complexity encourages capture, conflictuality does not.

Upset by high energy rates and other public policies, a variety of interest groups intervene in public utility commission proceedings. Commercial and industrial customers challenge utility company rate hike requests. Labor groups raise similar objections. Grassroots advocacy groups complain about high rates, environmental degradation, nuclear power, and policies that fail to protect the poor. Yet utility customers have less of a stake in these disputes than utility companies. Business and labor groups, with considerable resources at their disposal, have other obligations and concerns. Grassroots advocacy groups, with keener interests in utilities issues, have fewer resources. The complexity of utilities issues handicaps those who lack resources or the will to spend them. Despite considerable activity by interest groups other than utility companies, their effectiveness is limited.

In contrast, proxy advocacy groups are capable of mounting a sustained assault on utility companies. A response to the problem of public underrepresentation in regulatory agency proceedings, proxy advocacy is a new force in American politics. More than the ombudsman, who seeks "quick fixes" for aggrieved individuals, the proxy advocate seeks more permanent solutions for consumers as a class. Proxy advocates have the resources and the incentives to influence public policy. However, proxy advocacy groups are less common than grassroots advocacy groups. Also, proxy advocates are easily intimidated by issues that pit one segment of consumers against another. If their existence is usually enough to prevent capture, it is seldom enough to solve the problem of public underrepresentation.

All of these forces combine to strengthen the role of the regulatory staff. From the vantage point of commissioners, the staff offers an unusual combination of expertise, experience, detachment, and dedication. As a result, the attitudes of staff members are extremely important. Indeed, whether one looks at issue priorities, value priorities, or policy preferences, commissioners agree more with staff members than with anyone else.

Sources of regulatory attitudes, though diverse, can be specified to some degree. The data indicate that regulators are influenced by their professional training, that lawyers differ from nonlawyers on several issues. The data also indicate that Democrats differ from Republicans, at least outside the South. However, the proposition that people with industry experience differ from those without such experience is not supported by the data. This is not to minimize the influence of utility companies, only to suggest that the companies, like other intervenors, influence regulators through mechanisms other than the "revolving door." In fact, intervenors sometimes influence regulatory behavior without affecting regulatory attitudes. For example, the threat to challenge a public utility commission decision in court may be disconcerting enough to extract concessions from reluctant regulators.

What, then, can we conclude about the politics of public utility regulation? It is a visible process that frustrates participants who lack political support. It is a technical process that frustrates participants who lack expertise. It is an expensive process that frustrates participants who lack resources. It is a controversial process that frustrates participants who make authoritative decisions. In the patois of the deep South, the politics of public utility regulation is the politics of "flustration."

Although it is useful to generalize about the politics of public utility regulation, it is also important to recognize a considerable amount of variability. To argue that utilities issues are generally complex and conflictual is not to argue that all utilities issues are complex and conflictual. This suggests the need for a different focus, though not necessarily a different framework for analysis. If complexity and conflict can be used to characterize an issue area, they can also be used to characterize issues within that issue area.

Thus, the lifeline issue is highly conflictual but not very complex. Under such circumstances, grassroots advocates can be effective, although proxy advocates are unlikely to get involved. Revenue requirements issues, on the other hand, are highly complex but less conflictual (most consumers, at least, are united in their opposition to rate hikes). When such issues are at stake, proxy advocates are likely to be active and effective, whereas grassroots advocates, if active, are unlikely to be effective. In contrast, issues involving the allocation of costs between business and residential customers are highly complex and highly conflictual. Under such circumstances, grassroots advocates lack the resources to be effective, and proxy advocates lack the incentives to get involved (since consumers have divergent interests here).

The impact of regulatory resources also varies from issue to issue. In general, the effects of regulatory resources are greater when complexity is greater and expertise is essential. Thus, resource-rich commissions are more likely to adopt rate structure reforms that promote energy conservation, despite opposition from utility companies. Such commissions are also more likely to adopt rate designs favorable to residential customers. However, they are more willing to give utility companies a larger share of the rate hike requested. If resource-rich commissions are capable of withstanding pressure from regulated industries, they are also capable of withstanding pressure from consumers!

Policy responses to complexity and conflictuality also vary from state to state. Complexity and conflictuality do not guarantee a fixed set of policy responses; rather, they challenge a political system in a certain way. The political system's response will depend on its political culture (traditionalistic, moralistic, individualistic), its recruitment processes (whether commissioners are appointed or elected), the extent of public advocacy (including both grassroots and proxy advocacy), and the level of commission professionalism (resources, expertise).

Thus, in Mississippi, North Dakota, and Wyoming, relatively low rates and elected commissions (in Mississippi and North Dakota) have discouraged public intervention in public utility commission proceedings. These states have no proxy advocacy office and very little grassroots advocacy. Also, they have small regulatory staffs with small budgets. They would be hard pressed to challenge utilities if they wished to do so. As a result, one is not surprised to discover a pattern of incremental decision-making. For example, none of the three states has adopted time-of-day rates, rates for interruptible service, or lifeline rates.

In contrast, in Massachusetts, Michigan, and New York, relatively high rates and appointed commissions have encouraged public intervention in public utility commission proceedings, by both grassroots and proxy advocates. These states also have highly professional commissions. Not surprisingly, one finds greater evidence of innovation here. For example, all three states have adopted time-of-day rates and rates for interruptible service, and two of the three states (Massachusetts and Michigan) have adopted lifeline rates.

In short, complexity and conflictuality do not directly determine policy outputs. Rather, they encourage certain political responses that may or may not materialize. Conflictuality encourages public advocacy, though it does not guarantee that it will occur. Complexity encourages regulatory professionalism, though it does not guarantee that either. Ultimately, policy responses are determined in part by political forces which are shaped in part by complexity and conflictuality. It is in that sense that complexity and conflict make a difference.

Complexity and conflict also play a crucial role in structuring normative choices. Specifically, they bring latent tensions between accountability and expertise into bold relief. Accountability and expertise are not incompatible, but they often seem so when issues are high in conflict and complexity. Indeed, as we have seen, the choice between accountability and expertise surfaces in debates over direct election of public utility commissioners, the legislative veto, public advocacy in public utility commission proceedings, and the use of the initiative.

The Progressive solution to this dilemma was to pursue both values but in different contexts. Thus, with one hand, the Progressives promoted direct primary elections and the extension of the suffrage; with the other, they created expert commissions on public utilities and worker's compensation. While democratizing electoral institutions, they professionalized nonelectoral institutions. Conflictual issues would be resolved by electoral institutions; complex issues would be resolved by nonelectoral institutions; science and democracy would be kept in their respective places.

Unfortunately, the Progressives failed to foresee that nonelectoral politics would increase in importance and that nonelectoral issues would become more conflictual without becoming less complex. This is the crucial dilemma of public utility regulatory politics. When issues are complex, participation without expertise can be useless; when issues are conflictual, professionalism without accountability can be manipulative; when issues are complex and conflictual, there is a special need for institutions that promote expertise and accountability simultaneously.

The worst kind of solution to this dilemma is a reform that offers the illusion of greater accountability, the reality of lesser expertise (direct election of public utility commissioners).

Somewhat better are reforms that offer the realistic expectation of greater accountability (citizen initiatives) or greater expertise (larger commission staffs). Best of all are reforms that simultaneously promote both accountability and expertise (intervenor funding, the declassification of the higher civil service).

The cure for the problems of public utility regulation is not more politics or less politics but a different kind of politics which recognizes the importance of both accountability and expertise. The choice between accountability and expertise, like the choice between peace and honor, is one that should be avoided. If we reach the point where that choice must be made, then we are guilty of a failure of the imagination. Complexity and conflict do not require more painful choices, but they do require more painful thinking.

Appendices
Notes
Index

: Appendix A :
Research Design

This book is the outgrowth of a research project whose central purpose was to assess the policy impacts of public advocacy in public utility commission proceedings. However, the scope of the research project was much broader than this capsule summary suggests. To appreciate the importance of the public utility commission as a forum, it is necessary to understand the more limited roles of the governor, the state legislature, and the courts. To measure the influence of public advocates, it is necessary to control for other variables, such as political culture, public utility commission professionalism, and the method of selecting commissioners. To place the influence of public advocates in perspective, it is necessary to understand the influence of other actors, such as utility companies and the public utility commission staff. In practice, the distinction between a study of public advocacy in public utility commission proceedings and a study of the politics of public utility regulation is one of emphasis rather than one of coverage. This book places less emphasis on public advocacy than the research project as a whole, although public advocacy receives considerable attention here as well.

PLANNING

The research project began with a series of hypotheses concerning the policy impacts of public advocates. At the outset, it was recognized that it might be difficult to disentangle the effects of different public advocates, especially if they intervened in the same cases in pursuit of similar objectives. Interviews and agency documents might help to sort out these effects, but it was unclear how useful they would be. Accordingly, a pilot study was arranged in Michigan, a state reputed to have highly active public advocates, both governmental (proxy advocates) and nongovernmental (grassroots advocates). During October 1978, interviews were conducted in Lansing, Michigan, with public utility commissioners, public utility commission staff members, assistant attorneys general, and representatives of citizens' groups. Public utility commission documents were also examined, especially decisions in major rate cases.

The Michigan pilot study, which lasted one week, was extremely useful, as it helped to redefine problems, sharpen questions, and modify research strategies. For example, interviews revealed that public advocates often intervene in the same cases but in pursuit of different objectives. Interviews also underscored the importance of regulatory attitudes and resources. Overall, it appeared that it would be less difficult to disentangle the effects of different public advocates than to control for other important variables. One result of this discovery was the development of an extensive series of twenty specific questions about policy preferences to identify differences of opinion among participants in the public utility regulatory process. Another result was the development of an index to measure public utility commission resources.

More generally, the pilot study led to greater emphasis on interviews, less emphasis on a content analysis of agency documents. Interviews provided relatively consistent and comprehensive accounts of public utility commission cases and controversies. In contrast, agency records often failed to specify the positions of the various parties on key issues. Furthermore, agency records shed little light on the conversion processes by which policy proposals were translated into policy outputs.

A direct result of the Michigan pilot study was the preparation of a new interview protocol, with more attitudinal questions, more historical probes, and more queries about the regulatory process. The new interview protocol was pretested on respondents in Virginia and North Carolina before being used in the field. A tape recorder was also introduced on a trial basis, to see whether it inhibited frank responses. After concluding that candor was unaffected, it was decided to use the tape recorder in the field.

Although interviews offered the hope of in-depth understanding, the need for breadth was also recognized. This led to a questionnaire survey of all 188 state public utility commissioners, conducted in January and February 1979. In that survey, described more fully in Appendix B, commissioners estimated activity levels of different types of intervenors in their state's electric, natural gas, and telephone proceedings over the previous five years. The survey, which produced responses from all fifty states and the District of Columbia, was later used in conjunction with data on policy outputs and other political variables to assess the policy impacts of public advocates in different issue areas.

The questionnaire survey also resulted in a fourfold typology of states: (1) *grassroots advocacy states*, characterized by high levels of activity by grassroots advocates, low levels of activity by proxy advocates; (2) *proxy advocacy states*, characterized by high levels of activity by proxy advocates, low levels of activity by grassroots advocates; (3) *dual advocacy states*, characterized by high levels of activity by both grassroots and proxy advocates; and (4) *acquiescent states*, characterized by high levels of activity by neither. This typology served as the basis for a stratified sample of twelve states, also described in greater detail in Appendix B. The states included three grassroots advocacy states (California, Illinois, Wisconsin), three proxy advocacy states (Florida, Georgia, New Jersey), three dual advocacy states (Massachusetts, Michigan, New York), and three acquiescent states (Mississippi, North Dakota, Wyoming).

FIELD WORK

Interviews in each of the twelve states were arranged through a combination of letters and telephone calls. A letter was mailed approximately three weeks in advance of the interview date, followed by a telephone call two weeks later. The letter, from the principal investigator, explained the purpose of the project, indicated a preference for a tape-recorded interview, and offered assurances that responses would be treated on a not-for-attribution basis. The telephone call, from the chief research assistant, Carole Carlin, clarified uncertainties and set up a mutually convenient time for an interview.

Occasionally, it was necessary for the principal investigator to talk with a reluctant respondent over the telephone to offer assurances concerning objectivity, confidentiality, or some other matter. In one instance, the intervention of a well-respected third party helped to allay the fears of a commission chairman who initially balked at allowing access to his staff. In another instance, a congressional staff member attempted to assure an anxious constituent that the principal investigator was not affiliated with either the CIA or the FBI. Although some parties refused to cooperate, as noted in Appendix B, the overwhelming majority of those contacted agreed to an interview. Overall, 284 interviews were conducted as part of this study (see Appendix B for a detailed breakdown by type of respondent and by state).

The interviews, which lasted approximately forty-five minutes each, took place between September 1979 and February 1980. Approximately two-thirds of the interviews were conducted by the principal investigator; approximately one-third were conducted by Professor Charles Williams of the University of Illinois—Chicago Circle. Only a handful of respondents refused to be tape-recorded. The recorder, small and inconspicuous, did not seem to undermine candor. Some respondents were nervous, but the tape-recorder did not appear to account for their nervousness.

The interview protocol, reproduced in full in Appendix C, consisted of both open-ended and closed-ended questions. When closed-ended questions were used, however, respondents were normally encouraged to elaborate for the sake of texture and detail. The interview began with an open-ended question about issue priorities, which seemed to put most respondents at ease, since it allowed them to discuss whatever they wished. To help establish trust, questions about substantive policy preferences and value priorities were asked prior to more sensitive questions about political influence, policy impacts, and personal characteristics.

Occasionally, respondents expressed annoyance at a particular question. However, persistence usually paid off, as in the following exchange with a utility company executive:

Q: Which of the following most closely approximates your current annual personal income? (furnishes card)

A: Oh, come on. What do you need that for?

Q: Well, one of the questions we're looking at . . . is: What sort of incentives does an organization have to attract talented people? And so the extent to which money is an inducement to get good people to work for one type of organization rather than another is something of importance to us.

A: Well, I think rate managers generally earn in the $40,000 to $50,000 bracket.

Q: Is that how you would characterize yourself?

A: Yes.

In addition to the interviews, public utility commission documents were gathered in each of the twelve states. The documents included commission opinions and orders in "major" rate cases during the 1974–1979 period. Major rate cases were normally defined as ones involving electric, natural gas, or telephone companies serving more than 5 percent of the state's residential customers. In Florida and Massachusetts, which are served by large numbers of relatively small companies, a 25 percent threshhold was used. Overall, data on 246 major rate cases were obtained.

Securing public utility commission documents was no more difficult than securing access to public utility commission officials, although it was sometimes expensive. One commission insisted on adding labor costs to copying and mailing costs. Another commission would have charged $1 per page for copies of agency records, were it not for the intervention of the chairman, who agreed that such charges were exorbitant. With these exceptions, public utility commissions were very cooperative and efficient in providing necessary documents at reasonable rates.

These documents were subsequently used to test the validity of the questionnaire survey and its estimates of public advocacy activity levels during the 1974–1978 period. A comparison of actual and estimated activity levels during the same time periods revealed extremely high correlations between the two. The Pearson's correlation coefficient between estimated and actual activity levels was .878 for grassroots advocates, .964 for proxy advocates. Commission documents for the entire 1974–

1979 period were used to measure changes in rate case length (regulatory lag) over time.

CODING

The coding of commission documents to measure regulatory lag was relatively straightforward. Over a two-month period, a research assistant sifted through agency records and identified the filing date and decision date for each rate case. When in doubt about either date, he contacted the public utility commission or the utility company. With a complete list of docket numbers and dates in hand, he then obtained data on judicial review, again by contacting either the commission or the company.

The coding of interviews was much more time-consuming, as was the transcribing of those interviews—an unenviable task that should be performed only by people of sound mind and body. All tape-recorded interviews were transcribed, with the original syntax preserved for accuracy's sake. Since handwritten notes were available for all interviews, garbled passages were usually decipherable. Other interviews were also transcribed, after being reconstructed from handwritten notes.

The actual coding was done primarily by three students, who worked part time from October 1979 through June 1980. The coders were trained over a two-week period, during which time they consulted frequently with the chief research assistant, who impressed upon them the limits of Emerson's adage about a foolish consistency. The coding proceeded more or less routinely after that point, although coders were encouraged to consult with the chief research assistant as often as they wished. An exercise in which all three coders coded the same transcript revealed very high levels of inter-coder reliability.

Coding categories were kept as specific as possible, on the assumption that they could subsequently be collapsed into broader categories. For example, the issue priorities question included 151 separate coding categories, which were subsequently collapsed into nineteen categories and a relatively small "other" category. In general, it was assumed that respondents meant what they said. Thus, when a commissioner asserted that his commission was primarily accountable to God, a category for God was created. As it turned out, that decision was fortunate, since God received almost as many mentions as the Department of Energy. A complete set of coding categories is on file with the Inter-University Consortium for Political Research at the University of Michigan.

: Appendix B :
Sample Design

CHOICE OF STATES

The sample of twelve states was chosen by merging the results of a questionnaire survey of public utility commissioners in all fifty states and the District of Columbia with the observations of a panel of five experts on public utility regulation. The aim was to include states with different patterns of public advocacy in the sample. Of special interest were two kinds of public advocates: grassroots advocacy groups (citizens' groups, legal aid societies) and proxy advocacy groups (attorneys general, consumer counsel offices).

The survey, conducted during January and February 1979, involved mailing a questionnaire to all 188 public utility commissioners in the United States. Commissioners were asked to furnish estimates (on a scale of 1 to 10) of the level of activity of different types of intervenors in their state's electric, natural gas, and telephone rate cases during the 1974–1978 period. Responses were obtained from 83.5 percent of the commissioners after one letter and a reminder letter three weeks later. At least one response was obtained from all fifty states and the District of Columbia.

A tabulation of survey results suggested that there are four types of states, relatively equal in number: (1) grassroots advocacy states, characterized by high levels of activity by grassroots advocates, low levels of activity by proxy advocates; (2) proxy advocacy states, characterized by high levels of activity by proxy advocates, low levels of activity by grassroots advocates; (3) dual advocacy states, characterized by high levels of activity by both; and (4) acquiescent states, characterized by low levels of activity by both.

Without being apprised of the questionnaire survey results, five experts on state public utility regulation were asked to identify three states in each of the four categories. The panel of experts included two grassroots advocates, two proxy advocates, and one Department of Energy official familiar with public advocacy at the state level. The three states cited most frequently by the panel for each category were included in the sample, unless a particular state was rated differently by commissioners and panelists, in which case the panel's next most frequent mention was included. This process yielded the following sample: (1) grassroots advocacy states—California, Illinois, and Wisconsin; (2) proxy advocacy states—Florida, Georgia, and New Jersey; (3) dual advocacy states—Massachusetts, Michigan, and New York: and (4) acquiescent states—Mississippi, North Dakota, and Wyoming.

CHOICE OF CITIES

The choice of cities was influenced by the location of public utility regulators, public advocates, and utility company executives in different states. In general, public utility regulators tend to be located in the state capital; grassroots advocates tend to be located in the state capital or the largest city; and utility company executives tend to be dispersed throughout the state. All twelve state capitals were included in the sample of cities. Since information on grassroots advocates cannot be obtained from other sources, a special effort was made to visit cities where grassroots advocates are located. Wherever feasible, an effort was also made to interview utility company executives close to the primary interview sites.

In states with high levels of grassroots advocacy (grassroots advocacy and dual advocacy states), it was normally assumed that interviews should be conducted in the state capital and the state's largest city. Three exceptions should be noted. In California, where the public utility commission is located outside the state capital, interviews were conducted in the state capital (Sacramento), the largest city (Los Angeles), and the site of the public utility commission (San Francisco). In Massachusetts, where the state capital (Boston) is also the largest city, interviews were conducted in Boston and in two nearby communities (Westboro and Canton) to afford an opportunity to interview additional utility company executives. In New York, where most of the interviews were conducted in Albany and New York City, interviews were also conducted on Long Island, (Mineola and Bellmore) to increase the number of grassroots advocates and utility company executives in the sample.

In states with low levels of grassroots advocacy (proxy advocacy and acquiescent states), it was normally assumed that interviews in the state capital would suffice. However, three exceptions should be mentioned. In Florida, interviews were conducted in Tallahassee and Miami, since the only active grassroots advocacy groups were based in Miami. In New Jersey, interviews were conducted in Trenton and Newark, since the public utility commission and the proxy advocacy office are both located in Newark. An interview was also conducted in nearby Elizabeth, to increase the number of utility company executives in the sample. Finally, in Wyoming, interviews were conducted in Cheyenne and Riverton, since two of the three active grassroots advocacy groups were based in Riverton. Also, interviews were conducted in Denver, since the chief executive officers of the Cheyenne Light, Fuel, and Power Company (a wholly owned subsidiary of Public Service Company of Colorado) are based in Denver.

Thus, interviews were conducted in twenty-seven cities:

California: Sacramento, San Francisco, Los Angeles
Florida: Tallahassee, Miami
Georgia: Atlanta
Illinois: Springfield, Chicago
Massachusetts: Boston, Canton, Westboro
Michigan: Lansing, Detroit
Mississippi: Jackson
New Jersey: Trenton, Newark, Elizabeth
New York: Albany, New York, Mineola, Bellmore
North Dakota: Bismarck

Wisconsin: Madison, Milwaukee
Wyoming: Cheyenne, Riverton, Denver (Colorado)

CHOICE OF RESPONDENTS

In all twelve states, a stubborn effort was made to interview the following people: (1) all public utility commissioners; (2) public utility commission staff members—the executive director, general counsel, chief engineer, chief economist, director of policy analysis, chief administrative law judge, and directors of the electric, natural gas, and telephone divisions; (3) utility company executives—the vice-president for finance and the vice-president for regulatory affairs of at least one major electric, natural gas, and telephone company; (4) grassroots advocates—at least one professional staff member of every grassroots advocacy group active in public utility commission proceedings over the previous year; and (5) proxy advocates—all professional staff members active in public utility commission proceedings over the previous year. More selective interviews were conducted with representatives of business and labor.

Of course, these respondents did not always exist. In several states, there was no proxy advocacy office and hence no proxy advocates. In one state (Mississippi), there were no grassroots advocacy groups active in public utility commission proceedings (although some individual citizens participated). In many states, particular staff positions did not exist; in other states, positions were vacant. Thus, the number of respondents in each category varied from state to state.

By and large, all five groups of respondents were exceptionally cooperative. Of forty-seven public utility commissioners to whom letters were sent, 81 percent were interviewed. Of seventy-five commission staff members to whom letters were sent, 84 percent were interviewed or arranged for an assistant to be interviewed. Of seventy-three utility company officials to whom letters were sent, 73 percent were interviewed or arranged for an assistant to be interviewed. Of ninety-seven grass-roots advocates to whom letters were sent, 88 percent were interviewed in person and an additional 4 percent were interviewed over the telephone. Of thirty-eight proxy advocates with whom interviews were sought, 95 percent were interviewed.

It should be added that a noninterview was normally the result of a scheduling problem rather than a refusal to cooperate. One serious access problem did arise. In California, the executive director of the Public Utilities Commission, citing time constraints, permitted only one staff member to be interviewed. For the most part, however, cooperation was remarkably high. Overall, 284 people were interviewed in the twelve states, as table B-1 indicates:

Table B-1
Breakdown of Respondents by State
(N = 284)

	Grassroots advocates	Proxy advocates	Utility company officials	PUC staff members	PUC commis- sioners	Other	Total
California	19	0	6	1	5	2	33
Florida	2	8	2	7	5	0	24
Georgia	3	3	4	4	3	1	18
Illinois	15	1	5	7	3	1	32
Massachusetts	8	4	8	6	2	1	29
Michigan	6	3	3	7	2	1	22
Mississippi	0	0	3	5	3	0	11
New Jersey	2	10	4	5	2	0	23
New York	18	7	4	7	6	0	42
N. Dakota	2	0	2	2	3	0	9
Wisconsin	11	0	8	8	1	0	28
Wyoming	2	0	3	5	3	0	13
Total	89	36	52	63	38	6	284

: Appendix C :
Interview Protocol

INTRODUCTION

This is a scientific study, funded entirely by the National Science Foundation. Your responses to the questions I ask will be treated on a not-for-attribution basis. Thus, nothing you say will be attributed to you personally. For accuracy's sake, I would like to tape-record the interview. However, in case the tape-recorder should malfunction, I would also like to take notes. Is this arrangement agreeable to you? Good.

The purpose of this study is to understand how organizational characteristics are related to policy decisions. The focus of this study is on the role played by public intervenors in public utility commission proceedings, but we are also interested in the broader decision-making process, of which public intervention is a part. With few exceptions, the same questions are being asked of all persons being interviewed. These questions have been developed in consultation with social scientists, public utility commissioners, intervenors, and others.

Is there anything else you would like to know before we begin? If not, let's proceed.

1. Values
   a. To begin with, I'd like to ask you to try to forget for the moment the specific issues the public utility commission happens to be facing at the present time. In your opinion, what are the three most important substantive issues the PUC ought to be confronting today, in the order of their importance, from most important to least important?
   b. Here is a list of goals or values widely regarded as desirable elements of public utility commission decisions (fur-

nish card). Perhaps you regard all of these goals as desirable. However, if you had to rank them, on the basis of your own system of values, from extremely desirable to just very desirable, how would you rank them?

____Clean air

____Economic development

____Energy conservation

____Energy supply sufficient for demand

____Fair return for utility company investors

____Low rates for residential consumers

____Low rates for business consumers

____Special protection for the very poor

c. Are there any other values you would add to this list?

2. Policy preferences

Next I'd like to read a list of statements concerning issues, both broad and specific. Please tell me if you agree or disagree with each statement. If you feel strongly or somewhat either way, please tell me that as well (furnish card).

In answering, you should consider those utility companies, or commissions, with which you are familiar, whether in your state or elsewhere.

____Strongly disagree

____Disagree

____Somewhat disagree

____No opinion

____Somewhat agree

____Agree

____Strongly agree

____Not sure

a. General Issues

(1). Investor-owned utilities are generally more efficient than publicly owned utilities.

(2). There is already enough citizen involvement in public utility commission decisions.

(3). Investor-owned utilities have a tendency to provide misleading information to regulators.

(4). Utility companies should be allowed flexibility to design rates, provided that they are not discriminatory.

(5). Construction work in progress should not be included in the rate base of utility companies.

(6). Direct popular election of public utility commissioners is not a good idea.

(7). Utility companies are allowed excessive rates of return on common stock equity.

(8). Some environmental damage must be tolerated for the sake of economic prosperity.

(9). Citizens' groups that participate in public utility commission proceedings ought to be reimbursed for the costs of their participation.

(10). Residential ratepayers pay less than their fair share of the costs of service.

(11). Public utility commissions move too slowly in making decisions.

b. Energy issues

(12). Public utility commissions should promote greater competition in the sale of electric power to large industrial customers and to retail distribution systems.

(13). Public utility commissions should not rely on utility company estimates of future energy demand.

(14). An inverted rate structure, with residential customers paying more per kilowatt-hour as they consume more, is a good idea.

(15). The desirability of alternative modes of electricity generation is best determined by utility company management.

(16). Mandatory time-of-day rates for residential customers should not be implemented at the present time.

(17). Electric and gas companies should not be allowed to shut off service during the winter to apartment buildings whose landlords refuse to pay their bills.

(18). Rates for interruptible service are impractical for residential customers.

(19). A fuel adjustment clause is a good idea.

(20). Seasonal rates should be adopted for both residential and business customers.

3. Accountability (question 3a—public utility regulators and public advocates only; questions 3b–3e—public utility regulators only)

   a. To whom is your organization accountable?

   b. How active is your governor in the public utility policy area?

   c. Is your public utility commission sufficiently independent from the governor in practice?

   d. How active is your state legislature in the public utility policy area?

   e. Is your public utility commission sufficiently independent from the state legislature in practice?

4. Decision-making (question 4a—public utility regulators and public advocates only; question 4b—public utility regulators only; questions 4c–4f—public advocates only)

   a. I would like to get a clearer idea of the extent to which power is centralized or decentralized within your organization. On a scale of 1 to 10, with 1 representing a very centralized decision-making process and 10 representing a very decentralized decision-making process, how would you characterize your organization? (furnish card)

   In answering, you should refer to the actual, as opposed to the theoretical, diffusion of power within your organization.

1	2	3	4	5	6	7	8	9	10
Centralized									Decentralized

   b. I am interested in knowing how responsive public utility commissioners are to the chairman's leadership at your public utility commission. Would you characterize that responsiveness as high, moderate, or low? Does the degree of responsiveness depend on whether substantive or administrative matters are at stake?

   c. How does your organization decide on which issues it will focus its attention? Please elaborate.

   d. Who are your organization's leaders? How are they chosen?

   e. Does your organization have an executive board? If yes,

who sits on the executive board? What is the relationship between the executive board and the professional staff? Please elaborate.

f. Does your organization have members as such? If so, how much influence do members have in the policy-making of your organization? Please elaborate.

5. Mass media

a. How much attention do the mass media pay to utilities issues in your state?

b. What utilities issues do the mass media tend to focus on?

c. Could you characterize mass media coverage of utilities issues in your state as generally good or bad? Do you see any differences between newspapers and television stations in this regard?

6. Impacts (questions 6d, 6e—public utility regulators only; question 6f—public utility regulators and utility company executives only; questions 6g–6j—public advocates only)

a. For a variety of reasons, some participants in the political process have more of an impact on public policy decisions than others. On a scale of 1 to 10, how would you rate the overall impact of each of the following on your state PUC's decisions over the past year, with 1 representing a very low impact and 10 representing a very high impact? (furnish card)

____Attorney general (or consumer counsel)

____Business groups (other than utility companies)

____Citizens' groups

____Individual citizens

____Labor groups

____Municipalities

____Public utility commission staff

____Utility companies

b. Let me ask you more specifically about the impact of particular citizens' groups. On a scale of 1 to 10, how would you rate the overall impact of each of the following on PUC decisions over the psat year, with 1 representing a very low impact and 10 representing a very high impact? (furnish card, containing list of citizens' groups active in state over previous year)

c. Does the impact of different groups vary from issue area to issue area? Please elaborate.

d. Could you give me two or three examples of cases where a citizens' group had a major impact on a PUC decision? Please name the citizens' group in each instance and elaborate.

e. Could you give me two or three examples of cases where the attorney general (Office of Public Counsel) had a major impact on a PUC decision? Please elaborate.

f. What are the benefits and costs of citizen participation in PUC proceedings? Do the benefits outweigh the costs?

g. Could you give me two or three examples of cases where your organization had a major impact on a PUC decision? Please elaborate.

h. How would you describe your organization's role? By and large, do you see your organization as representing all consumers or as representing those consumers who are least able to represent themselves? Please elaborate.

i. As you assess the contribution of your organization to PUC decisions, what single factor best summarizes your organization's ability to shape the course of public policy? (furnish card) Please elaborate.
___Organization applies political pressure
___Organization provides a different point of view
___Organization provides useful information
___Other

j. Can you think of a recent case in which your organization found itself opposing another consumer group on a particular issue? Which case? What was the nature of the disagreement? How did the PUC resolve the disagreement?

7. Allocation of resources (questions 7a, 7b—public utility regulators and public advocates only; questions 7c–7e—utility company executives only)

a. Approximately what percentage of your organization's total budget is allocated to electric, natural gas, and telephone issues combined?

b. Approximately what percentage of this amount is allocated to each of the following? (furnish card)

___Quality of service issues
___Rate design issues
___Revenue requirements issues
___Other issues

c. What is your company's total budget for the current fiscal year?

d. Approximately what percentage of your company's budget is allocated to each of the following? (furnish card)
___Quality of service issues
___Rate design issues
___Revenue requirements issues
___Other issues

e. I'd like to get a better idea of how expensive a rate case tends to be. How much money did your company spend in the most recent rate case decided by your state's PUC? Was this more or less than usual? Please elaborate.

8. Diffusion of innovations (public utility regulators only)

a. Are there any state PUCs other than your own to which you look for ideas or innovations? Please name any that come to mind.

b. How do you keep informed about innovations in public utility regulation in other states?

c. Can you cite any specific policies adopted by your commission as a result of another commission's pioneering efforts?

9. Informal contacts (public utility regulators only)

a. How frequently would you say you are visited by citizens' group members in your office? (furnish card)
___Once a day
___Once a week
___Once a month
___Once a year

b. How frequently would you say you are visited by utility company employees in your office? (furnish card)
___Once a day
___Once a week
___Once a month
___Once a year

10. Recruitment and turnover (public utility regulators and public advocates only)
    a. When did you join your organization?
    b. Why did you join your organization?
    c. What incentives are there for you to remain within your organization?
11. Background (question 11e—public utility regulators only; question 11h—public utility regulators and utility company executives only; question 11i—public advocates only)
    a. What is your profession?
    b. What is the highest educational degree you have obtained?
    c. What is your political party?
    d. If you had to describe your political philosophy in ideological terms, how would you characterize yourself? (furnish card)
       ____Very liberal
       ____Moderately liberal
       ____Middle of the road
       ____Moderately conservative
       ____Very conservative
    e. Have you ever worked for a utility company or represented a utility company through a law firm?
    f. Have you attended any special training programs in the utilities area?
    g. What is your age?
    h. Which of the following most closely approximates your current annual personal income? (furnish card) Please check one.
       ____Less than $10,000
       ____$10,0000–$19,999
       ____$20,000–$29,999
       ____$30,000–$39,999
       ____$40,000–$49,999
       ____$50,000–$59,999
       ____More than $59,999
    i. Which of the following most closely approximates your annual personal income? (furnish card) Please check one.

_____Less than $5,000
_____$5,000–$9,999
_____$10,000–$14,999
_____$15,000–$19,999
_____$20,000–$24,999
_____$25,000–$29,999
_____$30,000–$39,999
_____$40,000–$49,999
_____$50,000–$59,999
_____More than $59,999

Note: Unless otherwise noted, questions were asked of all respondents, including public utility regulators (commissioners and staff members), public advocates (grassroots advocates and proxy advocates), and utility company executives.

Notes

Chapter 1. Policy Dilemmas in a Political Context

1. For interesting accounts of this period, see Robert LaFollette, *A Personal Narrative of Political Experiences* (Madison: The Robert LaFollette Co., 1913); Forrest MacDonald, *Insull* (Chicago: University of Chicago Press, 1962), pp. 102–32; and Douglas Anderson, *Regulatory Politics and Electric Utilities* (Boston: Auburn House Publishing Co., 1981), pp. 33–60.

2. Edward Berlin, Charles Cicchetti, and William Gillen, *Perspective on Power* (Cambridge, Mass.: Ballinger Publishing Co., 1975).

3. See, for example, Connecticut Public Utilities Control Authority et al., *Connecticut Peak Load Pricing Test* (Hartford, May 1977); Allen Miedema et al., *Time-of-Use Electricity Price Effects: Arizona* (Research Triangle Park, N.C., December 1978); and U.S. Department of Energy, *Electric Rate Demonstration Conference: Papers and Proceedings* (Denver, April 1–3, 1980).

4. Under the terms of an agreement between AT&T and the Justice Department, announced in January 1982, AT&T will divest itself of its twenty-two local operating companies, with assets of about $80 billion. In return AT&T will be permitted to enter markets from which it had previously been barred, including the lucrative data processing, cable television, and electronic publishing markets.

5. One approach is to allocate costs based on the proportion of total sales attributable to each customer class. Another approach determines the proportion of demand attributable to each class during peak consumption periods and allocates costs accordingly. A third approach, advocated by many economists, bypasses the cost allocation stage and sets prices equal to marginal costs for all customers, regardless of class.

6. Robert Stobaugh and Daniel Yergin, eds., *Energy Future: Report of the Energy Project at the Harvard Business School* (New York: Random House, 1979).

7. U.S. Energy Information Administration, *Typical Electric Bills—January 1, 1980* (Washington, D.C.: U.S. Government Printing Office, 1980).

8. U.S. Bureau of Labor Statistics, *Retail Prices and Indexes of Fuel and Utilities* (Washington, D.C.: Department of Labor, 1974); and idem, *Consumer Prices: Energy and Food* (Washington, D.C.: Department of Labor, 1980).

9. Larry Kramer, "President Pledges Continued Support for Consumer Efforts," *Washington Post,* December 20, 1978, p. D4.

10. Unfortunately, no organization computes national averages of local message unit telephone rates. However, the National Association of Regulatory Utility Commissioners (NARUC) annually publishes telephone rate data for communities of various sizes in all fifty states. The NARUC data were used to compute national yearly averages. The rate used in each state was the independent one-party exchange service rate for residents of the state's largest city. NARUC, *Exchange Service Telephone Rates* (Washington, D.C., 1974–1980).

11. Eunice Grier, "Social Equity Responsibilities of Utility Regulators," in *Summary of Proceedings*, State Utility Consumer Advocates Conference, University of Chicago, June 19–20, 1979, pp. 94–103.

12. Barry Commoner, *The Politics of Energy* (New York: Alfred Knopf, 1979), p. 29.

13. Gregory Skwira, "Power Cut Off at Flat: Blaze Kills 2 Children," *Detroit Free Press,* January 17, 1980, p. 1.

14. Robert Roach and Douglas Ilka, "Gas Shut Off: Baby Dies as Home Burns," *Detroit News,* December 5, 1979, p. 1.

15. Doug Shuit, "Changes on Unpaid Utility Bills Sought: Council Wants to Avoid Events that Led to Shooting Death," *Los Angeles Times,* February 16, 1979; Pam Moreland, "She Paid Her Bill and Then She Died," *Los Angeles Herald Examiner,* January 5, 1979.

16. Paul Joskow and Paul MacAvoy, "Regulation and the Financial Condition of the Electric Power Companies in the 1970s," *American Economic Review,* May 1975, pp. 295–301.

17. Concerned about this problem, Congress has offered tax incentives to utility investors who reinvest in utility company stock. Under the Economic Recovery Tax Act of 1981, utility shareholders may exclude dividends of up to $750 on an individual tax return if those dividends are reinvested in utility company stock.

18. Anderson, *Regulatory Politics,* p. 73.

19. Robert McFadden, "Businessmen Angry as Beame Inspects City's Looted Areas," *New York Times,* July 17, 1977, p. 1; "Blackout: New Paralysis, New Symptoms: Much Uglier," *New York Times,* July 17, 1977, p. 4.

20. Some utilities have reserve margins substantially above normal. Georgia Power, for example, has a reserve margin of approximately 32 percent. The Wisconsin Electric Power Corporation has a reserve margin of approximately 30 percent.

21. Griffith Morris and Richard Levin, "Addressing the 'Excess Capacity' Issue," *Public Utilities Fortnightly,* March 12, 1981, pp. 23–25.

22. Stobaugh and Yergin, *Energy Future,* p. 80.

23. Dorothy Nelkin, "Some Social and Political Dimensions of Nuclear Power: Examples from Three Mile Island," *American Political Science Review,* March 1981, p. 136.

24. "Alabama Reactor Licensed; End to Delays Sought Elsewhere," *Public Utilities Fortnightly,* April 9, 1981, pp. 50–51.

25. Commoner, *Politics of Energy,* p. 45.

26. In April 1980, a federal district court judge voided California laws and administrative regulations concerning nuclear power plants on the grounds that the Nuclear Regulatory Commission has exclusive jurisdiction over nuclear plants. However, in October 1981, the 9th Circuit Court of Appeals upheld California's ban on new nuclear plants *(Pacific Gas & Electric and Southern California Edison Co.* v. *State Energy Resources Conservation and Development Commission).*

27. Joan Aron, "Intergovernmental Politics of Energy," *Policy Analysis,* Fall 1979, p. 461.

28. Amory Lovins, *Soft Energy Paths* (Cambridge, Mass.: Ballinger Publishing Co., 1977).

29. For an interesting discussion of the utility company's potential role in promoting solar energy, see Eric Brown, "Should Utilities Finance Solar Systems?" *Public Utilities Fortnightly,* March 12, 1981, pp. 26–30.

30. Stobaugh and Yergin, *Energy Future,* p. 183.

31. Samuel Schurr et al., *Energy in America's Future: The Choices Before Us* (Balti-

more: Johns Hopkins University Press, 1979), pp. 531–32; Paul Joskow, "America's Many Energy Futures—A Review of Energy Futures, Energy: The Next Twenty Years, and Energy in America's Future," *Bell Journal of Economics and Management Science,* Spring 1980, pp. 377–98.

32. A number of universities also produce electricity through cogeneration.

33. Stobaugh and Yergin, *Energy Future,* pp. 157–61.

34. Thomas Casten and Harold Ross, "Cogeneration and the Regulations," *Public Utilities Fortnightly,* March 26, 1981, pp. 18–21.

35. Neal Peirce and Carol Steinbach, "Utilities Turn to Conservation—With Little Help from the Feds," *National Journal,* August 2, 1980, pp. 1260–65.

36. Stobaugh and Yergin, *Energy Future,* p. 136.

37. Joskow, "America's Many Energy Futures," p. 381.

38. Charles Cicchetti and Rod Shaughnessy, "Is There a Free Lunch in the Northwest? (Utility-sponsored Energy Conservation Programs)," *Public Utilities Fortnightly,* December 18, 1980, pp. 11–15.

39. Henry Friendly, *The Federal Administrative Agencies: The Need for Better Definition of Standards* (Cambridge: Harvard University Press, 1962); Theodore Lowi, *The End of Liberalism,* 2d ed. (New York: W. W. Norton & Co., 1979).

40. Jackson Diehl, "Utility Lobbies Keep Power Turned On in Annapolis," *Washington Post,* March 30, 1980, p. 1.

41. Charles Jones, *Clean Air: The Policies and Politics of Pollution Control* (Pittsburgh: University of Pittsburgh Press, 1975), pp. 175–311.

42. Theodore Lowi, "American Business, Public Policy, Case Studies, and Political Theory," *World Politics,* July 1964, pp. 677–715.

43. James Landis, *Report on Regulatory Agencies to the President-elect* (Washington, D.C.: U.S. Government Printing Office, 1960); U.S. Senate Government Operations Committee, *The Regulatory Appointments Process* (Washington, D.C.: U.S. Government Printing Office, 1977).

44. Robert Cushman, *The Independent Regulatory Commissions,* rev. ed. (New York: Octagon Books, 1972), p. 751.

45. U.S. Senate Commerce Committee, *Appointments to the Regulatory Agencies: The Federal Communications Commission and the Federal Trade Commission (1949–1974)* (Washington, D.C.: U.S. Government Printing Office, 1976).

46. Lincoln Smith, "State Utility Commissioners—1978," *Public Utilities Fortnightly,* February 16, 1978, pp. 9–15.

47. Richard Fenno, "U.S. House Members in Their Constituencies: An Exploration," *American Political Science Review,* September 1977, p. 915.

48. David Hilder, "Diluted PSC Forced to Cancel Hearing," *Atlanta Journal,* February 28, 1980, p. D18.

49. Fenno, "U.S. House Members," p. 915.

50. James Fesler, *The Independence of State Regulatory Agencies* (Chicago: Public Administration Service, 1942).

51. James Q. Wilson, ed., *The Politics of Regulation* (New York: Basic Books, 1980), p. 391.

52. For a concise summary of the Ash Council's report, see Roger Noll, *Reforming Regulation* (Washington, D.C.: The Brookings Institution, 1971), pp. 4–14.

53. David Welborn, *The Governance of Federal Regulatory Agencies* (Knoxville: University of Tennessee Press, 1977), p. 63.

54. Frederick Mosher, "Professions in Public Service," *Public Administration Review,* March/April 1978, p. 147.

55. These impressions are based on comparisons of NARUC annual reports for the years 1973 and 1979. Given the amount of missing data and varied reporting practices, a comprehensive description of staff changes is impossible. Nevertheless, in those states where comparisons are possible, the number of economists and lawyers almost always increases. Although the number of accountants and engineers increases in some states, it decreases in others.

56. Anderson, *Regulatory Politics,* pp. 96–115.

57. NARUC *Annual Reports,* 1973, 1974, 1978, 1979.

58. Paul Joskow, "Inflation and Environmental Concern: Structural Change in the Process of Public Utility Price Regulation," *Journal of Law and Economics,* October 1974, p. 313.

59. Murray Edelman, *The Symbolic Uses of Politics* (Urbana: University of Illinois Press, 1964); George Stigler, "The Theory of Economic Regulation," *Bell Journal of Economics and Management Science,* Spring 1971, pp. 3–21; Theodore Lowi, *The End of Liberalism,* 2d ed. (New York: W. W. Norton & Co., 1979).

60. Samuel Huntington, "The Marasmus of the ICC: The Commission, the Railroads and the Public Interest," *Yale Law Journal,* April 1952, pp. 467–509; Marver Bernstein, *Regulating Business by Independent Commission* (Princeton: Princeton University Press, 1955).

61. Grant McConnell, *Private Power and American Democracy* (New York: Alfred Knopf, 1966), p. 289.

62. Common Cause, *Serving Two Masters: A Common Cause Study of Conflicts of Interest in the Executive Branch* (Washington, D.C.: Common Cause, 1976).

63. William Gormley, Jr., "A Test of the Revolving Door Hypothesis at the FCC," *American Journal of Political Science,* November 1979, pp. 665–83. For similar findings concerning regulatory attitudes, see Paul Quirk, *Industry Influence in Federal Regulatory Agencies* (Princeton: Princeton University Press, 1981), pp. 62–69.

64. Roger Cramton, "The Why, Where and How of Broadened Public Participation in the Administrative Process," *Georgetown Law Journal,* February 1972, pp. 525–46.

65. U.S. Senate Committee on Governmental Affairs, *Public Participation in Regulatory Agency Proceedings* (Washington, D.C.: U.S. Government Printing Office, 1977).

66. Common Cause, *With Only One Ear: A Common Cause Study of Industry and Consumer Representation Before Federal Regulatory Commissions* (Washington, D.C.: Common Cause, 1977).

67. Wisconsin Administrative Procedure Act, chap. 227, sec. 13.

68. Ernest Gellhorn, "Public Participation in Administrative Proceedings," *Yale Law Journal, January 1972, pp. 359–*404; Cramton, "Why, Where and How"; U.S. Senate Committee on Governmental Affairs, *Public Participation.*

69. Andrew McFarland, *Public Interest Lobbies: Decision Making on Energy* (Washington, D.C.: American Enterprise Institute, 1976).

70. Mancur Olson, *The Logic of Collective Action,* rev. ed. (New York: Schocken Books, 1971).

71. Jon Van Til, "Becoming Participants: Dynamics of Access Among the Welfare Poor," *Social Science Quarterly,* September 1973, pp. 345–58.

72. Michael Lipsky, "Protest as a Political Resource," *American Political Science Review,* December 1968, p. 1157.

73. Note, "The Office of Public Counsel: Institutionalizing Public Interest Representation in State Government," *Georgetown Law Journal,* March 1976, pp. 895–923.

CHAPTER 2. GRASSROOTS ADVOCATES AND PROXY ADVOCATES

1. John Stuart Mill, *Representative Government* (New York: Oxford University Press, 1946); Jean-Jacques Rousseau, *The Social Contract* (New York: Dutton, 1941).

2. Joseph Schumpeter, *Capitalism, Socialism and Democracy,* 2d ed. (New York: Harpers, 1947); Robert Dahl, *A Preface to Democratic Theory* (Chicago: University of Chicago Press, 1956); Seymour Martin Lipset, *Political Man* (Garden City, N.Y.: Doubleday, 1963).

3. Hanna Pitkin, *The Concept of Representation* (Berkeley and Los Angeles: University of California Press, 1967); Carole Pateman, *Participation and Democratic Theory* (Cambridge: Cambridge University Press, 1970).

4. See, for example, D. Stephen Cupps, "Emerging Problems of Citizen Participation," *Public Administration Review,* March/April, 1977, pp. 478–87; Joel Aberbach and Bert Rockman, "Administrators' Beliefs About the Role of the Public: The Case of American Federal Executives," *Western Political Quarterly,* December 1978, pp. 502–22.

5. Pitkin, *Concept of Representation,* p. 211.

6. Dorothy Nelkin and Michael Pollak, "Public Participation in Technological Decisions: Reality or Grand Illusion?" *Technology Review,* August/September, 1979, p. 64.

7. Dennis Thompson, *John Stuart Mill and Representative Government* (Princeton: Princeton University Press, 1976), pp. 13–53.

8. Ibid, pp. 54–90.

9. Pitkin, *Concept of Representation,* pp. 232–33.

10. This convention presupposes that estimated public advocacy activity is an interval-level variable—a proposition defended shortly.

11. The five experts consisted of a Department of Energy official, a national citizens' group leader, a legal services attorney, a lawyer for a state attorney general, and a lawyer for a local citizens' group, all of whom were intimately familiar with public advocacy in public utility commission proceedings in a number of states.

12. There were two discrepancies, both apparently due to changes over time in public advocacy activity, which made it difficult to assess "average" activity over a five-year period.

13. In Massachusetts and Florida, which are served by a large number of relatively small utility companies, a major rate case was defined as one involving a utility company that serves more than 25 percent of the residential customers in the state.

14. Given the high correlation coefficients between actual activity levels (interval-level data) and estimated activity levels, it seems appropriate to regard the latter as interval-level data.

15. E. E. Schattschneider, *The Semi-Sovereign People: A Realist's View of Democracy in America* (New York: Holt, Rinehart & Winston, 1960), p. 23.

16. At first, it might be thought that a legal aid society should be classified as a proxy advocacy organization. Legal aid societies do receive most of their funds from the national Legal Services Corporation, which is funded by Congress. Nevertheless, legal aid societies are not government organizations and legal aid attorneys are not public officials. There is admittedly a sense in which legal aid societies serve as "proxies" for the poor. However, the distinction between legal aid societies and their clients breaks down because the two typically speak with one voice. Indeed, legal aid societies lack the authority to intervene in administrative proceedings except on behalf of their clients, who usually lack the resources to intervene except through legal aid societies.

To label legal aid societies "proxy advocates" and their clients "grassroots advocates" would be misleading because the two are not entirely discrete.

17. Under federal law, utility companies may reduce their income tax liability in various ways—for example, through accelerated depreciation and investment credits. Yet in most jurisdictions, utility companies are permitted to charge ratepayers for the taxes they would have paid in the absence of such tax breaks. Thus, most utilities keep two sets of books—one for "normal" financial accounting, the other for federal tax purposes. Differences in tax obligations between the two are sometimes referred to as "phantom taxes." Critics complain that this results in overcharging ratepayers. Defenders argue that, without phantom taxes, utilities would have to raise revenue through other more expensive means, to the detriment of ratepayers.

18. An inverted rate charges more per unit as consumption increases. It stands in stark contrast to declining block rates, which charge less per unit as consumption increases.

19. For each state, the relevant one-year period was defined as the twelve months immediately preceding the site visit. Since site visits were conducted between September 1979 and February 1980, each state's one-year period consisted of most of 1979 and a portion of either 1978 or 1980.

20. Mancur Olson, *The Logic of Collective Action,* rev. ed. (New York: Schocken Books, 1971).

21. Peter Clark and James Q. Wilson, "Incentive Systems: A Theory of Organizations," *Administrative Science Quarterly,* September 1961, pp. 129–66; Robert Salisbury, "An Exchange Theory of Interest Groups," *Midwest Journal of Political Science,* February 1969, pp. 1–32.

22. Paul Joskow, "Electric Utility Rate Structures in the U.S.: Some Recent Developments," in *Public Utility Rate Making in an Energy-Conscious Environment,* ed. Werner Sichel (Boulder, Colo.: Westview Press, 1979), pp. 1–22; Douglas Anderson, "State Regulation of Electric Utilities," in *The Politics of Regulation,* ed. James Q. Wilson (New York: Basic Books, 1980), pp. 3–41.

23. Jon Van Til, "Becoming Participants: Dynamics of Access Among the Welfare Poor," *Social Science Quarterly,* September 1973, pp. 345–58.

24. For a more sanguine view of the ombudsman's role, see Larry Hill, *The Model Ombudsman* (Princeton: Princeton University Press, 1976); also, Walter Gellhorn, *Ombudsmen and Others: Citizens' Protectors in Nine Countries* (Cambridge: Harvard University Press, 1966).

25. W. Wheeler Bryan, "State Offices for Utility Consumer Intervention" (Paper prepared for the U.S. Office of Consumers' Education, January 27, 1978), pp. 3–4.

26. The attorney general is appointed by the governor in Alaska, Hawaii, New Hampshire, New Jersey, and Wyoming. The attorney general is selected by the state legislature in Maine and by the Supreme Court in Tennessee. Council of State Governments, *The Book of the States 1980–1981* (Lexington, Ky.: Council of State Governments, 1980), p. 195.

27. As of March 1982, sixteen states had a governor and an attorney general who belonged to different parties: Arizona, Arkansas, California, Idaho, Iowa, Kansas, Louisiana, Minnesota, Nevada, Ohio, Tennessee, Texas, Utah, Virginia, Wisconsin, and Wyoming.

28. National Association of Attorneys General, *Attorney Generals' Intervention Before Regulatory Agencies* (Raleigh, N.C., January 1975), p. 15.

29. Ibid., pp. 7–15.

30. Bryan, "State Offices," pp. 3–4.

31. The previous attorney general, Louis Lefkowitz, also intervened in New York Public Service Commission cases prior to 1974, when the Consumer Protection Board began participating in utility rate cases.

32. "Shevin: Firm May Settle Overcharges for $5.5 Million," *Miami Herald,* July 12, 1978, p. 3B; "PSC Counsel Seeks $8-Million Refund by Florida Power," *Miami Herald,* October 27, 1978.

33. Daniel Elazar, *American Federalism: A View from the States* (New York: Thomas Crowell Co., 1972), pp. 79–116.

34. Ira Sharkansky, "The Utility of Elazar's Political Culture," *Polity,* Fall 1969, pp. 66–83.

35. V. O. Key, Jr., *Southern Politics* (New York: Alfred Knopf, 1949); Anthony Downs, *An Economic Theory of Democracy* (New York: Harper & Row, 1957); Lester Milbrath, "Political Participation in the States," in *Politics in the American States,* ed. Herbert Jacob and Kenneth Vines (Boston: Little, Brown & Co., 1965), pp. 25–60.

36. Interparty competition has been defined as the average percentage of votes received by the losing party in gubernatorial elections between 1968 and 1976. This measure, which focuses exclusively in statewide elections, is particularly appropriate to a study of nonelectoral participation at the state level.

37. Political culture has been defined as the extent to which a state is moralistic, individualistic, or traditionalistic. In calculating political culture scores for all fifty states, I have used a nine-point scale, as suggested by Sharkansky ("Utility of Elazar's Political Culture"). I have applied this scale to Elazar's most recent political culture classifications (*American Federalism*). I am indebted to Professor Elazar for suggesting an appropriate classification for the District of Columbia's political culture (traditionalistic/individualistic).

38. Susan B. Hansen, "Participation, Political Structure, and Concurrence," *American Political Science Review,* December 1975, pp. 1191–92.

39. Ibid., p. 1181.

40. For a more detailed exposition of this argument, see William Gormley, Jr., "Nonelectoral Participation as a Response to Issue-Specific Conditions: The Case of Public Utility Regulation," *Social Science Quarterly,* September 1981, pp. 527–39.

41. The index was created by calculating T scores, derived from z scores, as suggested by Sigelman and Yough. See Lee Sigelman and Syng Yough, "Some 'Trivial' Matters that Sometimes Matter: Index Construction Techniques and Research Findings," *Political Methodology* 5 (1978): 369–84.

42. Richard Stewart, "The Reformation of American Administrative Law," *Harvard Law Review,* June 1975, pp. 1789–93.

43. George Stigler and Claire Friedland, "What Can Regulators Regulate? The Case of Electricity," in *The Crisis of the Regulatory Commissions,* ed. Paul MacAvoy (New York: W. W. Norton & Co., 1970), pp. 39–52.

44. Milbrath, "Political Participation"; Thomas Dye, *Politics, Economics, and the Public: Policy Outcomes in the American States* (Chicago: Rand McNally & Co., 1966).

45. Hansen, "Participation, Political Structure."

46. Salisbury, "Exchange Theory."

47. Clark and Wilson, "Incentive Systems."

48. Salisbury uses similar categories, although he refers to purposive incentives as expressive benefits.

49. Because of their vagueness, "interesting work" and "personal convenience" have not been categorized as material, purposive, or solidary incentives. Some might disagree with this decision. Zald and Jacobs, for example, treat "task satisfaction" as a

solidary incentive (see Mayer Zald and David Jacobs, "Compliance/Incentive Classifications of Organizations," *Administration and Society,* February 1978, pp. 403–24). Perhaps they would also characterize interesting work as a solidary incentive. Yet, work may be interesting or satisfying because it permits someone to serve the community (a purposive incentive) or because it permits someone to develop marketable skills (a monetary incentive). Indeed, the "interesting work" response is often a conversation-starter and nothing more. Respondents who refer to interesting work frequently do so at the outset, prior to more specific and more substantive comments. To treat "interesting work" as a solidary incentive would be to invest this response with more meaning than it probably has.

50. Jeffrey Berry, *Lobbying for the People* (Princeton: Princeton University Press, 1977), pp. 42–43.

51. Olson, *Logic of Collective Action;* Downs, *Economic Theory.*

52. Note, "Federal Agency Assistance to Impecunious Intervenors," *Harvard Law Review,* June 1975, pp. 1815–37.

53. Roger Cramton, "The Why, Where and How of Broadened Public Participation in the Administrative Process," *Georgetown Law Journal,* February 1972, p. 538.

54. Richard Fenno, *The Power of the Purse: Appropriations Policies in Congress* (Boston: Little, Brown & Co., 1966).

55. During the course of an interview, respondents were permitted to identify as many as three funding sources. Although each funding source was coded separately, responses were subsequently recoded to create a more parsimonious set of categories. In the process, some previously separate categories were merged. For example, under the revised coding scheme, a group that receives funds from the Department of Energy, the Department of Labor, and the Community Services Administration is treated as receiving funds from only one source—the federal government. This coding scheme is more manageable than one with a larger number of categories. However, it does tend to understate the extent to which grassroots advocacy organizations in particular receive funds from more than one source. The original limitation of three responses has a similar effect. Thus, table 9 does a better job of reflecting the diversity of funding sources at the aggregate level than the number of funding sources at the individual level.

56. In Massachusetts and New Jersey, proxy advocacy offices receive funds from utility companies under a fee system mandated by their respective state legislatures.

57. During the period under investigation, proxy advocacy offices in Georgia, Michigan, and New York received grants from the U.S. Department of Energy's Office of Utility Systems. Under the Reagan administration, that program has been terminated.

CHAPTER 3. POLITICAL EXECUTIVES AND CAREER EXECUTIVES

1. Samuel Huntington, "Political Development and Political Decay," *World Politics,* April 1965, pp. 386–430; Anthony King, "Overload: Problems of Governing in the 70s," *Political Studies,* September 1975, pp. 284–96.

2. King, "Overload," p. 286.

3. See, for example, B. Guy Peters, "The Problem of Bureaucratic Government," *Journal of Politics,* February 1981, pp. 56–82.

4. Top-level staff members were defined to include the executive director, general counsel, heads of the electric, gas, and telephone divisions, chief economist, chief engineer, chief administrative law judge, head of the office of policy analysis, and other

key personages with similar titles. In each of the twelve states, an effort was made to interview all of these individuals, provided, of course, that each position existed and was filled.

5. See, for example, Saul Alinsky, *Rules for Radicals* (New York: Random House, 1971).

6. James David Barber, *The Lawmakers: Recruitment and Adaptation to Legislative Life* (New Haven: Yale University Press, 1965), pp. 116–62.

7. Ned Breathitt of Kentucky and Brendan Byrne of New Jersey went on to become governors of their respective states; Jon Cartwright of Oklahoma became state attorney general; Michael Barnes of Maryland and Arlen Erdahl of Minnesota became members of Congress; Alfred Kahn of New York became chairman of the Civil Aeronautics Board. However, these examples are noteworthy because they are so unusual.

8. According to a comprehensive, though possibly dated, study, the median tenure of federal regulatory commissioners is 4.5 years. David Stanley, Dean Mann, and Jameson Doig, *Men Who Govern: A Biographical Profile of Federal Political Executives* (Washington, D.C.: The Brookings Institution, 1967), pp. 68–69.

9. Lincoln Smith, "State Utility Commissioners—1978," *Public Utilities Fortnightly,* February 16, 1978, pp. 9–15.

10. National Association of Regulatory Utility Commissioners (NARUC), Bulletins 16, 17, 18—April 20–May 4, 1981.

11. According to NARUC, twenty-four states provide for minority party representation by law or by practice. NARUC, *1979 Annual Report on Utility and Carrier Regulation* (Washington, D.C., 1980), pp. 732–36.

12. Anthony Downs, *Inside Bureaucracy* (Boston: Little, Brown & Co., 1967), pp. 223–24.

13. Joel Aberbach and Bert Rockman, "Clashing Beliefs Within the Executive Branch: The Nixon Administration Bureaucracy," *American Political Science Review,* June 1976, pp. 456–68.

14. Richard Cole and David Caputo, "Presidential Control of the Senior Civil Service: Assessing the Strategies of the Nixon Years," *American Political Science Review,* June 1979, pp. 399–413.

15. Paul Quirk, *Industry Influence in Federal Regulatory Agencies* (Princeton: Princeton University Press, 1981), p. 67.

16. John P. Plumlee, "Lawyers as Bureaucrats: The Impact of Legal Training in the Higher Civil Service," *Public Administration Review,* March/April 1981, p. 226.

17. Everett Ladd, Jr., and Seymour M. Lipset, "Professors Found to Be Liberal but Not Radical," *Chronicle of Higher Education,* January 16, 1978, p. 9.

18. In differentiating between lawyers and nonlawyers I do not mean to imply that there are no interesting differences within the nonlawyer category. In fact, the data suggest that engineers are more conservative than accountants, who are more conservative than economists, who are more conservative than lawyers. However, this rank-ordering should be regarded as tentative rather than definitive, since the number of respondents in each subcategory is quite small.

19. Since political party and profession are nominal-level variables, it is important to measure their effects through methods appropriate for such variables. The technique employed here is multivariate contingency table analysis. For a discussion of how such analysis may be used to analyze nominal-level data, see Herbert Kritzer, "An Introduction to Multivariate Contingency Table Analysis," *American Journal of Political Science,* February 1978, pp. 187–226.

20. All six relationships remain statistically significant if one also controls for interaction effects between political party and profession.

21. For a critical view of the legal profession, see Jerold Auerbach, "A Plague of Lawyers," *Harper's,* October 1976, pp. 37–44.

22. See, for example, Claude Vaughan, Jr., and James Sharpe, "The Public Utility Regulatory Policies Act: Implications for Regulatory Commission Reform," *Public Administration Review,* May/June 1981, pp. 387–91.

23. Marver Bernstein, *Regulating Business by Independent Commission* (Princeton: Princeton University Press, 1955), pp. 184–85; Murray Edelman, *The Symbolic Uses of Politics* (Urbana: University of Illinois Press, 1967), p. 53; Louis Kohlmeier, *The Regulators: Watchdog Agencies and the Public Interest* (New York: Harper & Row, 1969), pp. 48–73; Common Cause, *Serving Two Masters: A Common Cause Study of Conflicts of Interest in the Executive Branch* (Washington, D.C.: Common Cause, 1976).

24. Quirk, *Industry influence,* p. 66.

25. William T. Gormley, Jr., "A Test of the Revolving Door Hypothesis at the FCC," *American Journal of Political Science,* November 1979, pp. 665–83.

26. Quirk, *Industry Influence,* p. 66; Gormley, "Revolving Door Hypothesis," pp. 679–81.

27. If one also controls for interaction effects between political party and industry experience, the findings remain the same.

28. Quirk, *Industry Influence,* pp. 143–74.

29. Downs, *Inside Bureaucracy,* p. 224.

30. For an excellent discussion of the pros and cons, see James Fesler, *The Independence of State Regulatory Agencies* (Chicago: Public Administration Service, 1942). Fesler's personal conclusion is that independence from the governor and the state legislature is more appropriate for service agencies than for regulatory agencies.

31. Herbert Kaufman, "Emerging Conflicts in the Doctrines of Public Administration," *American Political Science Review,* December 1956, pp. 1057–73.

32. Thad Beyle and J. Oliver Williams, eds., *The American Governor in Behavioral Perspective* (New York: Harper & Row, 1972), p. 2.

33. Larry Sabato, *Goodbye to Good-Time Charlie* (Lexington, Mass.: D. C. Heath, 1978).

34. Deil Wright, "Executive Leadership in State Administration," *Midwest Journal of Political Science,* February 1967, pp. 1–26.

35. Martha Wagner Weinberg, *Managing the State* (Cambridge: MIT Press, 1977).

36. For further details on appointment and removal procedures, see NARUC, *1979 Annual Report,* pp. 228–32, 732–36.

37. Wright, "Executive Leadership."

38. Alan Rosenthal, *Legislative Life: People, Process, and Performance in the States* (New York: Harper & Row, 1981), p. 343.

39. Barber, *Lawmakers,* p. 20.

40. For a discussion of the legal foundations of public utility regulation in the states, see Martin Farris and Roy Sampson, *Public Utilities: Regulation, Management, and Ownership* (Boston: Houghton Mifflin Co., 1973), pp. 18–45.

41. For a discussion of recent developments in fuel adjustment clauses, see Harry Trebing, "Motivations and Barriers to Superior Performance Under Public Utility Regulation," in *Productivity Measurement in Regulated Industries,* ed. Rodney Stevenson and Thomas Cowing (New York: Academic Press, 1981), pp. 385–87.

42. Lifeline rates have been adopted in California, the District of Columbia, Maine, Massachusetts, Michigan, Minnesota, and South Dakota.

43. NARUC, *1979 Annual Report,* pp. 767–69.

44. Rosenthal, *Legislative Life,* pp. 321–22.

45. For accounts of congressional inattention to federal regulatory commissionership appointments, see U.S. Senate, Committee on Commerce, *Appointments to the Regulatory Agencies: The Federal Communications Commission and the Federal Trade Commission (1949–1974)* (Washington, D.C.: U.S. Government Printing Office, April 1976); and U.S. Senate, Committee on Government Operations, *The Regulatory Appointments Process* (Washington, D.C.: U.S. Government Printing Office, January 1977).

46. William Grigg, "Regulatory Lag Currently," *Public Utilities Fortnightly,* June 23, 1977, pp. 13–18; John Thornton, "Expediting Regulatory Decision Making," *Public Utilities Fortnightly,* February 28, 1980, pp. 9–14.

47. Richard Stewart, "The Reformation of American Administrative Law," *Harvard Law Review,* June 1975, pp. 1770–76.

48. Ibid., p. 1771.

49. A major rate case was defined as a general rate case involving a company that serves more than 5 percent of the state's residential customers. Due to an unusually large number of small utility companies in Florida and Massachusetts, only companies serving more than 25 percent of the residential customers in those states were included.

50. A final decision should be differentiated from an interim decision, which may precede a final decision, and a supplemental decision, which may follow a petition for reconsideration or judicial remand.

51. The total number of rate cases does not equal the sum of cases in each category, because thirty-five cases were both electric and gas cases.

52. Merrill Lynch, Pierce, Fenner & Smith, Inc., "Utility Research: A Statistical Analysis of Regulatory Trends," November 1980, p. 19. The Merrill Lynch estimates are based on a larger but less carefully drawn sample of rate cases from across the country. Although Merrill Lynch regards these estimates as reliable, it does not guarantee their accuracy.

53. NARUC, *1979 Annual Report,* pp. 737–41.

54. In a review of the cost of service index (COSI) used by New Mexico's largest electric utility (the Public Service Company of New Mexico), the New Mexico Public Service Commission concluded that COSI had reduced capital costs and enhanced the company's ability to attract capital. However, the commission also concluded that incentives to minimize costs were inadequate under COSI and that stronger regulatory oversight was needed. See New Mexico Public Service Commission, Decision and Order No. 1419, Santa Fe, N.M., December 29, 1978.

55. William Tucker, "Environmentalism and the Leisure Class," *Harper's,* December 1977, pp. 49–80.

56. Stewart, "American Administrative Law," p. 1772.

57. Stephen Frank, "The Oversight of Administrative Agencies by State Supreme Courts: Some Macro Findings," *Administrative Law Review,* Summer 1980, pp. 477–99.

58. *Louis Lefkowitz et al.* v. *Public Service Commission of New York and Consolidated Edison,* New York State Supreme Court, October 1, 1974.

59. *Mississippi Public Service Commission* v. *Mississippi Valley Gas Co.,* 327 So. 2d 296.

60. *Wisconsin's Environmental Decade* v. *Public Service Commission,* 81 Wis. 2d 344; *Wisconsin's Environmental Decade* v. *Public Service Commission,* 84 Wis. 2d 504.

61. On September 30, 1975, the Chicago Area Recycling Group appealed an Illinois Commerce Commission decision in a Peoples Gas Light and Coke Company rate case. That appeal was rejected by the Circuit Court of Cook County on August 17, 1976. However, the Chicago Area Recycling Group appealed that decision to the Appellate Court. On March 27, 1978, the Appellate Court reversed the Circuit Court and remanded the case to the commission with instructions.

62. See, for example, *Citizens to Preserve Overton Park, Inc.* v. *Volpe,* 401 U.S. 402 (1971); *Environmental Defense Fund, Inc.* v. *Ruckelshaus,* 439 F. 2d 584 (D.C. Cir. 1971); *United States* v. *SCRAP,* 412 U.S. 669 (1973).

CHAPTER 4. POLITICAL ATTITUDES

1. Hanna Pitkin, *The Concept of Representation* (Berkeley and Los Angeles: University of California Press, 1972), pp. 60–91.

2. See, for example, Sidney Verba and Norman Nie, *Participation in America: Political Democracy and Social Equality* (New York: Harper & Row, 1972), pp. 299–308; Susan B. Hansen, "Participation, Political Structure, and Concurrence," *American Political Science Review,* December 1975, pp. 1181–99.

3. Robert Weissberg, "Collective vs. Dyadic Representation in Congress," *American Political Science Review,* June 1978, pp. 535–47.

4. Warren Miller and Donald Stokes, "Constituency Influence in Congress," *American Political Science Review,* March 1963, pp. 45–56; Verba and Nie, *Participation;* Hansen, "Participation, Political Structure"; and Helen Ingram et al., *A Policy Approach to Political Representation: Lessons from the Four Corners States* (Baltimore: Johns Hopkins University Press, 1980).

5. Weissberg, "Collective vs. Dyadic Representation"; and Susan B. Hansen, "Linkage Models, Issues, and Community Politics," *American Politics Quarterly,* January 1978, pp. 3–28.

6. Miller and Stokes, "Constituency Influence."

7. Verba and Nie, *Participation.*

8. Roger Cobb and Charles Elder, *Participation in American Politics: The Dynamics of Agenda Building* (Baltimore: Johns Hopkins University Press, 1972).

9. Verba and Nie, *Participation,* p. 328.

10. E. E. Schattschneider, *The Semi-Sovereign People: A Realist's View of Democracy in America* (New York: Holt, Rinehart & Winston, 1960), p. 68.

11. Peter Bachrach and Morton Baratz, "Decisions and Non-decisions: An Analytical Framework," *American Political Science Review,* September 1963, pp. 632–42.

12. Although respondents were asked to identify only three issues, some mentioned more. To avoid losing valuable information, as many as four responses were coded.

13. William T. Gormley, Jr., "Newspaper Agendas and Political Elites," *Journalism Quarterly,* Summer 1975, pp. 304–08.

14. See Verba and Nie, *Participation,* pp. 412–14.

15. An alternative way to measure concurrence would be to divide the number of agreements by the number of separate issues mentioned by either party. Thus, if a utility executive and a commissioner mention five issues between them and they agree on only one, their concurrence score would be 1/5, not 1/3. The principal consequence of this approach is to lower concurrence scores across the board.

16. The difference between the concurrence scores of proxy advocates and utility executives would also be statistically significant at an acceptable level (.05) if a one-

tailed significance test were used. However, such a test is appropriate only when direction is predicted in advance.

17. Milton Rokeach, *Beliefs, Attitudes, and Values* (San Francisco: Jossey-Bass, 1972), p. 157.

18. Donald Searing, "Measuring Politicians' Values," *American Political Science Review,* March 1978, p. 71.

19. The value priorities question used in this study differed from Searing's in two respects: first, respondents were asked to rank eight values, as opposed to four lists of nine values each; second, respondents were asked to rank values of special importance to their particular subsystem. The more parsimonious value list reduced the likelihood that respondents would be overwhelmed by the task at hand. The more familiar value list reduced the likelihood that respondents would be threatened by questions outside their realm of expertise.

20. The number of ties is relatively small. Otherwise, Kendall's tau might be a more appropriate measure.

21. If one is willing to use a one-tailed test, then the following differences are also statistically significant at the .05 level: commissioners are more likely to agree with staff members than with proxy advocates, and commissioners are more likely to agree with proxy advocates than with grassroots advocates.

22. For a detailed discussion of the distinction between "structural" and "allocative" decisions, see Robert Salisbury and John Heinz, "A Theory of Policy Analysis and Some Preliminary Applications," in *Policy Analyses in Political Science,* ed. Ira Sharkansky (Chicago: Markham Publishing Co., 1970), pp. 39–59.

23. These ideas are adapted from Murray Edelman, *The Symbolic Uses of Politics* (Urbana: University of Illinois Press, 1964).

24. For a discussion of the withering away of vigorous regulation, see Samuel Huntington, "The Marasmus of the ICC: The Commission, the Railroads, and the Public Interest," *Yale Law Journal,* April 1952, pp. 467–509.

25. Bachrach and Baratz, "Decisions and Non-decisions."

26. For a discussion of the distinction between "terminal" and "instrumental" values, See Rokeach, *Beliefs,* pp. 156–78.

CHAPTER 5. POLITICAL INFLUENCE

1. Samuel Huntington, "The Marasmus of the ICC: The Commission, the Railroads and the Public Interest," *Yale Law Journal,* April 1952, pp. 467–509; Marver Bernstein, *Regulating Business by Independent Commission* (Princeton: Princeton University Press, 1955).

2. Roger Noll, *Reforming Regulation* (Washington, D.C.: The Brookings Institution, 1971).

3. Murray Edelman, *The Symbolic Uses of Politics* (Urbana: University of Illinois Press, 1967).

4. Theodore Lowi, *The End of Liberalism,* 2d ed. (New York: W. W. Norton & Co., 1979).

5. Murray Weidenbaum, *Business, Government, and the Public* (Englewood Cliffs, N.J.: Prentice-Hall, 1977); Paul MacAvoy, *The Regulated Industries and the Economy* (New York: W. W. Norton & Co., 1979).

6. Paul Sabatier, "Social Movements and Regulatory Agencies: Toward a More Adequate—and Less Pessimistic—Theory of 'Clientele Capture,' " *Policy Sciences,* September 1975, pp. 301–42.

7. Sam Peltzman, "Toward a More General Theory of Regulation," *Journal of Law and Economics,* August 1976, pp. 211–40.

8. James Q. Wilson, ed., *The Politics of Regulation* (New York: Basic Books, 1980), pp. 357–94.

9. David Welborn, *The Governance of Federal Regulatory Agencies* (Knoxville: University of Tennessee Press, 1977); Judy Rosener, "Citizen Participation in an Administrative State" (Ph.D. dissertation, Claremont Graduate School, 1979), pp. 120–59; Daniel Mazmanian and Paul Sabatier, "A Multivariate Model of Public Policy-Making," *American Journal of Political Science,* August 1980, pp. 439–68; Robert Katzmann, "Federal Trade Commission," in *Politics of Regulation,* ed. Wilson, pp. 152–87.

10. Bernstein, *Regulating Business*; Edelman, *Symbolic Uses*; George Stigler, "The Theory of Economic Regulation," *Bell Journal of Economics and Management Science,* Spring 1971, pp. 3–21.

11. For an empirical assessment of the "life cycle" theory of capture, see John P. Plumlee and Kenneth Meier, "Capture and Rigidity in Regulatory Administration: An Empirical Assessment," in *The Policy Cycle,* ed. Judith May and Aaron Wildavsky (Beverly Hills: Sage Publications, 1978), pp. 215–34.

12. David Truman, *The Governmental Process* (New York: Alfred Knopf, 1951); Sabatier, "Social Movements"; Erwin Krasnow and Lawrence Longley, *The Politics of Broadcast Regulation,* 2d ed. (New York: St. Martin's Press, 1978); Steven Kelman, "Occupational Safety and Health Administration," in *Politics of Regulation,* ed. Wilson, pp. 236–66.

13. J. Leiper Freeman, *The Political Process,* rev. ed. (New York: Random House, 1965), p. 5.

14. Herbert Simon, *Administrative Behavior,* 3d ed. (New York: The Free Press, 1976); Anthony Downs, *Inside Bureaucracy* (Boston: Little, Brown & Co., 1967); and Graham Allison, *Essence of Decision: Explaining the Cuban Missile Crisis* (Boston: Little, Brown & Co., 1971), pp. 67–100; Welborn, *Governance of Federal Agencies.*

15. Max Weber, *The Methodology of the Social Sciences*, trans. and ed. Edward Shils and Henry Finch (Glencoe: The Free Press, 1949), p. 64.

16. Angus Campbell and Philip Converse, "Social Change and Human Change," in *The Human Meaning of Social Change,* ed. idem (New York: Russell Sage Foundation, 1972), p. 10.

17. By this definition, the "reputational" approach and the "decisional" approach to measuring influence both rely on the perceptual method. Indeed, in retrospect, one is struck more by the similarities than by the differences between these alternative approaches, which polarized social scientists for years.

18. Floyd Hunter, *Community Power Structure* (Chapel Hill: University of North Carolina Press, 1953); Robert Dahl, *Who Governs? Democracy and Power in an American Community* (New Haven: Yale University Press, 1961); Nelson Polsby, *Community Power and Political Theory* (New Haven: Yale University Press, 1963).

19. Robert Friedman, "Representation in Regulatory Decision Making: Scientific, Industrial, and Consumer Inputs to the F.D.A.," *Public Administration Review,* May/June 1978, pp. 205–14.

20. Richard Cole, *Citizen Participation and the Urban Policy Process* (Lexington, Mass.: D. C. Heath, 1974); W. R. Derrick Sewell and Susan Phillips, "Models for the Evaluation of Public Participation Programmes," *Natural Resources Journal,* April 1979, pp. 337–58.

21. Friedman, "Representation," p. 207.

22. An alternative approach would be to exclude self-evaluations from analysis. This approach would modify the overall results somewhat, most notably with respect to proxy advocates (who see themselves as more influential than others do) and utility companies (who see themselves as less influential than others do). Without self-evaluations, the average estimated influence of proxy advocates would decline from 7.03 to 6.79, while the average estimated influence of utility companies would increase from 7.43 to 7.79. However, if self-evaluations were excluded, the overall rank-ordering of groups would still remain the same.

23. The figures in table 23 (sample sizes, means, and standard deviations) may be used in paired-sample comparisons to determine whether any given difference of means is statistically significant at an acceptable level (.05, using a two-tailed t test). In North Dakota, with the smallest sample size (N = 9), 10 of 21 comparisons are statistically significant. In New York, with the largest sample (N = 42), 27 of 28 comparisons are statistically significant. In Florida, a fairly typical state (N = 23), 23 of 28 comparisons are statistically significant.

24. Business groups appear to be less influential in states with a weak industrial base, such as North Dakota and Wyoming.

25. Barry Checkoway and Jon Van Til, "What Do We Know About Citizen Participation?" in *Citizen Participation in America*, ed. Stuart Langton (Lexington, Mass.: D. C. Heath, 1978), pp. 33–34.

26. Labor groups are judged largely ineffective in eleven of the twelve states. In only one state (Illinois) is labor judged moderately effective. In that state, the United Mine Workers has been somewhat successful in convincing the Illinois Commerce Commission to promote the use of Illinois coal by electric utilities.

27. Municipalities own and operate public utilities in a substantial number of communities, including Los Angeles, Cleveland, and Jacksonville. Municipally owned utilities are generally free from the authority of the public utility commission, although the commission is sometimes empowered to determine their rate designs. Most municipalities, however, do not own an electric, natural gas, or telephone company; rather, they are customers of privately owned utilities, which means that they pay rates determined by the public utility commission for municipal buildings, street lights, and so forth. If a municipality fails to provide its own utility service, residents of the municipality also purchase utility services from privately owned utilities. With such interests at stake, municipalities often intervene in public utility commission proceedings in an effort to keep rate hikes as low as possible and to secure rate designs favorable to municipal governments.

28. Wilson, *Politics of Regulation*, p. 391.

29. An alternative approach would be to treat capture as one of several possible outcomes of an interest group struggle, in which case the capture model and the interest group model would be compatible. However, differences between capture theorists and group theorists are sufficiently sharp that it seems inadvisable to blur these distinctions. If capture occurs, as capture theorists predict, then something is fundamentally wrong with the classic interest group model.

30. For a similar argument, see Barry Mitnick, *The Political Economy of Regulation* (New York: Columbia University Press, 1980), p. 210.

31. Jeffrey Berry, *Lobbying for the People* (Princeton: Princeton University Press, 1977), p. 254.

32. Public utility commission staffs in Mississippi, North Dakota, and Wyoming are among the smallest in the country. The Mississippi commission has such a severe staff shortage that commissioners often wind up writing press releases themselves. Indeed,

the Mississippi commission recently argued before the U.S. Supreme Court that it lacks the financial resources to implement the Public Utility Regulatory Policies Act, even if it wished to do so (which it does not). See Brief for State of Mississippi and the Mississippi Public Service Commission, *FERC* v. *The State of Mississippi et al.*, argued before U.S. Supreme Court, January 19, 1982.

33. The situation in Illinois has changed somewhat since the time period under investigation. The statewide Office of Consumer Services, established to disburse Department of Energy funds to Illinois citizens' groups, now participates directly in certain Illinois Commerce Commission proceedings.

34. Although Florida respondents characterize grassroots advocacy groups overall as moderately effective, they place no single grassroots advocacy group in that category. Rather, they characterize the effectiveness of the two grassroots advocacy groups active during the time period under investigation as low.

35. These findings should be qualified to some extent. In New York, grassroots advocacy groups as a whole are judged to be relatively ineffective, but several grassroots advocacy groups are judged to be moderately effective. Thus grassroots advocacy groups do make some difference in New York. As for Michigan, it should be kept in mind that respondents were asked to assess the effectiveness of grassroots advocacy groups over a one-year period. Interviews with Michigan respondents suggest that grassroots advocacy groups there were more effective several years earlier and could be still more effective in the future.

36. See Mancur Olson, *The Logic of Collective Action,* rev. ed. (New York: Schocken Books, 1971).

37. The concept of institutionalized governmental consumer advocates who participate in the proceedings of other agencies has not yet been embraced by the federal government. However, at least two regulatory agencies, the Civil Aeronautics Board and the Interstate Commerce Commission, have an in-house consumer counsel office. See U.S. Senate Committee on Governmental Affairs, *Public Participation in Regulatory Agency Proceedings* (Washington, D.C.: U.S. Government Printing Office, 1977), pp. 72–90.

38. Theodore Lowi, "American Business, Public Policy, Case Studies, and Political Theory," *World Politics,* July 1964, pp. 677–715.

CHAPTER 6. POLICY IMPACTS

1. E. E. Schattschneider, *The Semi-Sovereign People* (New York: Holt, Rinehart & Winston, 1960), p. 63.

2. Theodore Lowi, "Four Systems of Policy, Politics, and Choice," *Public Administration Review,* July/August 1972, pp. 298–310; see also Lowi, "American Business, Public Policy, Case Studies, and Political Theory," *World Politics,* July 1964, pp. 677–715.

3. James Q. Wilson, *Political Organizations* (New York: Basic Books, 1973), pp. 327–46.

4. Robert Salisbury and John Heinz, "A Theory of Policy Analysis and Some Preliminary Applications," in *Policy Analysis in Political Science,* ed. Ira Sharkansky (Chicago: Markham Publishing Co., 1970), pp. 39–60; Paul Sabatier, "Social Movements and Regulatory Agencies: Toward a More Adequate—and Less Pessimistic—Theory of 'Clientele Capture,'" *Policy Sciences,* September 1975, pp. 301–42; Michael Hayes, "Semi-Sovereign Pressure Groups," *Journal of Politics,* February 1978, pp. 134–61; and David Price, "Policy Making in Congressional Committees: The Impact of 'Environmental' Factors," *American Political Science Review,* June 1978, pp. 548–74.

5. For an excellent collection of articles that exemplify this approach, see *State and Urban Politics,* ed. Richard Hofferbert and Ira Sharkansky (Boston: Little, Brown & Co., 1971).

6. Sabatier, "Social Movements."

7. Dorothy Nelkin and Michael Pollak, "Public Participation in Technological Decisions: Reality or Grand Illusion?" *Technology Review,* August/September 1979, p. 62.

8. Harmon Zeigler, "The Effects of Lobbying: A Comparative Assessment," in *Public Opinion and Public Policy,* ed. Norman Luttbeg (Homewood, Ill.: Dorsey Press, 1968), pp. 193–95.

9. The Illinois Office of Consumer Services, recipient of a grant from the U.S. Department of Energy's Office of Utility Systems, ran afoul of the Illinois State Legislature when it awarded subgrants to citizens' groups openly critical of key legislators. The legislature responded by severely limiting the extent to which a state government office can subsidize citizens' groups.

10. Legal aid societies are not the only grassroots advocacy groups that receive federal funds. However, other groups are seldom required to represent a particular constituency. For example, the Department of Energy's program of assistance to state and local public advocacy groups requires that they spend their funds on electric or gas cases only but does not insist that they represent a particular constituency.

11. To receive money from the Legal Services Corporation, which is funded by Congress, legal aid societies must represent clients on the basis of their "financial ability to afford legal assistance." See *The Legal Services Act as Amended 1977* (Public Law 95–222).

12. See *Florida Statutes 1979,* chap. 350; *Michigan Compiled Laws 1970,* sec. 14.28; *New Jersey Statutes Annotated,* chap. 52, sec. 27E–18; *New York Statutes,* art. 20, sec. 553.

13. See *Annotated Laws of Massachusetts,* chap. 12.

14. See *Georgia Code Annotated,* chap. 93–3A.

15. Daniel Elazar, *American Federalism: A View from the States* (New York: Thomas Crowell Co., 1966).

16. Lee Sigelman and Roland Smith, "Consumer Legislation in the American States: An Attempt at Explanation," *Social Science Quarterly,* June 1980, pp. 58–70.

17. Ira Sharkansky, "The Utility of Elazar's Political Culture," *Polity,* Fall 1969, pp. 66–83.

18. Marver Bernstein, *Regulating Business by Independent Commission* (Princeton: Princeton University Press, 1955).

19. William Berry, "Utility Regulation in the States: The Policy Effects of Professionalism and Salience to the Consumer," *American Journal of Political Science,* May 1979, pp. 263–77.

20. Robert Lineberry and Edmund Fowler, "Reformism and Public Policies in American Cities," *American Political Science Review,* September 1967, pp. 701–16.

21. For conflicting evidence on this point, see Robert Hagerman and Brian Ratchford, "Some Determinants of Allowed Rates of Return on Equity to Electric Utilities," *Bell Journal of Economics and Management Science,* Spring 1978, pp. 46–55; Peter Navarro, "Electric Utility Regulation and National Energy Policy," *Regulation,* January/February 1981, pp. 20–27.

22. Richard Dawson and James Robinson, "Inter-Party Competition, Economic Variables, and Welfare Policies in the American States," *Journal of Politics,* May 1963, pp. 265–89; Thomas Dye, *Politics, Economics, and the Public: Policy Outcomes in the American States* (Chicago: Rand McNally, 1966); Jack Walker, "The Diffusion of Inno-

vations Among the American States," *American Political Science Review,* September 1969, pp. 880–99; Brian Fry and Richard Winters, "The Politics of Redistribution," *American Political Science Review,* June 1970, pp. 508–22.

23. Edward Tufte, *Data Analysis for Politics and Policy* (Englewood Cliffs, N.J.: Prentice-Hall, 1974), p. 162.

24. Ordinary least squares regression analysis assumes that the range of the dependent variable is unrestricted and that the conditional variances for all joint values of the independent variables are equal. Neither condition is met when the dependent variable is dichotomous.

25. D. J. Finney, *Probit Analysis* (Cambridge: Cambridge University Press, 1952); Henri Theil, *Principles of Econometrics* (New York: John Wiley & Sons, 1971), pp. 628–36; Richard McKelvey and William Zavoina, "A Statistical Model for the Analysis of Ordinal Level Dependent Variables," *Journal of Mathematical Sociology* 4 (1975): 103–20; John Aldrich and Charles Cnudde, "Probing the Bounds of Conventional Wisdom: A Comparison of Regression, Probit, and Discriminant Analysis," *American Journal of Political Science,* August 1975, pp. 579–85.

26. The relationship between public advocacy and the rate granted/rate requested ratio could be misleading if utility companies deliberately requested more in states with highly active consumer advocates, to give consumer advocates an easy victory and satisfy consumers through "symbolic politics." However, it is equally plausible to argue that utility companies are especially unlikely to "pad" a rate hike request in such states. Where consumer advocates are highly active, padding is more likely to be detected. Once detected, it severely damages a utility's credibility. Until future research suggests otherwise, it seems appropriate to treat a utility's rate hike request as a reasonably reliable indicator of the utility's perceived needs.

27. For each firm, a 1978 rate decision, if available, was used; otherwise, a 1977 rate decision was used. If no information was available for either year, the firm was excluded from the analysis.

28. It is not at all unusual for a public utility commission to grant a utility company less than the full rate hike requested. However, public utility commissions tend to grant electric utilities at least 60 percent of what they ask for. Thus, when the state attorney general convinced the Massachusetts Department of Public Utilities to grant Boston Edison less than 42 percent of its rate hike request, this was widely considered a victory for the attorney general.

29. Principal source: Electric Power Research Institute (EPRI) et al., *Reference Manual and Procedures for Implementing PURPA,* Palo Alto, March 1979. Since then, lifeline rates have also been adopted by South Dakota.

30. For a more detailed account of the California lifeline rate case, see Douglas Anderson, "State Regulation of Electric Utilities," in *The Politics of Regulation,* ed. James Q. Wilson (New York: Basic Books, 1980), pp. 26–32.

31. National Association of Regulatory Utility Commissioners, *1978 Annual Report* (Washington, D.C., 1979), p. 493.

32. U.S. Department of Energy, Office of Consumer Affairs, *The Energy Consumer* (Washington, D.C., October 1979), pp. 9–19.

33. Charles Williams, "Determinants of State Economic Regulatory Policy: The Case of Electric Utility Rates" (Paper presented at the Annual Meeting of the Midwest Political Science Association, Chicago, Ill., 1979).

34. Although a consensus has yet to emerge, there is substantial support for energy conservation at the mass level. See, for example, the Eagleton Poll, "New Jersey Residents and Energy Conservation: A Survey of Citizens' Attitudes," New

Brunswick, October 23, 1978. Also see Claire Knoche Fulenwider, "Conservation Among Wisconsin Residents: Behavior and Motivation," Wisconsin Center for Public Policy, Madison, July 17, 1980.

35. Principal source: EPRI et al., *Reference Manual.*

36. Marginal cost pricing principles usually justify the adoption of time-of-day rates, seasonal rates, and rates for interruptible service. They may or may not justify the adoption of inverted rates.

37. For similar accounts of the EDF's efforts in support of marginal cost pricing, see Paul Joskow, "Electric Utility Rate Structures in the United States: Some Recent Developments," in *Public Utility Rate Making in an Energy Conscious Environment,* ed. Werner Sichel (Boulder: Westview Press, 1978), pp. 1–22; and Douglas Anderson, "State Regulation," pp. 32–38.

38. Joskow, "Electric Utility Rate Structures," p. 13.

39. Walker, "Diffusion of Innovations," pp. 880–99.

40. Alfred Light, "Intergovernmental Sources of Innovation in State Administration," *American Politics Quarterly,* April 1978, p. 159.

CHAPTER 7. REGULATORY REFORM

1. Duncan MacRae, *The Social Function of Social Science* (New Haven: Yale University Press, 1976); Charles Anderson, "The Place of Principles in Policy Analysis," *American Political Science Review,* September 1979, pp. 711–23.

2. See, for example, Arthur Okun, *Equality and Efficiency: The Big Tradeoff* (Washington, D.C.: Brookings Institution, 1975).

3. Herbert Kaufman, "Emerging Conflicts in the Doctrines of Public Administration," *American Political Science Review,* December 1956, pp. 1057–73.

4. For powerful challenges to the concept of neutral competence, see Frank Marini, ed., *Toward a New Public Administration* (Scranton, Pa.: Chandler Publishing, 1971).

5. Roger Cramton, "The Why, Where and How of Broadened Public Participation in the Administrative Process," *Georgetown Law Journal,* February 1972, pp. 525–46; Ernest Gellhorn, "Public Participation in Administrative Proceedings," *Yale Law Journal,* January 1972, pp. 359–404.

6. Robert Leflar and Martin Rogol, "Consumer Participation in the Regulation of Public Utilities: A Model Act," *Harvard Journal on Legislation,* February 1976, pp. 235–97.

7. The eleven states are Alabama, Arizona, Georgia, Louisiana, Mississippi, Montana, Nebraska, North Dakota, Oklahoma, South Dakota, and Tennessee. In Texas, members of the Public Utility Commission are not popularly elected, although members of the Railroad Commission are.

8. Jeff Brummer, "No Regulation Without Representation!" *Power Line,* June 1981, p. 1–11.

9. Thomas Pelsoci, "Commission Attributes and Regulatory Discretion: A Longitudinal Study of State Public Utility Commissions" (Paper presented at the Annual Meeting of the American Political Science Association, New York, N.Y., August 31–September 3, 1978).

10. Robert Hagerman and Brian Ratchford, "Some Determinants of Allowed Rates of Return on Equity to Electric Utilities," *Bell Journal of Economics and Management Science,* Spring 1978, pp. 46–55.

11. Robert LaFollette, *A Personal Narrative of Political Experiences* (Madison: The Robert LaFollette Co., 1913), pp. 348–49.

12. For a more detailed discussion of these alternatives, see William Gormley, Jr., "Statewide Remedies for Public Underrepresentation in Regulatory Proceedings," *Public Administration Review,* July/August 1981, pp. 454–62.

13. Donald Pfarrer, "Citizen Utility Group Making a Big Splash," *Milwaukee Journal,* October 13, 1981, p. 4.

14. Utility Consumer Protection Board members are chosen by the governor from lists of names submitted by the attorney general (one vacancy) and the Michigan Consumers' Council (four vacancies). The Council is a nine-member body which advises the State Legislature on consumer issues.

15. Hanna Cortner, "Formulating and Implementing Energy Policy: The Inadequacy of the State Response," *Policy Studies Journal,* Autumn 1978, pp. 24–29; Claude Vaughan, Jr., and James Sharpe, "The Public Utility Regulatory Policies Act: Implications for Regulatory Commission Reform," *Public Utilities Fortnightly,* May/June 1981, pp. 387–91.

16. Lincoln Smith, "State Utility Commissioners—1978," *Public Utilities Fortnightly,* February 16, 1978, pp. 9–15.

17. National Association of Regulatory Utility Commissioners, Bulletins 16, 17, and 18, April 20–May 4, 1981.

18. Henry Geller, "A Modest Proposal for Modest Reform of the FCC," *Georgetown Law Journal,* February 1975, p. 722.

19. Among commissioners with shorter terms of office (five years or less), 61.1 percent have an advanced degree. Among commissioners with longer terms of office (six years or more), 53.1 percent have an advanced degree. National Association of Regulatory Utility Commissioners, Bulletins, 16–18.

20. Glen Robinson, "The FCC: An Essay on Regulatory Watchdogs," *Virginia Law Review,* March 1978, p. 213.

21. National Association of Regulatory Utility Commissioners, Bulletins 16–18.

22. Among commissioners interviewed for this study, 43 percent of the elected commissioners and 25 percent of the appointed commissioners agree that "there is already enough citizen involvement in public utility commission proceedings." These differences are especially noteworthy, since there is actually less citizen participation in states with elected commissioners.

23. The state of Mississippi recently challenged the constitutionality of PURPA. A federal district court judge, Harold Cox, agreed that PURPA violated the Commerce Clause and the 10th Amendment. The U.S. Supreme Court, however, found PURPA to be constitutional. See *FERC* v. *Mississippi* (1982), Slip Opinion, #80-1749.

24. The National Electric Reliability Council (NERC), a utility-run research organization, estimates reserve margins on a regional basis and (more selectively) on a statewide basis. See NERC, "Assessment of the Overall Adequacy of the Bulk Power Supply Systems: Summer of 1980" and "Assessment of the Overall Reliability and Adequacy of the Bulk Power Supply Systems: Winter of 1980/81."

25. Paul Van Riper, *History of the U.S. Civil Service* (Evanston: Row, Peterson & Co., 1958).

26. According to Tolchin and Tolchin, there is a great deal of state government patronage in New York and Illinois, relatively little in California and Wisconsin. See Martin Tolchin and Susan Tolchin, *To the Victor . . . Political Patronage from the Clubhouse to the White House* (New York: Random House, 1971), pp. 88–130. In all four states, the public utility commission's practices coincide with broader state practices.

27. Daniel Elazar, *American Federalism: A View from the States* (New York: Thomas Crowell Co., 1972), 2d ed., pp. 84–126.

28. John Fenton, *Midwest Politics* (New York: Holt, Rinehart and Winston, 1966), pp. 1–7, 219–31.

29. Among top-level public utility commission staff members, career executives have worked an average of 13.5 years for their commission, while political executives have worked an average of 11.7 years.

30. Bruce Owen and Ronald Braeutigan, *The Regulation Game: Strategic Use of the Administrative Process* (Cambridge, Mass.: Ballinger Publishing Co., 1978).

31. Thomas Morgan, "Toward a Revised Strategy for Rate-making," *University of Illinois Law Forum,* 1978, pp. 21–78.

32. See, for example, *Consumers Lobby Against Monopolies* v. *Public Utilities Commission,* 25 Cal. 3d 891, 603 P. 2d 41, 160 Cal. Rptr. 124 (1979). In that case, the California Supreme Court held that rate-making is quasi-legislative because it has numerous legislative features, including multiple intervenors and an outcome that cannot be viewed as a clear victory for any one party. For an interesting discussion of the CLAM decision, see Linda Ross, "Consumers Lobby Against Monopolies v. Public Utilities Commission: The PUC's Power to Award Attorney Fees," *California Law Review,* July 1981, pp. 969–1000.

33. Owen and Braeutigan, *Regulation Game,* pp. 1–42.

34. Morgan, "Toward a Revised Strategy;" p. 78.

35. For a discussion of the Ash Council's report, see Roger Noll, *Reforming Regulation* (Washington, D.C.: The Brookings Institution, 1971), pp. 4–14.

36. Roger Cramton, "Regulatory Structure and Regulatory Performance: A Critique of the Ash Council Report," *Public Administration Review,* July/August 1972, p. 286.

37. Bruce Ackerman and William Hassler, *Clean Coal/Dirty Air* (New Haven: Yale University Press, 1981), pp. 79–103.

38. Charles Goodsell, "Collegial State Administration: Design for Today?" *Western Political Quarterly,* September 1981, pp. 447–60.

39. Morgan, "Toward a Revised Strategy," p. 42.

40. Peter Schuck, "Litigation, Bargaining, and Regulation," *Regulation,* July/August 1979, p. 34.

41. Kenneth Davis, *Administrative Law Treatise,* vol. 1, 2d ed. (San Diego: K. C. Davis, 1978), p. 448.

42. *SEC* v. *Chenery Corp.,* 332 U.S. 194 (1947); *National Petroleum Refiners Assn.* v. *FTC,* 482 F. 2d 672 (D.C. Cir. 1973). More generally, see Bernard Schwartz, *Administrative Law* (Boston: Little, Brown & Co., 1976), pp. 185–90.

43. For example, the Wisconsin Supreme Court invalidated emissions limits established by the state Department of Natural Resources on the grounds that the agency should have formulated an emissions policy through rule-making. See *Wisconsin Electric Power Company* v. *Department of Natural Resources* (1980), 93 Wis. 2d 222.

44. Richard Stewart, "Vermont Yankee and the Evolution of Administrative Procedure," *Harvard Law Review,* June 1978, pp. 1813–14.

45. Richard Neustadt, *Presidential Power* (New York: John Wiley & Sons, 1960); Theodore Lowi, *The End of Liberalism* (New York: W. W. Norton & Co., 1969); James MacGregor Burns, *Leadership* (New York: Harper & Row, 1978).

46. Louis Fisher, *The Constitution Between Friends* (New York: St. Martin's Press, 1978), pp. 128–32.

47. *Youngstown Sheet & Tube Co.* v. *Sawyer,* 343 U.S. 579 (1952).

48. Susan King, "Comment: Executive Orders of the Wisconsin Governor," *Wisconsin Law Review,* 1980, p. 333.

49. In Massachusetts, for example, the governor has the authority to reorganize the

bureaucracy on his own initiative, subject to a legislative veto. Despite that fact, governors have presented their reorganization proposals to the state legislature as ordinary statutory proposals. See the discussion of Massachusetts by Victoria Schuck in Duane Lockard, ed., "The Strong Governorship: Status and Problems," *Public Administration Review,* January/February 1976, p. 91.

50. *Buckley* v. *Valeo,* 424 U.S. 1, 286 (1976).

51. Richard Cohen, "The Specter of the Legislative Veto," *National Journal,* September 30, 1978, p. 1561.

52. National Conference of State Legislatures, "Restoring the Balance: Legislative Review of Administrative Regulations," Washington, D.C., 1979, p. 17.

53. Wayne Francis, *Legislative Issues in the Fifty States* (Chicago: Rand McNally & Co., 1967), pp. 51–59.

54. See, for example, E. E. Schattschneider, *Party Government* (New York: Rinehart & Co., 1942); Austin Ranney, *The Doctrine of Responsible Party Government* (Urbana: University of Illinois Press, 1954); James MacGregor Burns, *The Deadlock of Democracy: Four Party Politics in America* (Englewood Cliffs, N.J.: Prentice-Hall, 1963); and Sarah McCally Morehouse, *State Politics, Parties and Policy* (New York: Holt, Rinehart and Winston, 1981).

55. Sarah McCally (Morehouse), "The Governor and His Legislative Party," *American Political Science Review,* December 1966, pp. 923–42.

56. David Price, "Policy Making in Congressional Committees: The Impact of 'Environmental' Factors," *American Political Science Review,* June 1978, pp. 548–74.

57. Ibid., pp. 571–72.

58. Interview in National Governors' Association, *Reflections on Being Governor* (Washington, D.C.: National Governors' Association, 1981), p. 188.

59. Eric Herzik, "Governors and Issues: A Typology of Concerns" (Paper presented at the Annual Meeting of the Southern Political Science Association, Memphis, Tenn., November 6, 1981).

60. Michael Nelson, "Power to the People," *Saturday Review,* November 24, 1979, pp. 12–17.

61. Ibid., p. 12.

62. John Snyder, "Note: The Proposed National Initiative Amendment: A Participatory Perspective on Substantive Restrictions and Procedural Requirements," *Harvard Journal on Legislation,* Spring 1981, pp. 429–69.

63. For a broader discussion of initiatives in different issue areas, see David Magleby, *Direct Legislation: Voting on Ballot Propositions in the United States* (Baltimore: Johns Hopkins University Press, 1982).

64. Nelson, "Power to the People," p. 17.

65. Jerry Gillam, "Three Nuclear Safety Bills Okayed," *Los Angeles Times,* June 2, 1976, p. 1; Richard Bergholz, "Brown Pauses to Sign Three Nuclear Power Bills," *Los Angeles Times,* June 4, 1976, p. 3; Robert Jones and Larry Pryor, "Prop. 15—The Why and How of Its 2-1 Defeat," *Los Angeles Times,* June 10, 1976, p. 1.

66. For a summary of arguments for and against plebiscites, see *Referendums: A Comparative Study of Practice and Theory,* ed. David Butler and Austin Ranney (Washington, D.C.: American Enterprise Institute, 1978), pp. 23–37.

67. Hugh Bone and Robert Benedict, "Perspectives on Direct Legislation: Washington State's Experience, 1914–1973," *Western Political Quarterly,* June 1975, pp. 339–40.

68. Charles Price, "The Initiative: A Comparative State Analysis and Reassessment of a Western Phenomenon," *Western Political Quarterly,* June 1975, pp. 256–57.

Index